BOOKS AND BEYOND:

THEMATIC APPROACHES FOR TEACHING LITERATURE IN HIGH SCHOOL

BOOKS AND BEYOND:

THEMATIC APPROACHES FOR TEACHING LITERATURE IN HIGH SCHOOL

Edited by
Gail P. Gregg
Florida International University
and
Pamela S. Carroll
Florida State University

Christopher-Gordon Publishers, Inc.

Norwood, Massachusetts

Credits

Every effort has been made to contact copyright holders for permission to reproduce borrowed material where necessary. We apologize for any oversights and would be happy to rectify them in future printings.

Christopher-Gordon Publishers, Inc.
1502 Providence Highway, Suite #12
Norwood, MA 02062
Tel: 781-762-5577

Copyright © 1998 by Christopher-Gordon Publishers, Inc.

All rights reserved. Except for review purposes, no part of this material protected by this copyright notice may be reproduced or utilized in any form or by any means, electronic or mechanical, including photocopying, recording, or any information and retrieval system, without the express written permission of the publisher or copyright holder.

Printed in the United States of America

10 9 8 7 6 5 4 3 2 1   03 02 01 00 99 98

ISBN: 0-926842-72-2

Acknowledgments

The authors wish to thank the following teachers and prospective teachers for their contributions to the chapters, and for their enthusiasm for this project:

Jeannie Adams, Sara Alston, Alexandria Alverez, Karly Askeland, Jennifer Boegli, Deborah Christy, Beth Clayton, Emily Eichoff, Cory Espinar, Yolanda Franklin, Rick G. Funes, Maria Fernandez, Christina Gonzales-Yip, Allison Love, Amy K. Powell, Eric Sanders, Paul A. Satty, Eric Schlichenmaier, Christine Wagner, Joe Wilk.

Dedication

For our finest teachers,
Barbara Goleman, Grace O'Haren, Beth Nysewander, and Terry C. Ley,
for our husbands,
Bill Gregg and Joe Donoghue,
and for our mothers,
Grace Duganne and Wyleen Carroll

Table of Contents

Authors' Introduction ... xi

Chapter One
I AM: Coming to Know Thyself through Literature
by Elizabeth L. Watts

"He Knows Now"—Gail P. Gregg	1
Helping High School Students Find Themselves: Goals and Rationale	2
Introducing a Unit on Identity	3
Books as the Core	4
Shabanu	5
Before Reading *Shabanu*	6
During Reading of *Shabanu*	7
After Reading *Shabanu*	8
Supplemental Work: Other Resources to Complement Study of *Shabanu*	11
Antigone	11
Before Reading *Antigone*	12
During Reading of *Antigone*	13
After Reading *Antigone*	16
Supplemental Work for *Antigone*	18
Conclusion	18
Works Cited	19
Supplemental Resources	20

Chapter Two
John Wayne, Where Are You? Everyday Heroes and Courage
by Pamela S. Carroll

"Feeding the Birds"—Belkis L. Cabrera	27
Do We Really Need Another Hero? Implementing this Unit in High School Classes: Goals and Rationale	29
Initial Decisions for Each Teacher	30
Books as the Anchor	31
Book from the School Canon	31
Five Fictional Young Adult Books	32
Nonfiction	33
Popular Movies and Electronic Media: Instructional Core or Supplement?	34

Using the World Wide Web as a Complement	36
Beginning the Unit—Short Preview Activities	37
Preview One	38
Preview Two	39
Sustaining the Unit—Language Activities to Use During Reading	41
Mid-Unit Activity One	41
Mid-Unit Activity Two	42
Completing the Unit—Activities to Use After Reading	44
Works Cited	45
Supplemental Resources	49

Chapter Three
A Teen-age Crisis: Gangs and Violence
by Gail P. Gregg

"Did You Know the Boy?"—Belkis L. Cabrera	61
Why Study Gangs and Violence in the Language Arts Classroom?	62
Exploring the Many Causes of Violence	63
A Bridge from Violence to the Topic of Gangs	67
Gang Members: Who Are They? Why Do They Join?	68
Some Classic Options	70
Suggested Young Adult Novels	71
Works Cited	73
Supplemental Resources	75

Chapter Four
Growing Strong Family Trees
by Pamela S. Carroll

"Morning Noon and Night"—Belkis L. Cabrera	81
Selecting a Family-Oriented Topic and Literary Texts for Your Students	83
Suggestions for Whole-Class or Small-Group Reading	84
Growing Strong Family Trees: Teaching and Learning Activities	87
Planting and Nourishing the Tree with an Oral History Project	87
Guidelines for Beginning the Oral History Project	88
Conducting Oral History Interviews	90
Culminating Activity: Presenting Oral Family Histories	92
Other Activities to Include During the Growing Strong Family Trees Unit	93
Popular Music	93
Tableaux as Response for Literature, Songs, Television, Movies/Videos	96
Tune in to See Yourself: A Television Family Project	98

Other Suggested Resources to Use When Presenting a Unit on Family
    Relationships   101
Works Cited   110

Chapter Five
Homelessness in Literature, the Media, and in Our Minds
by Gail P. Gregg and Michelle Tollentino-Davidson

"Lola in a Cardboard Box"—Belkis L. Cabrera   113
Do Our Students See This Problem? Homelessness as a Topic and Theme:
    Goals and Rationale   115
Into Our Consciousness: Developing the Theme   116
From the Eyes of the Homeless: Introducing the Topic and Theme with
    Music, Videos, and Photography   116
Our Eyes on the Homeless—Introducing the Unit   117
Others' Perspectives on the Homeless   119
Teenage Homelessness and the Runaways   121
Homelessness and Families: An Activity to Increase Empathy and
    Introduce a Classic American Film in an Academic Context   123
  The Films   124
  The Activity   126
Creating Lasting Impressions and Memories: Activities that Extend
    the Classroom into the Community   128
Visiting   128
Writing   128
Visual Art: Billboard-Sized Murals   129
Interdisciplinary Connections   130
Works Cited   131
Supplemental Resources   132

Chapter Six
America: Mother of Exiles
by Gail P. Gregg, Melinda Miller, and Nan Vollbracht

"Big Green Lady"—Belkis L. Cabrera   137
A Bridge Across Early and Recent Arrivals   139
The Harsh Journey   139
Their Arrival   142
Life in Their New "Home"   143
Disappointment, Disillusionment, and Loss of Identity   145
Young Adult Novels Depicting Immigrant Life in America   146

A Final Activity or Two	149
Works Cited	149
Supplemental Resources	151

Chapter Seven
The Middle Passage
by Linda Spears-Bunton

"Mamma Says"—Iman Bunton, age 14	157
No One Can Forget the Road to Her House: Goals and Rationale for Teaching a Unit on The Middle Passage	158
The Middle Passage: A Difficult Yet Essential Feature of the Secondary School Curriculum	159
The Middle Passage: A Teacher's Beginning	160
The Middle Passage: Opening Students' Eyes, Ears, and Minds	162
A Final Word	164
Works Cited	165
Supplemental Resources	166

Chapter Eight
Aging: Our Understandings and Attitudes
by Larry S. Gordon

"He Knew Hemingway"—Belkis L. Cabrera	169
My Students are So Young: Why Should I Teach a Unit on Aging? Goals and Rationale	171
Creating Empathy	171
Introducing the Theme of Aging with Songs, Literature, Movies, and Television	172
Examining Attitudes about Aging and the Elderly	177
Exploring the Aging Process: Activities Using Literature, Graphs, and Community Involvement	178
Using the Canon and other Resources	182
Facing the Inevitable: Literature and Activities that Deal with Death	183
Works Cited	185
Supplemental Resources	187

Author Index	193
Subject/Title Index	197
About the Editors	209
About the Contributors	210

Introduction

We are delighted that you have opened our book. We had you in mind as we wrote it. A few years ago, we asked teachers of secondary English to tell us about their classroom practices. The survey results reflected your enthusiasm for teaching literature from and beyond the traditional school canon, but also your frustration—there are so many print and non-print materials that finding those that are appropriate for your students and implementing them into your curricula is a daunting task. You asked for information about how to select and incorporate materials that will appeal to the students who sit in your classes; you asked for help in arranging instruction that would fully engage your students. As teachers of middle and high school English/language arts, and now as English Education professors who work with prospective and practicing teachers, we are aware of many of your dilemmas.

You would like to spend hours poring over professional articles that discuss the theories and research that inform the ways that literature and written composition, as well as the other language arts, are viewed and taught today. You would like to have time to sit in on one colleague's wild sixth period or another's brilliant class of sophomores. Let's face it: you'd even like to read the billboards that you pass on your way to work. But you do not have time, because you are a teacher!

You want to break the pattern of teaching your literature courses chronologically, because you find that your students respond most enthusiastically to contemporary writers and ideas. Your textbooks, however, are arranged by major periods or by genres, and the department requires that you "cover" all of the important authors in the canon. You are also a bit nervous about teaching authors whose names you don't recognize from your college literature courses.

Your students are bored and reluctant when you ask them to read. When you ask them write, they play it safe and turn in clean but uninspired papers. You know that they are interested in the world around them, but you sometimes have trouble helping them make connections between their worlds and your classes.

You would like to incorporate available technologies in your classroom, but wonder where to begin. You have not yet figured out how to track down the information that will enhance your students' learning, while separating chaff from the grain. The enormity of the Web gives you the jitters.

We think we can help.

In this book, colleagues who are secondary school teachers and university teachers join us to present ideas for turning classrooms into places where students explore issues that are important to them. Within his or her chapter, each contributing author integrates traditional and contemporary literary works, popular music, television, movies and videos, the World Wide Web, and student creations.

A thematic approach to instruction provides you with an opportunity to individualize instruction without isolating students at either end of the classroom success spectrum. Thematic instruction allows students of varying abilities to focus on a common issue, through texts that differ in genre and difficulty. Using thematic units, you can organize lessons that bring the contemporary world into your classroom; instead of teaching only short stories, poems, or novels for six weeks before moving to another genre, you are able to blend print and non-print materials in a natural way, using a theme as the common frame of reference. Students can work at their own ability levels; all can participate in sophisticated thinking activities related to a common theme.

We have found that students are likely to participate in learning when they see connections between the classroom and their own lives. Too often, what is presented in the classroom seems detached from the rest of their worlds. They see homeless and exiled people, torn families, aging and neglected adults, and friends who look to gangs and violence for heroes and identities. We suggest ways to address these issues in the following chapters.

Using this Text: A Few Notes

You need not worry that the technological aspects of this text require computer sophistication. We do not pretend to be experts in the use of technology in the classroom, but we have found ways to use the Web to enhance our instruction, and in each chapter we recommend specific sites that we have found to be useful. If you have not had many opportunities to learn about using the Internet and its resources in your classroom, you might find these simplified definitions and suggestions helpful:

Definitions:

Internet: the Internet is a collection of computerized data resources that are joined together. To take advantage of the Internet, you will need to use a computer that is linked to an online service; check with your school media specialist if you are not sure that your computers are linked. If you do not have access to computers in your school, we recommend that you visit your public library; many are now connected to the Internet and are available for use by the public. The only real problem we find with the Internet, and one of its stars, the World Wide Web, is that the computer connection will not distinguish between reliable information and junk. That job is still yours.

World Wide Web: a part of the Internet, "the Web" offers information using graphics, including clips from videotapes, photographs of works of art, and so on. It also allows users to be interactive; students in your classroom can exchange questions and answers, pictures and video clips, and so on with users at NASA, the White House, the British Museum, a classroom in Amsterdam, the Netherlands, and so on. The Web expands your classroom walls. Again, though, the teacher must keep an eye on the sites that students find; there is no automatic filter that rids the screen of garbage, including pornography, hate-group diatribes, and so on.

Search Engines: a search engine is a special site that allows you to enter key words, then sit back and wait while the computer does the work of finding resources that are related to your key words. Two search engines that we use regularly, and which we find in many schools, are "Yahoo" and "WebCrawler." Following is an example of how we used Yahoo to lead us to a site dedicated in some way to the Civil Rights Movement: At the prompt for "open location," we typed in "Yahoo" then chose "Society and Culture" from the Yahoo screen, which lists general topic headings. Once we clicked the mouse at Society and Culture, a new screen appeared, from which we chose to click on "Civil Rights." On the Civil Rights page we clicked on "National Civil Rights Museum"; once there, we went deeper, into the "Virtual Tour" then further to "Martin Luther King, Jr." Our favorite link at that particular site was the text of King's "I Have a Dream" speech.

Suggestions

We have done searches and "browsed," which means we have looked around the data resources related to our theme topics, and have included representative sites in the chapters within this book. We realize, however, that sites are added daily; when you use this text, start with our sites, then search for yourself, perhaps using Yahoo or WebCrawler to help. You may find the need to limit the time you allow yourself for Web browsing; if you are looking for information on topics that are of contemporary interest, such as the ones addressed in this book, there may be thousands of related sites. We recommend seeking out sites that are supported by nationally and internationally recognized organizations, for example, a site created and supported by the American Medical Association if you want information on drug abuse among teens. We also recommend bypassing sites created and supported by individuals; you have no way of knowing how well-informed Sam Smug is, and thus the reliability of the information in his Web page, in which he extols the virtues of cocaine use, is suspect, at best. The Web, and the Internet in general, make our jobs much easier—and much more difficult.

For much more thorough information, we refer you to an excellent teacherly resource, Bard Williams' *The World Wide Web for Teachers* (Foster City, CA: IDG Books Worldwide, 1996, ISBN 1-56884-604-5), which is a volume in the simply and directly written For Dummies computer book series, available widely in book and computer stores.

There is no need to read this book from cover to cover. Choose a theme that interests you and your students, and begin there. You might start by incorporating into your existing curriculum some of the books, popular music, movies and videos, and Web sites that we suggest. We have not included any materials that are difficult to find. We have purposely suggested contemporary movies (the videos that have followed) that have been box office hits, with the hope that students who study movies and other media in your class will develop habits of mind that will make it natural for them to study movies and other media beyond your class, as well. The strategies that we recommend blend traditional classroom practices, such as whole-class reading of a single text, with newer approaches, including student creation of multimedia projects and performances. Our goal is to have students use language in real ways—to crystallize and communicate their ideas, and to make sense of the expressions of others.

Dig in, have fun and let us know what you think.

G. G. *and* S. C.

CHAPTER ONE

I AM:
COMING TO KNOW THYSELF THROUGH LITERATURE

Elizabeth L. Watts

He Knows Now
Gail P. Gregg

A gift from a failed marriage
Who never crawled or walked
Just got up and ran twenty some odd years ago
Trying to find it
Thick blonde hair a ray of sun
Whose face was always bathed in a smile
As he searched endlessly through great pain
Silently, bravely
Contacts, not glasses
Sports, not books
Excitement and chatter, reflection and solace
Is it outside or inside?
Little boy pursuits, manly passions
Sensitivity grows
A little boy, a man
A son, my soul.

Helping High School Students Find Themselves: Goals and Rationale

High school students in our English classrooms are seeking their individual identities as they come of age. These adolescents attempt to answer two questions: (1) Who am I? (2) Who am I in relation to others? Adolescents, especially high school age adolescents, may feel caught "in the middle" between childhood, where they are dependent upon adult rules and perceptions as they form their own, and adulthood, where they make moral choices that reflect the personal value and knowledge they may or may not have developed growing up. The English/language arts classroom provides the opportunity for adolescents to develop the capacity to think critically while honing their literacy abilities. Literature is a lens through which students may examine the choices of others and use similar experiences evoked by the text to evaluate their own decisions and influence future ones. Literature explored through integrated language study allows students to read, write, and discuss their reactions to literature, and to build upon those reactions to interpret what they read and to apply their interpretations to their own experiences.

When we explore individuality thematically with our students through the language arts, students may

(1) understand how choices shape who we are and who we become;
(2) learn how one's values affect decision-making;
(3) understand who they are as individuals in relation to others;
(4) understand how one's identity, or selfhood, is dynamic, changing as we go through our lives.

Discussion of individuality issues in literature, such as identity, conformity, and coming of age, may prompt students to discuss similar situations in their own lives. By engaging in reading, discussion, writing, and acting to explore individuality, students may challenge their perceptions of what it means to become an individual who makes informed decisions, who sometimes pushes the boundary or goes against the grain. Reading literature on individuality encourages students to examine their selfhood in relation to others. They can explore their own values, experiences, and perceptions about selfhood through the kaleidoscope of characters' lives in the literary works.

This chapter discusses what exploring individuality as a theme may involve in the English/language arts classroom by suggesting texts and other media you may use to explore individuality with your students. We provide prereading, reading, and postreading language arts activities for use with literature on individuality, and we suggest other language arts activities to enhance the study of this theme. The end of the chapter provides a list of resources for teachers who wish to incorporate this theme into their English/language arts classrooms.

Introducing a Unit on Identity

You might begin this unit by asking your students to consider the question, "What do you think it means to be an individual?" You and your students could engage in freewriting on this subject while listening to a portion of "Adagio for Strings," a modern piece by Samuel Barber. Freewriting (Elbow, 1973) involves writing thoughts down about any subject without censoring them and without editing for grammar, usage, or mechanics. Freewriting allows students to see what they think and to think through ideas that come to mind. To get involved in freewriting as an introduction to the unit, you may do the following:

1. Have students freewrite an answer to the question, "What do you think it means to be an individual?" on a piece of notebook paper. This involves writing an uncensored answer to the question, just writing down their thoughts. Students must keep their pens moving, even if they scribble when they lose a thought.
2. Let your students know that they will use this response for class discussion and that the discussion will occur immediately after the freewriting.
3. Begin the music recording, and tell students to write. Sit in a conspicuous place, and write along with your students, looking up periodically to monitor their progress. Freewrite with your students.
4. After four minutes, tell students to finish up their last thought. At five minutes, stop the recording and give students one minute to read their responses silently.
5. Pose the question to students once again, "What do you think it means to be an individual?" Ask students to refer to their written responses to answer the question. Write key phrases from

volunteer students' answers on the board; afterward, share your own definition as that of another individual.

Questions that you might ask in order to require students to further probe their ideas about individual identity include these:

- What is your definition of individuality?
- Do you think it is possible to be an individual and be a valuable part of a community? Explain.
- Do you think American society promotes a particular definition of individuality? Explain.
- Do you think gender-based definitions of individuality exist in our society? Explain.
- Do you think our society has definitions of individuality in childhood, adolescence, and adulthood? Explain.
- Do you think your ethnic culture affects your definition of yourself as an individual? Explain.

You could use the questions above or particular questions you come up with as a class exercise for journal entries during thematic study. You and your students might complete freewrites on these individual questions while listening to songs such as, "You Gotta Be" by Des'ree and "This Is Your Life" by En Vogue. You could ask students to keep a journal throughout the unit to record their responses to literature, thoughts about characters in the literature, thoughts about themselves during the unit, and preliminary writings for assignments on individuality. "Journaling" helps students to get their thoughts down about a subject and may help them understand their own experiences in conjunction with the literature they read.

Books as the Core

You may design your unit around two core pieces of literature and use songs, poetry, short stories, movies, and websites to round out your study of individuality. Two literary works that hold possibilities for discussion of individuality are *Shabanu* (1989) by Suzanne Fisher Staples, a novel about a Pakistani adolescent coming of age, and *Antigone* by Sophocles, a traditional member of the high school canon.

Shabanu

Adolescents may benefit from reading and exploring several issues of individuality in *Shabanu* (1989) by Suzanne Fisher Staples, a novel about an eleven-year-old Pakistani girl coming of age in the desert. This novel is a 240 page book suitable for in-class and at-home reading. The story is told from Shabanu's point of view, providing an adolescent's perception of family relationships and new experiences to which adolescent readers can relate.

Shabanu and her family are desert people, nomads who follow the water supply throughout the year. Shabanu is the younger of two girls in a family with no sons and has been allowed freedom normally forbidden to most Muslim girls. Though Shabanu exudes independence and a lack of interest in woman's work, such as cooking and cleaning, she is devoted to her family. Shabanu ponders her role as a woman in Muslim society over the course of two years during which the action takes place. According to tradition, their father has betrothed Shabanu and her older sister, Phulan, to their male first cousins, Murad and Hamir, respectively. Shabanu accepts her betrothal even though it will bring an end to her freedom. When a tragic encounter with a wealthy landowner ruins the marriage plans of Phulan, Shabanu is called upon to sacrifice the life she has dreamed of with her future husband. She must choose between upholding her family's honor or following her own inner voice.

This novel sheds light upon one Muslim family's life, the relationships between men and women, and the powerful community of Muslim women with their own inner circle of strength, tradition, and belief. Phulan embodies family honor, following the wishes of her parents and the community, willing to perform her duties as a Muslim female and wife. Shabanu's cousin Sharma embodies Shabanu's inner voice of independence. Sharma left her husband because he began beating her and then their girlchild only because Sharma did not bear him a son; she refused to be beaten and lives on her own with her daughter Fatima in the desert. Sharma also embodies the secret of personhood for Shabanu in a society that appears to subordinate women to men. She tells Shabanu that the secret to pleasing one's husband is "keeping your innermost beauty, the secrets of your soul, locked in your heart so that he must always reach out for it" (240). Shabanu must decide where she fits into society as a woman.

For Shabanu's family to remain safe, she must marry the brother of the landowner who killed Phulan's fiancé. The landowner's brother is very wealthy, around age fifty, and already has three wives, who will look upon Shabanu with disdain because she is from the desert. She will marry him when she begins menstruating, a sign of her coming of age.

Throughout the novel, Shabanu has significant experiences which are mile markers on her journey from girlhood to womanhood. First, her father sells her prized camel at the marketplace. Second, her sister Phulan marries Shabanu's fiancé. Third, she must choose between a life with Sharma and Fatima, hiding from the landowner's brother or marrying him to keep her family safe. In the end, Shabanu runs away from her parents with Mithoo, a young camel, following behind her. She decides she will go to live with Sharma and Fatima and risk being killed by her father for dishonoring the family. When Mithoo breaks his leg by stepping in a foxhole, she knows she cannot leave him and resolves that she will hold Mithoo and other secret joys inside her heart so that the landowner's brother, her new husband, will love her forever.

Staples uses Shabanu's voice to portray the desert setting along with Shabanu's culture and to help readers understand Shabanu's struggle to figure out where she fits into adult society. While reading this novel, your students could examine gender-based definitions of individuality in Shabanu's society and in our own, how ethnic culture affects self-perception, and how individuality differs in adolescence and adulthood.

Before Reading *Shabanu*

You may want to read, respond, and discuss "Thumbprint," a poem by Eve Merriam, with your students prior to reading *Shabanu*. The speaker of this poem writes about her thumbprint, how its unique design reflects her personhood, and how she makes her own "interior weather" (17). Students studying individuality may understand their own uniqueness by exploring this poem. First, discuss the significance of fingerprints. Second, pass out copies of the poem "Thumbprint" or display it on the overhead. Third, have a volunteer read the poem aloud to students. Fourth, assign sentences to particular students and have each assigned student read those sentences from the poem aloud in succession. This allows students to hear lines in this poem about individuality in different voices. Fifth, ask students to write a response to the poem. Sixth, ask volunteers to share their responses and discuss the advantages and disadvantages of being an individual. You could also extend this activity and have students write a short poem of four to seven lines about another sign of identity, such as a signature, using similes and metaphors as Merriam does to create descriptions that celebrate individuality. Students may understand their own individuality while learning how to use descriptive language to depict an image and communicate an idea. You might use this activity to lead into a work of literature on individuality, such as *Shabanu*, where the protagonist attempts to understand her uniqueness and the society around her.

During Reading of *Shabanu*

By engaging in activities while reading *Shabanu*, students may understand their own struggle to find themselves and to understand sociocultural influences on identity. Issues of conformity and individuality in Shabanu's culture may be puzzling to American students who grow up in a society where females seem to have the same opportunities and rights as males.

One activity to help students understand the context of Shabanu's quest to learn her identity is to have students keep a running record of clues or incidents in the novel that show how the Muslim society in which Shabanu lives defines the female identity. Your students could keep this record in the form of a timeline, on which they note (1) the page(s) where they find the clue or incident; (2) Shabanu's age at the time; (3) a one or two sentence summary of the event or clue; (4) Shabanu's feelings; and (5) how this clue or event contributes to Shabanu's growth or awareness of her role as a female in Muslim society. You could also allow students to make an image journal (King, 1996, 250) of these clues or incidents, noting the same information for the timeline journal on the back of each image. The image could be made on paper with crayons, fingerpaint, or pencil. Images could be kept in a folder or loose-leaf notebook. This would allow those students who learn better visually to use images to reflect their initial thoughts on the clues and incidents they find. Artistic quality should not be the focus of these images; the point is for students to "get their thoughts down" immediately so that they may reflect on how the image relates to the text. Students keep a journal of key events in Shabanu's growth and their interpretations of them; thus, your students have a record that reflects their process of making meaning, which they may revisit when making future conjectures and interpretations.

The clues and incidents students include in their timeline journals may be sociocultural in nature; you may want to review student lists individually, or in class discussion every two to three chapters, or as you deem necessary. The class could keep a running list on banner paper posted in the classroom. If you assign reading for homework, you might allow student volunteers to come into class and write phrases identifying clues or incidents they found in the reading on the chalkboard; you could use these events to begin your initial discussion of the assigned reading.

After Reading *Shabanu*

At the end of the novel, Shabanu accepts the responsibility of upholding her family honor by marrying the wealthy older man, the brother of the landowner who killed her sister's fiancé. She comes to terms with her role in the Muslim culture in which she lives, vowing to keep her innermost joys and treasures private. Our students might think that Shabanu has "sold out" to others' expectations by marrying the older man and not running away with her cousin Sharma. You may want students to complete one or more postreading activities to help them understand the novel's resolution and their interpretations of the novel, to reconcile their feelings about characters, and to learn how sociocultural expectations may influence their individuality.

After finishing *Shabanu*, students could read and respond to "Choices" by Nikki Giovanni. The poem's speaker talks about the significance of choosing a path we do not want to take but resolve to follow. This poem may help students understand Shabanu's growth into womanhood and her choice to marry the wealthy older man to ensure the safety and honor of her family. It may also give students the opportunity to discuss their own choices. First, pass copies of the poem out to students or display a transparency of the poem on the overhead projector. Second, read the poem aloud to students and then allow them to read the poem to themselves silently. Third, assign five students to read the poem aloud to the class, one reader per stanza. Your students will "listen" to the poem three times in different voices before responding to it; the emphasis different readers place on particular words in the poem may enrich the experiences it evokes and in turn the interpretations students make. Fourth, ask students to write a response to these questions: (1) What personal experiences do you think of when you read "Choices"? What does this poem mean to you? (2) How do you think this poem relates to Shabanu? Students are using writing to make connections between personal experiences and the texts they read, helping them to process their interpretation of the poem and of Shabanu's choices. Fifth, allow students to share their responses in pairs; this gives your students the opportunity to share their interpretations with another reader, who may help clarify misunderstandings and validate conjectures. Sixth, you could return to the all-class setting and use student responses as a framework for discussing postreading issues of individuality in *Shabanu*.

The "I Am" poem (Mee, 1986) is another activity you may consider using after reading works on individuality like *Shabanu*. This is a formula poem providing the first two words of each sentence; the first sentence of the poem is repeated at the end of each stanza. All the students could write an "I Am" poem about themselves and then about a character in the novel they identify with or about a character who puzzles or angers them. Writing from the point of view of the character may help students understand the character as an individual. We provide a personal example, and then one based on the character of Shabanu, below:

Personal Example*
Elizabeth Watts

I am independent and focused.
I wonder what will become of me.
I hear others telling me to live up to my name.
I want to be known as a caring person.
I am independent and focused.
I pretend I am joyful in times of trouble.
I feel that I am loved and respected by those around me.
I touch others with my teaching.
I worry about my parents growing old and how I will deal with it.
I cry when others suffer.
I am independent and focused.
I understand that I cannot save every student I meet.
I say, "I love you."
I dream that I can heal others, conquer the world, and save the weak.
I try to love others unconditionally.
I hope that I leave a legacy of learning for new teachers.
I am independent and focused.

---

*E. Watts is the author of this chapter and of this poem, prepared specifically as an "I Am..." poem for this chapter.

Shabanu's Poem

I am determined and steadfast.
I wonder why I cannot lead my own life.
I hear my father saying I carry family honor.
I want my sister to stand up for herself.
I am determined and steadfast.
I pretend I am obedient to my father's wishes.
I feel like I cannot save my family by marrying another.
I touch my sister's hand and wish her well in marriage.
I worry about Mithoo and my family once I am gone.
I cry because I have to choose between my life and a life of servitude.
I am determined and steadfast.
I understand that I can run away and live on my own if I so choose.
I say, "I love you, Father."
I dream of a life of freedom, living alone in the desert.
I try to find myself and understand my womanhood as a Muslim.
I hope my new husband will love me.
I am determined and steadfast.

Students could share these poems in small groups according to the character they choose. These poems may help them to understand themselves and may cause them to rethink their interpretations of characters' motivations and choices.

Another activity you may consider using relates to society's gender-based definitions of individuality. Students may use their timeline journals on Shabanu to get an idea of what gender-based definitions of individuality entail. First, have students meet in triads to discuss how Muslim society dictated female individuality for Shabanu; students use their timeline journals to discuss indicators of a prescribed Muslim female identity, how Shabanu learns of it, and how she reacts to it. Second, return to the all-class setting and discuss student findings. Third, discuss the issue of prescribed gender-based individuality in American culture. Fourth, in small groups students could create a portfolio of examples from websites, magazines, newspapers, and other media to show what gender-based definitions of individuality exist and how they are depicted. This portfolio could be made of samples from five websites, clippings from magazines and newspapers, and if possible video clips from commercials, movies, or television shows. Each student could also interview at least two individuals about gender-based individuality, depending on the gender the group chooses with a group-created questionnaire. Students could have time in class to work on this project. They could bring in magazines and newspapers; you could also check with the media specialist for these items. You may consider giving students a two-week time span to complete the project depending upon your schedule constraints and student accessibility to resources and one another outside of school. This project might help students to understand the issues with which fictional characters like Shabanu—and real people, too—deal. It may also help your students understand the pressures they face while coming of age, deciding who they are as males or females in a larger community that may appear to confine individuals with gender-based expectations.

Supplemental Work: Other Resources to Complement Study of *Shabanu*

Your students could find poems, songs, or characters in film and television that remind them of Shabanu's quest for self, or their own quest for self. They could also study literature about an individual's rights and duties to the community by reading essays in Ayn Rand's *Virtue of Selfishness: A New Concept of Egoism* (1964).

Students could view the film *Little Women* and analyze and respond to the gender-defined roles the protagonists face. As an extension of the postreading activity about gender and individuality, students could compare and contrast gender roles in *Shabanu*, *Little Women*, and in American culture. This may help them understand how culture affects prescribed gender roles and individuality.

Antigone

Antigone, by Sophocles, is a Greek tragedy about the daughter of the late Oedipus the king. Subject to rule by the new king, her uncle Creon, Antigone decides to bury her brother Polynices, an expatriate who had attempted to conquer the city. The gods' laws state that the dead must be buried, but Creon decrees that Antigone's brother is to be left outside the city walls, a victim of war, unburied. Anyone who buries Polynices will be stoned to death. Antigone decides where her allegiance lies, to her family and the gods' law as opposed to Creon's law, and appears determined to suffer the consequences.

Sophocles layers various issues through the central conflict in the play while presenting action in short episodes suitable for in-class reading and discussion. Seventy pages in length, *Antigone* offers readers hard-hitting dialogue containing literary elements that can be studied, such as the initial scene between Antigone and her sister Ismene, which addresses gender roles and individuality.

Antigone and Creon assert themselves as individuals at polarized positions. They have different definitions of loyalty. Creon defines loyalty as adhering to his laws, the laws of the state, whereas Antigone defines loyalty as fulfilling the wishes of the gods by burying her brother and remaining true to her family. Students may benefit from reading *Antigone*, which provides opportunities for discussion about the significance of individuality in relation to self and others. During adolescence, students try to figure out who they are and who they are in relation to others; by reading and exploring *Antigone*, they may understand their own definitions of individuality and that being an individual involves taking a stand with the group or against it according to one's values.

Students may also explore gender-based definitions of individuality by examining the actions of Creon, Antigone, and Antigone's sister Ismene. Ismene conforms to Creon's wishes; she loves her brother but fears punishment if she helps Antigone defy the king. Ismene attempts to convince Antigone to follow Creon's decree by reminding her, "Remember we are women, we're not born to contend with men" (62). Antigone chooses to follow her own course by burying her brother and going against Creon's law.

Before Reading *Antigone*

Before beginning *Antigone*, students may benefit from reading and responding to "The Road Not Taken" by Robert Frost. First, pass out copies of the poem to students, and read it aloud. Second, ask another student to read it aloud to the class. Third, have students read the poem to themselves silently again, writing down on the hard copy of the poem key words noting similar experiences and words or phrases that they associate with the poem while reading, what we call "associative jotting." The students will have "heard" the poem three times before responding to it, giving them time to process its literal meaning and evaluate prior experiences called up by it.

You might model the "associative jotting" by showing a transparency copy of the poem on the overhead projector, reading the first stanza aloud and noting your own thoughts as you read. Students then engage in "associative jotting" by writing their thoughts down on the hard copy of the poem while reading it, a practice that allows them to identify and record thoughts or experiences evoked by the text, which they may then use to inform their interpretation of the poem itself (Rosenblatt, 1978). You might ask students to use these notes to make a written response to the poem drawing upon their own background knowledge relative to the poem and its theme of individuality.

Fourth, have students use the notes they made about the poem in "associative jotting" to write a paragraph or more in response to the poem within ten minutes. This response may address one of two questions: (1) What do you think this poem says about individuality? (2) Have you ever taken "the road less traveled"? Inform students that they will be sharing their responses in pairs and afterward may volunteer to share their response with the class.

Fifth, place students in pairs and give them roughly seven minutes to read their partner's response to the poem, write comments or questions on their partner's response, and then discuss what the poem means to them. This gives each student the opportunity to discuss the poem with another reader, who may or may not have the same interpretation. Students may be more prone to ask questions about the poem or to discuss personal experiences evoked by it in a one-on-one peer setting. When you return to the all-class setting, you could have a volunteer read the poem aloud and then ask a few students to share their responses. Collect student poem copies and responses to find out how they processed the poem and responded to it. You may use this activity as a segue into introducing *Antigone*, a play about a young woman who takes a road less traveled.

During Reading of *Antigone*

Students may benefit from engaging in activities while reading *Antigone*. Through these activities, you may (1) focus on how the theme of individuality manifests itself in the play; (2) understand how students are processing the text; (3) find any gaps in their comprehension; and (4) give students the opportunity to voice their working interpretations of the text. Here, you are paying attention to how and what students understand about a text, what Langer (1992, 1995) calls a reader's envisionment: "the understanding a reader has about a text at a particular point in time; what a reader understands, the questions that develop, as well as the hunches that arise about how the piece might unfold" (1992, 39). To chronicle their envisionment while reading *Antigone* aloud in class, you could have students create a triple-entry or J3 journal, an extension of the double-entry journal, developed by Pamela Carroll. First, have students divide each page of the journal into three sections by drawing a line down the middle of the page two-thirds of the way down. Thus, there are two columns on the page, as in the double-entry format, and an additional space at the bottom. Students use the left column to jot down quotations, retell events, describe characters, and make observations about the literature. Then they record their corresponding questions or reflective comments in the right column. At the bottom of the page, a second reader responds to information contained in both columns of the first reader's double-entry. The second reader may respond with particular observations, questions, connecting experiences, or alternative interpretations of textual aspects the first reader commented upon.

With individuality being the focus of study in *Antigone*, students could note key events or thoughts about characters on the left side of the page, responding to these on the right side. For instance, after reading the prologue to the play, where Antigone and Ismene discuss the possibility of burying their brother, students may label Ismene's protest as weakness. They may also have questions about Creon's law and why Antigone considers breaking it to stay loyal to her family name. After reading the prologue, or first scene, you might model the triple-entry format and then have students complete their own triple-entry journal. You could ask students to complete triple-entry journals as collections of information about Creon, Ismene, and Antigone as individuals to be used for discussion, role-play, or formal essay writing. Not only does the triple-entry journal get students thinking about the text, but it gives them the opportunity to confirm, clarify, and perhaps question their thinking through response from another reader. You might act as the second reader or let another student do so. This way, students' questions and evolving interpretations of the text do not go unanswered, which may occur in an all-class discussion with one teacher and thirty other students. Each student gets a response from another reader who may have similar or contrasting conjectures and interpretations about the text.

Writing in conjunction with reading a text such as *Antigone* with format and language that may be new could help your students to focus on their evolving understanding of the text rather than on what they could interpret as its mind-boggling structure and style. Not only are students creating a record of what they understand, but they may be learning a strategy for reading that they can use with any type of text, expository or narrative.

Students may also learn to understand characters as individuals, and in turn learn about themselves as individuals by studying a character's motivation. Mitchell (1995) has her students write a monologue to be delivered to the character involved; students write monologues when the class reaches an especially puzzling or upsetting portion of a text. Students could discuss reactions to something a character did, give advice to the character, or impressions of the character and where the character seems to be heading. Adolescents studying individuality and reading a work such as *Antigone* could create one-minute monologues as a means of understanding a particular character as an individual and create monologues about their own experiences to understand themselves.

Your students could create a one-minute monologue immediately after reading any scene that they find troubling; the writing can become a vehicle for students to use as a way of making sense of the event and trying to understanding why the character acted a particular way. Give students a five-minute time limit to write the monologue; their initial writing is more prone to be genuine and reflective of their interpretations of the play at that moment. Next, give the students seven to ten minutes to create a one-minute monologue of the character, answering the original student monologue to or about the character (King, 1993). By writing from the character's point of view, students may consider the character's role in the plot of the text and may understand the character as a living, breathing entity with emotions, motivations, and loyalties. Third, give students about ten minutes to reread both monologues and then write a short response to, "What do you think (Creon, Antigone, Ismene) values most? Explain. Do you think he or she acts as an individual or conforms to others' expectations? Explain." As an extension, you could have students (1) recall a decision they made that puzzled or angered someone else; (2) write a monologue to and about them from the other person's point of view; (3) write a monologue responding to that person; and (4) respond to, "What did you value most in that situation? Explain. Did you act as an individual or conform to others' expectations? Explain. How did that experience affect your identity?" Students may better understand their actions, themselves, and better relate to characters in the play, portrayed by Sophocles as unique individuals in a crisis.

After Reading *Antigone*

At the end of *Antigone*, Creon decides to free Antigone from the tomb in which he sealed her as punishment for burying her brother. He arrives too late, only to find her dead. Students may question why Antigone hangs herself, why the playwright has Creon arrive too late, and what the play itself says about individuals standing up for their beliefs. To come to terms with their final envisionment of the literary work, which includes what they understand, do not understand, and questions they still have (Langer, 1995), you might have students complete one or more postreading activities.

You might use the triple-entry journal for students to write about an essay by Ayn Rand, "Doesn't Life Require Compromise?" in *The Virtue of Selfishness: A New Concept of Egoism* (1964), a collection of essays about individual rights and conformist ethics. Some adolescent readers of *Antigone* have particular difficulty understanding why Antigone chooses to die for her beliefs. Rand's three-page essay may help students understand why Antigone both refuses to compromise her loyalty to her family and sacrifices her life to uphold the law of the gods. It may also help students clarify their final envisionment of the play. Read Rand's "Doesn't Life Require Compromise?" aloud in class and have students respond to it in a triple-entry journal, choosing and commenting on aspects of the essay that help them to understand Antigone's decision. Then have students exchange the triple-entry journal with a partner, who responds to the reader's observations, questions, and key quotations on the left side of the page and reflective comments on the right side of the page. Have students return journals to their respective owners; then, in an all-class setting, discuss action in *Antigone* within the context of Rand's essay and allow students to use their triple-entry journals as a basis for their comments. By reading Rand's essay, "Doesn't Life Require Compromise?" students may raise questions and discuss the motives behind Creon and Antigone's conflict.

Imagemaking (King, 1993) is another way to help students understand their final envisionments of a literary work. King promotes imagemaking as a way to transcend words and express our thinking through pictures. When the class finishes reading *Antigone*, have students create images that reflect how they feel about the outcome of the plot at the end of the play. Provide students with fingerpaints or crayons in a variety of colors; students may create images with vivid color to express their thoughts. If you do not have access to these, allow students to use pens or pencils. Give them thirty seconds to one minute to do so. This way, students are most likely to draw or paint an image reflective of their gut responses.

After students create the images that reflect what they feel at the play's end, you might ask each student to share the images in small groups. You could have students discuss what the image says about their feelings, promoting dialogue about the play's outcome. When the students finish sharing in their groups, have them write down their questions about the play, questions they would pose to the playwright, and what they think the play says about being an individual on another sheet of paper. Then have students post their images on a bulletin board in the room or place them on a table for the class to view. When you return to the all-class setting, you and your students may discuss what you think this collection of images says about interpretations of the play's ending, focusing on color, dimension, and tone of the images as a group. You could use student questions and interpretations about individuality as a basis for discussion about the play.

You could also use collages as another activity to help students synthesize their thoughts about literature on individuality, such as *Antigone*. Each student could choose a major character from the text and create a collage about the character as an individual. First, you could have students bring in magazines; your media specialist may also let you have old magazines. Second, provide students with glue and scissors. Third, have students cut out pictures and words that they believe represent the character they chose and paste them on an eight and one-half by eleven sheet of paper. When students finish their collages, have them use their individual collages to write a short paper on one of the following topics:

(1) What do you think makes your character an individual? Why was it important for the author to include this character in the literary work?
(2) Write about how you think your character would approach two controversial issues in today's society. Would your character be a conformist or nonconformist? Explain.
(3) If your character could create an ideal society, what would it look like? Would there be inequality? Definitions of individuality according to gender?
(4) Create a conversation between you and your character that reflects your thoughts as portrayed in your collage.

You might want students to support their claims by referring back to the character's actions in the text. If students have been keeping a journal while reading the literary work, you might allow them to refer back to that record as a source for the collage and the essay.

Supplemental Work for *Antigone*

Students may do small-group research on persons in their community and in history who have distinguished themselves as individuals standing up for their beliefs; they could make oral presentations to the class about these figures. Persons such as environmental activists like Marjory Stoneman Douglas and John McPhee, and civil rights activists, such as Dr. Martin Luther King, Jr. and Gandhi, and current political leaders often intrigue high school students.

Students could also study artistic works about individuals like Antigone who maintained loyalty to their beliefs despite the consequences. Ayn Rand's *Anthem* and Lois Lowry's *The Giver* are two works that chronicle the quest of persons to understand society and their place within it. Mary E. Lyons' *Letters From a Slave Girl* chronicles the life of Harriet Jacobs through a series of letters she writes in a diary during her coming of age as an African-American woman enslaved.

Your students may also benefit from watching and discussing such films about individuality in the face of conformity as *Eleni*, about a Greek woman who tries to save her village, and *Separate but Equal*, the story of Thurgood Marshall, the attorney who handled the civil rights case for equal education of African Americans, Brown vs. the Board of Education of Topeka.

Conclusion

The activities we suggest could be used with literary works on individuality with modifications to suit your students' needs and the texts you read. By studying individuality, students may learn to appreciate their own beliefs, values, talents, and uniqueness by exploring the lives and choices of others on the same quest for selfhood. You may learn more about yourself as an English/language arts practitioner and person in the same exploration.

Works Cited

Barber, S. (1989). Adagio for strings. On *Orchestra music selections*. Performed by the St. Louis Symphony Orchestra. Leonard Slatkin, Conductor. EMI Records.

Des'ree. (1992). You gotta be. On *Mind adventures*. 550/Sony.

Elbow, P. (1973). *Writing without teachers*. London: Oxford University Press.

Eleni. (1985). (PG). CBS Productions. Directed by Peter Yates. Produced by Nick Vanoff, Mark Pick, and Nick Gage. Starring Kate Nelligan and John Malkovich.

En Vogue. (1992). This is your life. On *Funky divas*. Elektra.

Frost, R. (1965). The road not taken. In H. Felleman (Ed.), *Poems That Live Forever*. New York: Doubleday. 317.

Giovanni, N. (1978). Choices. In *Cotton candy on a rainy day*. Reprint in *Literature and Language* (1994). Evanston, IL: McDougal, Littell and Co., 49.

King, N. (1993). *Storymaking and drama*. Portsmouth, NH: Heinemann.

King, N. (1996). *Playing their part*. Portsmouth, NH: Heinemann.

Langer, J. (1992). Rethinking literature instruction. In J. Langer (Ed.), *Literature instruction: A focus on student response*. Urbana, IL: National Council of Teachers of English.

Langer, J. (1995). *Envisioning literature*. New York: Teachers College Press & Newark, DE: International Reading Association.

Little Women. (1994). (PG). Columbia Pictures. Directed by Gillian Armstrong. Produced by Denise Di Novi. Starring Winona Ryder, Claire Danes, and Susan Sarandon.

Lowry, L. (1993). *The giver*. New York: Bantam Doubleday.

Lyons, M. E. (1992). *Letters from a slave girl*. New York: Aladdin Paperbacks.

Mee, S. (1986), September 8. "I Am." *Scholastic voice*.

Merriam, E. (1964). Thumbprint. In *It doesn't always have to rhyme*. Reprint in *Understanding literature* (1984). New York: MacMillan, 217.

Mitchell, D. (1995). "Teaching ideas: Ways into literature." *English Journal, 84*, 5, 106–110.

Rand, A. (1964). "Doesn't Life Require Compromise?" In A. Rand (Ed.), *The virtue of selfishness: A new concept of egoism*. New York: Signet, 79–81.

Rand, A. (1995). *Anthem*. Fiftieth Anniversary Edition. New York: Signet.

Rosenblatt, L. (1978). *The reader, the text, the poem*. Carbondale, IL: Southern Illinois University Press.

Sophocles. (1982). *Antigone*. In R. Fagles (Ed.) *The three Theban plays: Antigone, Oedipus the king, Oedipus at Colonus*. New York: Penguin.

Staples, S. F. (1989). *Shabanu: Daughter of the wind*. New York: Random House.

Supplemental Resources

Books

Chopin, K. (1972). *The awakening*. New York: Avon Books.
> While vacationing at the beach with her husband and children, Edna Pontellier realizes that she has a need and a passion within her to be different from the other Creole women (whom she calls the "mother women") around her. The story takes place in late nineteenth century Louisiana. Upon returning home from vacation, Edna's feelings of entrapment and her inability to be who she desires to become intensify.
>
> Potentially controversial elements include adultery and suicide.

Cisneros, S. (1991). *The house on Mango Street*. New York: Random House.
> This is a story of a young girl growing up on Mango Street in the Latino section of Chicago. The young protagonist, Esperanza Cordero, wants more from life than the low expectations others have for her. Esperanza finds her individuality through writing and is able to invent herself.
>
> Some potentially controversial elements in this novel may be references to sexual abuse, physical abuse, and prejudice.

Hawthorne, N. (1965). *The scarlet letter*. New York: Bantam Books.
> Set in colonial New England, this novel is about a woman, Hester Prynne, who has a child out of wedlock and disgraces the community. The community forces her to wear a scarlet colored "A" on her clothing, announcing her sin to all. Despite the harassment and scorn she faces, Hester has the will to fight the rules of conformity.
>
> A possible controversial element in this novel is the topic of adultery.

Hurston, Z. N. (1973). *Their eyes were watching god.* New York: Harper and Row.
>
> This novel is about one woman's evolution through three marriages. Despite others' expectations and prejudices, this woman realizes that she must learn to enjoy life and live for herself.
>
> Language may be a controversial element in this novel.

Le Guin, U.K. (1968). *The wizard of earth and sea.* New York: Bantam.
>
> This novel is about Ged, a young wizard growing up in the multicultural world of Earthsea. He finds himself by slowly understanding his inner strength and by saving others. He learns to make informed choices while battling with his inner self in the course of the plot, portrayed by a threatening shadow he releases in an egotistical battle of magic.

Lowry, L. (1993). *The giver.* New York: Bantam Doubleday.
>
> This novel is about Jonas, a boy raised in a futuristic, controlled society in which there is no pain and no freedom. Everyone in the community has an assigned duty to make society function. As a twelve-year-old, Jonas is chosen to be the next Receiver for the community. He soon learns that this means he must receive all memories of life before "sameness." As he learns about pain, love, death, and freedom, he realizes that he wants to be an individual with the ability to make his own life choices.

Lyons, M.E. (1992). *Letters from a slave girl.* New York: Aladdin Paperbacks.
>
> Lyons writes the story of the author Harriet Jacobs as a young African-American slave coming of age through a series of letters Harriet writes to friends and family. She refuses to be enslaved and goes to drastic measures to ensure her freedom.
>
> One controversial element may be reference to a sexual relationship between Harriet and her slave master.

Rand, A. (1995). *Anthem.* Fiftieth Anniversary Edition. New York: Signet.
>
> This novel is set in a society where all individuality has been wiped out, decisions are made by committees, and all things exist in collectives. One man, Equality 7-2521 searches for some way to understand his longings to think and to make choices for himself. In this struggle to recognize himself, he comes close to losing his life before he escapes and finds the lost holy word, "I."

Salinger, J. D. (1945). *The catcher in the rye*. London: Little, Brown and Company.

This novel is told from the perspective of its protagonist, Holden Caulfield, a young man on the verge of a mental breakdown. He searches for his identity and reflects on his family life after the death of his younger brother.

Notable controversial elements in this novel are profanity, Holden's sexual experiences, and a potential homosexual encounter between Holden and his former teacher.

Twain, M. (1959). *The adventures of Huckleberry Finn*. New York: Signet.

This classic adventure story centers around the friendship between two outcasts, a young rebel named Huck and an African slave named Jim. The novel chronicles their trip down the Mississippi River in search for self-identity and destiny.

Controversial topics include racial slurs.

Movies

Braveheart. (1988). Paramount Pictures. Directed by Mel Gibson. Produced by Mel Gibson, Alan Ladd, Jr., and Bruce Davey. Starring Mel Gibson.

William Wallace leads Scotland to fight for its freedom against the English. Wallace stands up for his beliefs unto death.

Controversial elements are some violent scenes and profanity.

Dead poets' society. (1990). Touchstone Pictures. Directed by Peter Weir. Produced by Steven Haft, Paul Junger Witt, and Tony Thomas. Starring Robin Williams.

John Keating teaches English at an all-boys' prep school that encourages conformity. He inspires his students to be individuals and to live life to the fullest.

This contains some profanity and addresses suicide and the questioning of adult authority by young adults.

Eleni. (1985). CBS Productions. Directed by Peter Yates. Produced by Nick Vanoff, Mark Pick, and Nick Gage. Starring Kate Nelligan and John Malkovich.

A Greek woman tries to save her village from post-World War II Communists.

This contains some violent scenes.

Little women. (1994). Columbia Pictures. Directed by Gillian Armstrong. Produced by Denise Di Novi. Starring Winona Ryder, Claire Danes, and Susan Sarandon.

    This movie, based on the book by Alcott, is about four sisters growing up in New England during the 1860s. The film explores the relationships of these sisters and the female roles society prescribes for them. Jo, the most independent sister, becomes a writer and shatters the female stereotypes of her time.

Separate but equal. (1991). Picture Home Videos. Directed by George Stevens, Jr. Produced by Sidney Poitier, Burt Lancaster, and Richard Kiley. Starring Sidney Poitier.

    This is the story of the landmark civil rights case, Brown vs. the Board of Education of Topeka. Poitier stars as Thurgood Marshall, the prosecuting attorney who fought for equal education of African Americans.

Poems

Frost, R. (1965). The Road Not Taken. In H. Felleman (Ed.) *Poems that live forever*. New York: Doubleday, 317.

    This poem is about an individual's choice.

Giovanni, N. (1978). Choices. In *Cotton candy on a rainy day*. Reprint in *Literature and language* (1994) Evanston, IL: McDougal, Littell and Company, 49.

    The poem is about one person's views on making difficult life choices.

Merriam, E. (1964). Thumbprint. In *It doesn't always have to rhyme*. Reprint in *Understanding literature* (1984). New York: MacMillan. 217.

    Merriam describes a thumbprint to explore individuality.

Rich, A. (1989). Delta. In *Time's power: poems 1985-1988*. New York: W. W. Norton and Company, 32.

    This two stanza poem is about being a true individual.

Plays

Hansberry, L. (1994). *A raisin in the sun*. R. Nemiroff (Ed.) New York: Penguin.

    An African American family struggles in everyday life. Set in the 1940s, this play centers around the quest for identity.

Short Prose

Le Guin, U. K. (1988). The ones who walk away from Omelas. In P. Prescott (Ed.), *Norton book of American short stories*. New York: Norton, 566–571.

In this utopian society, everyone feels good and lives well all the time. One child is the sacrificial lamb for the community; the child endures suffering, misery, and unhappiness for the society. The child is kept locked in a small room with little light and just enough nourishment to remain alive. Every person in the society sees this person one time. This story is about those persons who choose to live in the society and those who leave.

Songs

Blues Traveler. (1994) Stand. On *Four*. A & M Records.

This song deals with facing opposition when trying to be an individual and not conforming to others' wishes.

Brooks, G. (1994) The Dance. On *Garth Brooks the hits*. Pearl Records.

The singer looks back on his life and decides that if he had to relive his life, he would not change anything. He understands that the pain and suffering he experienced have made him into who he is.

Bruce, T., and Wiseman, C. (1995) Someone else's dream. Sung by Faith Hill on *It matters to me*. Almo Music Corporation.

A young girl feels that her entire life has been lived to please others. She wants to live her life for herself and to celebrate her individuality.

Dave Mathews Band. (1994) Dancing nancies. On *Under the table and dreaming*. RCA Records, 1994.

This is about discovering self-identity and individuality.

Des'ree. (1992) You gotta be. On *Mind adventures*. 550/Sony.

Des'ree gives advice on how to face the world as an individual.

En Vogue. (1992) This is your life. On *Funky divas*. Elektra.

This deals with finding out who you are, following your dreams, and ignoring negativity.

Rush. (1990) Freewill. On *Rush chronicles*. Polygram.

This discusses relying on fate or actively choosing your own path. Potentially controversial as it addresses religious ideas.

Rush. (1990) Subdivisions. On *Rush chronicles*. Polygram.
>   This focuses on not fitting in. It specifically deals with high school, a time when being an individual is not always popular.

Web Sites

http://www.greatbasin.net/ dconnor/noframes/qind.html
>   This site features quotes from politicians, actors, actresses, and authors about individuality. These could be used as prompts for discussion or writing prompts.

http://people.delphi.com/~eccentric/eccentricity.html
>   This site is dedicated to individuality. Students could use this site to learn about famous people and their individuality.

http://www.bibble.org/quotes/individuality.html
>   This site offers quotes about the individual in society from authors, politicians, and other celebrities. These could be used to introduce the topic of individuality and conformity; they could also be used as writing prompts.

CHAPTER TWO

JOHN WAYNE, WHERE ARE YOU? EVERDAY HEROES AND COURAGE

Pamela S. Carroll

Feeding the Birds
Belkis L. Cabrera

She feeds the birds old Cuban bread
Breaking the ends into pieces
Crumbs piercing wrinkled veins
She calls them by name
And whispers to the cracks
Along the sidewalk
Beneath her tired bones
There is life
Vibrating as she tosses her gift
Over the hungry beaks that
Peck and squirm and gurgle
Mama
She wears the sun around
Her shoulders and her white hair
An iridescent cloak of light
Wraps her into a sweat
And she smiles
As the brief-cased men
Push their way and kick
Their black moccasins

And their low patterned socks
At the air
And at her children
The ladies with their Sunday
Skirts and dresses
And church-ridden faces
Toss their polished nails
Around their purses
Flash a red-mouthed "Crazy"
And as they cross themselves
Her back curves against their words
She laughs a broken laugh
And stares beyond their eyes and lips
At the sky
At her babies' wings
And in her mind
She flies.

Do We Really Need Another Hero?
Implementing this Unit in High School Classes: Goals and Rationale

Adolescence is, by definition, a time of physical, emotional, social, and intellectual change; for many adolescents, these changes are confusing and confounding. Fortunately, many teens emerge from this period of rapid changes with few if any lasting scars as evidence of the journey, but such is not the case for all adolescents. In *Adolescence: Guiding Youth Through the Perilous Ordeal* (1995), clinical psychologist Miller Newton notes that today's youth face unprecedented and life-threatening risks. The concerns of previous generations of adolescents may seem naive and benign—concerns such as facing physical maturation, changed relations with peers, and the tension of the need for independence from and dependence on parents. Adolescence today, laced as it is for many with gang violence, drugs, depression, and thrill-seeking, is often a "perilous ordeal." Perhaps now, more than ever before, our adolescent students need to find examples of heroic behavior and to develop definitions of courage that they can draw upon when they face serious challenges and temptations.

It is unrealistic to assume that any literature-based program will solve the problems that teachers, parents, and teens face in today's schools and society. However, reading and studying literature may help students develop perspectives and attitudes that will lead them to see that people can be heroic and virtuous, even at the edge of the twenty-first century. Through reading and studying literature, students may begin to develop or enhance their set of personal values, and thus empower themselves to establish high standards for themselves, and to resist negative pressure from those who encourage them toward dangerous or criminal activities.

This chapter suggests that we, as teachers, lead students in a consideration of heroes and courage from the different perspectives provided by books, movies, and other media. Through participation in this kind of literature-based study, our students will explore a range of human responses to serious challenges. Literature and other media provide no miracles for the teens of any generation, but perhaps lessons in which courage is a focus will help adolescents consider strong and positive options for dealing with the problems and frustrations they face.

Initial Decisions for Each Teacher

As an individual teacher, you will need to decide how to balance the focus on heroes and courage with attention to other issues that students determine to be important to them, as readers and thinkers, during the study of this unit. None of the works that we suggest immediately below, or in the annotated lists at the end of the chapter, is exclusively "about" courage, and we believe that students should be given the opportunity to find and focus on other important issues, topics, and themes within the texts as they read and study. Nevertheless, each of those listed herein presents courage as a significant theme.

This chapter suggests print and nonprint resources and teaching activities that include attention to everyday heroes and uncommon courage—people who seemed to be leading normal lives until they found themselves in situations that called for especially courageous behavior. But our focus can easily be modified according to your goals. Some of you might decide to have your students, in either a whole-class or small-group format, focus solely on one category of hero, such as heroes in sports, science, the performing arts, medicine, business, religion. Others might want to have students engage in a genre study of heroes, beginning perhaps with heroes in mythology and folk tales. Another option would be for students to study heroes and courage in groups, each with a particular genre to be explored; for example, one group might read and study romances, then come to conclusions about how heroes and courage are portrayed in romance novels, movies, stories, and poems, while another reads science fiction and then works together to define heroes and courage in terms of sci-fi novels, movies, stories, and drama. Each group could give attention to the heroic traits of the characters in their own genres. Possibilities are many.

As the teacher, you will also need to decide whether your students will approach the theme primarily through the academic study of literary texts, from within or beyond the school canon, through critical sessions in which they view and study movies/videos, and/or through careful examination of other contemporary print and non-print sources such as magazines, newspapers, and World Wide Web sites. The suggestions within this chapter are a starting place, a set of ideas from which you can select the ideas that appeal to you. We encourage you to modify our ideas for your own purposes, with the nature of your own teaching situation, and the interests and needs of your students, in mind.

Books as the Anchor

Books from the School Canon

You are best qualified to decide on the format for an instructional unit that focuses on heroes and courage. You might decide that the entire class will read a book in common, and use that text as the centerpiece of the unit of study. Another teacher might choose to use the "Book Club" idea so that several different texts are studied concurrently, followed by discussions involving first the small groups of students who have read the same texts, and next, the whole class of students, using the common themes they found in their different texts as the unifying thread. Whichever design for instruction you choose, one or more of the following selections, listed chronologically in terms of original publication dates, may be useful as anchors for the unit of study; these choices include books that you will recognize as standard secondary school fiction—works from the school canon:

Stephen Crane's *The Red Badge of Courage* (1895) is a story that pits boy-soldier Henry Fleming against others in war, and against himself in a psychological and spiritual battle as he attempts to make sense of the war and the inevitability of death, and his own (un)courageous reactions to the reality of war.

Zora Neale Hurston's *Their Eyes Were Watching God* (1937) is a story in which Janie severs ties with the only family she has known in order to travel into a world that is new and often cruel to her; she seeks love, respect, and a life that she can call her own, and must fight against others' judgments of her at almost each turn.

Ernest Hemingway's *The Old Man and the Sea* (1952) is a short novel in which the old fisherman, Santiago, triumphs over a giant fish and demonstrates to himself and a young boy that the value of the prize is second to the glory of an intense battle.

Harper Lee's *To Kill A Mockingbird* (1961) is a story in which racial hatred ignites in a Southern town when a Black man is accused of raping a White woman, and only one man, lawyer Atticus Finch, demonstrates the courage to seek justice for the accused through a fair, unprejudiced trial, and to try to quell the explosion.

Five Fictional Young Adult Books

The following five contemporary young adult books allow secondary students to explore the theme of everyday heroes and uncommon courage while also considering, from contemporary perspectives, issues that are important to them as adolescents. These books are particularly appropriate for those who are reluctant readers; if you find that you have a student who turns away from a thick literature textbook, perhaps overwhelmed by what seems to be an impossible amount of material, we recommend that you put one of these books in his or her hands. None is a work from the school canon, but each has the potential to speak to teen readers:

Lois Lowry's *The Giver* (1991) is a different kind of book—a troubling yet ultimately triumphant fantasy. In it, Jonas, who is appointed the job of his society's "Receiver of the Memory," becomes aware that the world has not always been colorless, flat, and tightly organized around a hierarchical structure. He learns, too, that the people whom he has trusted, including his own father, have deceived and betrayed him and the others. He makes the decision to run from the community in order to try to save it. Readers might examine the choices Jonas makes and decide whether or not he acts courageously; they may also focus on the consequences of each of those choices, then think about the consequences of their own assumptions, decisions, and actions.

Rodman Philbrick's *Freak the Mighty* (1993) deals with courage from the perspective, among others, of the courage it takes to be loyal as a friend. In this fine novel, two misfits befriend each other; Kevin is brilliant, but suffers from a condition that stunts his external growth. His internal organs outgrow his body, and the condition eventually leads to his early death. Kevin's friend, Max, is in many ways his opposite; Max is a physically huge adolescent whose intellectual growth seems stunted. Together, though, the misfits become "Freak the Mighty"; Max carries Kevin on his shoulders into the many adventures and challenges they face. In their ordinary and extreme experiences, the friends exhibit the courage to recognize their own limitations, to risk rejection by peers, to face the adults who have proven untrustworthy, as well as to depend on those who have proven they can be trusted and loved.

Mildred Taylor's *Roll of Thunder, Hear My Cry* (1976) is a Newberry Award winning novel that has earned praise from readers of all abilities and middle/secondary school levels. It is the story of the Logan family and their community in the Depression-era South. Young adolescent

Cassie Logan tries to make sense of racial prejudices and inequities; she observes enough of each to grow from innocence toward reluctant recognition of the existence of social evils. The love of the Logan family, their loyalty to the land, and their determination to make the community a better place become Cassie's sources of strength and courage. Many high school students will have read this novel while in middle school; we believe that the book is worth revisiting with an eye toward its courageous and heroic characters and actions.

Chris Crutcher's *Stotan!* (1986) allows the reader to feel like a participant with the other members of a high school swim team who are the protagonists in the novel. The swimmers learn from Coach Max that the courage to face one's challenges must come from a strong internal desire to succeed in the face of obstacles. His lesson transcends application to their intense training for swimming competition. When one swimmer's family is killed in a boating accident which was caused by a drunk friend, his courage to face each new day is severely tested; while he struggles to come to terms with his new life, his friends must fight to find ways to break through his barriers and reach out to him.

Walter Dean Myers' *Fallen Angels* (1988), told from the perspective of teenage soldiers in the Vietnam conflict, powerfully depicts the courage—and lack of courage—of teenage soldiers in war. This book does not glamorize war or its heroes; nor does it present John Wayne-type soldiers who are confident about their reasons for being involved in battles on foreign soil. Teen readers are pressed to examine their assumptions about the definition of courage in the face of such circumstances.

Nonfiction

We have found that the theme of courage and heroes lends itself well to cross-disciplinary study; when we deal with the theme in this way, planning lessons with social studies/history teachers so that the issues raised in one class are reinforced through study in the other class, we prefer to use literary nonfiction, or to combine fiction and nonfiction. We suggest having students read about a single incident from both fiction and nonfiction perspectives. The following four nonfiction texts are appropriate choices for many high school readers; they are intended as suggestions that may help you—and your social studies/history teacher colleagues—begin thinking toward other book-length works of nonfiction that would enhance your students' study of heroes and courage. Note that, again, our choices focus on everyday heroes who have shown uncommon courage.

Melba Patillo Beals' autobiographical *Warriors Don't Cry* (1996) (abridged edition) offers a first-hand picture of the violent and demeaning treatment endured by the "Arkansas Nine," a group of African-American students who were the first to integrate Central High School in Little Rock, Arkansas, in the mid 1950s. Beals, who was one of the nine, presents her story without flinching. For Beals, courage meant not only facing those who were prejudiced against her, but also transcending the hatred brewed by those who tormented her. This book is an ideal one to pair with Mildred Taylor's fictitious *Roll of Thunder, Hear My Cry* (1976) or Carolyn Meyer's *White Lilacs* (1994).

The Miracle Worker (1960) is William Gibson's drama about the early life of Helen Keller and her teacher, Annie Sullivan. A popular play for study by high school students, *The Miracle Worker* allows students to consider courage from the perspective of one with extreme physical challenges, and may encourage them to appreciate the accomplishments of those they know who are physically challenged.

Maggie's American Dream (1988) is an autobiography told by child psychologist James Comer and his mother, Maggie. With his mother's leadership and courage as a guide, Comer fought racial discrimination and poverty; he learned to depend on education as a means for transcending the negative aspects of his childhood. Comer is currently active in issues that bring attention to the needs and abilities of underprivileged minority youth.

Randy Shilts' *And the Band Played On: Politics, People, and the AIDS Epidemic* (1987) is the author's dark and serious chronicle of his life as an AIDS victim. Shilts, who succumbed to the disease, reveals the disturbing politics that have swirled around the epidemic. His fights against the disease and against the stigma associated with it are courageous. This is not a book for teachers or students who choose to avoid, or who are not allowed to study, controversial issues; it is a book for those who believe that we need to learn more about a misunderstood killer disease.

Popular Movies and Electronic Media: Instructional Core or Supplement?

The popular media, including movies that are available on videotapes, are replete with possibilities for works that might be used as the central or supplemental pieces for the study of heroes and courage. The study of movies works well, of course, when paired with the reading and studying of literature. For example, the 1995 Universal feature film, *Apollo 13* might be incorporated to introduce the primary theme of the "Heroes and Courage" unit of study. This movie depicts the Apollo 13 astronauts as the country's heroes, and allows viewers to see that each had his own set of heroic traits; it presents the wives and families of the astronauts as courageous and recognizes the valor of engineers who, through working as a team on the ground and with the men in the spacecraft, were able to solve life-threatening problems, and bring the astronauts home safely.

The 1994 Paramount Pictures feature, *Forrest Gump*, might be shown in the midst of the unit, in conjunction with the reading and study of any of the literature suggested herein, in order to allow students to explore expressions of the theme from differing perspectives. Based on a much more cynical novel of the same name, written by Winston Groom (1986), *Forrest Gump* follows the life of the innocent Forrest Gump from the time he was a poor child in leg braces, to his triumphant run across America, to his confused but valorous participation in the Vietnam conflict, to the death of his beloved mother and the struggles with the troubled friend whom he has loved since childhood, and finally to his success as an American businessperson—one who uses his popularity to enable a disabled veteran to regain his will to live. Gump is an everyman-hero; his belief in the good of others marks him as different; his willingness to act on that belief marks him as courageous.

The 1995 Hollywood Pictures film, *Mr. Holland's Opus*, might then be shown during the unit wrap-up, in order to allow students to compare and contrast the effectiveness of the literary and electronic genres in drawing attention to heroes and courage. In *Mr. Holland's Opus*, a composer must neglect his own artistry to support his wife and child by working as a music teacher. He becomes a dedicated and beloved teacher, but pulls away from his family, refusing to give his son, who cannot hear, the attention and caring that he desperately needs. In a stirring concert scene, Mr. Holland reconciles with his son and realizes that his life—and all the students' lives he has touched—are the great opus that he had always hoped he would be able to compose. This movie presents the theme of heroes and courage more subtly than *Apollo 13* and *Forrest Gump*, and, like the other two suggestions, it presents many other themes and issues for students to consider.

Some students might prefer to study movies in which superhumans are heroic, such as the *Batman* series; others will enjoy considering the heroics of those aboard Starship *Enterprise* in the *Star Trek* series of movies.

Either series might enhance the study of classic mythological heroes. Again, choices are myriad. When students have the freedom and responsibility to make their own selections, particularly where "their" media, movies and television, are concerned, they may be more willing to devote time and effort to the study of the work. Please see the Supplemental Resources list at the close of the chapter for suggested television series, as well as more suggestions in the other areas.

Using the World Wide Web as a Complement

The World Wide Web offers many possibilities for enhancing the study of heroes and courage. (Please see the Introduction, p. xii through xiii, for more details on how to use "search engines," and how to select high-quality Web sites.) We find that the Web is particularly useful as a means of locating biographical information on famous and little-known heroes and information on projects that bravely address social and environmental problems and which encourage those who are interested to work toward improvements. Following are two examples of how the Web might be used to enhance the study of movies, and one example of how the study of a book can be enriched with electronic research.

If students study *Apollo 13*, they might use the World Wide Web to seek information from NASA about how astronauts are trained, the current status of the space program, or many other space-related topics. We recently found, for example, an interesting site that presents information on the space shuttle. The steps we followed are these:

(1) Start by clicking onto Netscape;
(2) Click on "Open" and in the blank, type this address (to get into the Yahoo search engine): http://www.yahoo.com;
(3) From the choices provided, click on "Science";
(4) Click on "Astronomy";
(5) Click on "Space";
(6) Under the "Space" heading, many options will appear; we chose "Space Shuttle," and from there clicked on "NASA Shuttle Web."

It takes several minutes for this link to be established, but the results will be worth the wait for those who want information on the shuttle from the source itself, NASA.

If students study *Forrest Gump*, they might search the Web for information on any of the historic scenes that are incorporated into the movie, including the following ones in which people have displayed unusual courage or strength: integration of universities during the Civil Rights Movement, John F. Kennedy's tenure as president, the Vietnam conflict, and even college football rivalries.

Literary texts can also be enhanced by probing issues using Web resources. For example, if the class reads Hurston's *Their Eyes Were Watching God*, individual students might search the World Wide Web for electronic sites that span a range of topics such as the treatment of blacks in the first part of the twentieth century, history of black-only communities in the American South, the Everglades, or the ultimately tragic life of Zora Neale Hurston. By using the search engine Alta Vista, students can search the Web by topic; they can type in "heroes" or "courage" at the prompt to find links that focus on issues related to the theme. A student recently conducted a topic search using Alta Vista to arrive at a Web site that discusses the work of two *Los Angeles Times* reporters who won a Pulitzer Prize for the reports on courageous people who helped their neighbors put out house fires and clean up after the massive earthquake in the spring of 1994. He insists that he never would have known to try without the help of the search engine. The address he found, by following the links that began with Alta Vista, is this: http://www.pulitzer.org/winners/1995/works/spot-news-reporting/VALOR.html.

In all of these examples of Web resources, issues that are likely to emerge during this unit of study are probed electronically; the issues can then can be discussed by students in small-group or whole-class sessions. When Web-based research is paired with movies and books, students build a significant source of information and background from which they can discuss themes and other issues that arise. This informed base of discussion avoids one of the primary obstacles to serious classroom discussions: it moves students beyond the limitations of their own initial opinions.

Beginning the Unit —Short Preview Activities

Following are two suggested preview activities, each of which can be useful as an introduction to the study of heroes and courage. Both could be implemented regardless of whether the entire class will be reading the same text, or small groups are reading different ones; they can be implemented, too, if the unit anchor will be a movie or even episodes from a television series, as well as literature.

Preview One

Before you can begin this activity, you will need to have collected several copies of four or five editions of your local newspaper. We have found that we accomplish this with the least effort when we ask four or five of our colleagues to collect their newspapers for one week, then promise them a cup of gourmet coffee on the day we specify for the papers to be brought into the school. Their help saves us the trouble of asking for donations from the local newspaper office. However, if you are going to ask more than one class to engage in this activity concurrently, you might wish to call the newspaper office and seek donations. The goal is to compile several copies of four or five editions of the newspaper; if you normally have four groups during group work, save copies of four editions; if you use five groups, save copies of five days' editions, and so on.

Stage One: First, pass out a copy of the newspaper to all members of the class. Be sure that at least four different editions of the paper (copies from Monday through Thursday, for example) are randomly distributed around the room. Ask students to skim and scan the papers, and provide time for them to enjoy the simple yet rewarding feel of reading the paper. Then ask them to select one particularly compelling story from the edition they have just skimmed and scanned. Add one criterion: the story must feature a heroic or courageous act. Ask students to mark the story, then to write two or three sentences about the substance of the story, then two or three more sentences about why that story caught their attention. Creative students might begin to practice their journalistic-style writing at this point, being careful to write concisely and clearly in a way that grabs the reader's attention.

Stage Two: Divide the class into groups; those with the same editions of the paper will form groups. (For example, all those who have worked with the Monday edition will become the "Monday Group" and so on.) First allow the group members time to share the stories they have selected as compelling ones, and to discuss what their different choices suggest about their differing perspectives as readers and thinkers. Next, ask each group to work to reach consensus on the most compelling of all of the previously selected stories, those that have just been discussed. After they have decided on one story, ask each group to develop a dramatization of the story, or to rewrite the report so that it can be broadcast to their classmates by the group's "reporter." Ask them to omit the resolution of the story, because the class will try to supply a reasonable resolution, based on the facts as presented by the group's dramatic reenactment or by the reporter's broadcast.

Stage Three: Ask each group to present its dramatization or broadcast; after each group's presentation, the class audience will take about ten minutes to create and write resolutions to each story that is presented. (The teacher might require that all possibilities offered be positive in nature, since the focus of the introduction is on heroic and courageous actions.)

Stage Four: Audience volunteers will read aloud their story endings, then a member of the presenting group will read to the class the entire, actual newspaper story and allow the class to compare its responses with the facts of the story.

This introductory activity may open discussion of local heroes and the possibility of demonstrating courage in everyday situations. In this activity, students may begin to realize that "hero" and "courage" have myriad definitions and manifestations; this concept will be a necessary one for students to develop as they engage in the work of the unit, because each will be expected to respond to the literature and media from his or her own personal understanding of the issues and themes. As when you teach other response-based literature units, you will rarely have specific "right" and "wrong" responses in mind as your students discuss the subject matter of this unit.

Preview Two

During the introduction to the unit of study, you might also ask students to begin collecting articles from magazines and the newspaper, and/or to write brief summaries of televised news reports, of people who are in some way heroic or courageous. Students can donate articles and summaries to a class pool for a "Courage File," from which inspiring stories can be read aloud and used as either writing prompts during the unit of study, or merely as thought pieces to be discussed or reflected on by students when there are extra moments during the unit of study. If you find that more structure is necessary for your classes, you could determine a schedule in which each student is responsible for contributing to the Courage File on a specific day.

The primary purpose of such a file is to increase students' awareness that there are, in fact, heroes in today's world. It may encourage them to develop a mental habit of looking for heroic and courageous acts. The teacher can donate the first pieces to the Courage File and, as a unit preview, can share those pieces with the students as examples. A sampling of recent articles that we have culled from popular publications include these that focus on "everyday heroes":

- children who, despite being cancer patients, are seeking ways to make others happy (Alan Ebert, "Season's Greetings from the Heart," McCall's, December, 1996, pages 64–66);
- a 23-year-old man who was born as a nonverbal quadriplegic, but whose father carries him through the miles of swimming, biking, and running of competitive triathlons (Geoff Marchant, "He Ain't Heavy, He's My Son," FootNotes, Winter, 1996, pages 12–13);
- a Harvard honors student who lost the use of her body, but not the use of her mind, in a traffic accident when she was beginning seventh grade, attends the university with the constant help of an unusual roommate—her mother (Kim Painter, "The Ability to Tackle Harvard," USA Today, Section D, pages 1–2);
- a wealthy Georgia businessman rescues a small rural community from desperate poverty and racial division by building a factory there in order to provide the residents with a source of income, and by securing assistance from others, including former President Jimmy Carter and then-Georgia governor Joe Frank Harris (Robert Lamme, "The Employer," Sky, December, 1996, pages 124–129).

This selection of magazine articles demonstrates an important point about the kinds of units we are recommending in this book: materials for study of contemporary issues surround us; we encourage you to keep an eye open for them not only when reviewing teacherly texts, but as you read articles while waiting in doctors' offices and sitting on airplanes, when you glance through sports and fashion magazines while in the grocery store or car repair shop. You may be amazed, as we have been, with how many resources appear before your eyes when your attitude is receptive and expectant.

Sustaining the Unit—Language Activities to Use During Reading

Following are two suggestions for activities that will allow students to synthesize their understandings of the literature and/or movies being studied, and to expand on the issues that are emerging for them as they participate in the heroes and courage unit. Depending on time and interest, you might ask students to choose one or the two activities, or might assign only one. Because both move beyond the book or movie being studied, they are appropriate as homework assignments, even in situations in which books must remain in the classroom.

Mid-Unit Activity One

For this activity, you will ask that students to stop reading or studying a text at predetermined points and identify, at those points, the actions and attitudes of a character on a scale, or a continuum. Please see the example, in which we ask students to rate Henry Fleming's actions in *The Red Badge of Courage*, in the simple diagram below:

COWARDLY_____HEROIC

          1   2   3   4   5   6   7   8   9   10

By page 65, we see that Henry Fleming has acted in what way?

For the first pairing on the scale, students should rank Henry's actions 1 to 10, using "cowardly" and "heroic" as the opposite extremes. You can easily demonstrate this method by placing one word on the left side of the board or overhead transparency, and the other word opposite it, on the right side. Connect the words with a line that is divided into ten segments, and number the segments 1–10. The question asked will be the same for each word pair, but will refer to different points in the plot or to different characters. Ask students to add other word pairs that they feel are appropriate for the text they are currently studying; the only requirement is that each word pair must name an opposition that is significant in the story. For example, besides "cowardly" and "heroic" actions in *The Red Badge of Courage*, students might decide that "loyalty" and "disloyalty"; "competence" and "ineptness"; "order" and "chaos"; and "surety" and "confusion" are pairs that represent conflicts that are central in the first half of the novel.

After they have listed the number of oppositional word pairs that you require, ask students to mark the point on each continuum line at which they feel the protagonist (or any specified character) is acting at that point in the story. Below each marked line, ask them to write a brief explanation of the placement of the character on a continuum. Reading these comments will help you understand how well the student comprehends the role of the character within the story, and will also give you an informal indication of his or her level of engagement with the text.

Next, ask students to write a one-paragraph prediction about how the character will act in the remainder of the story. Remind them to base their predictions on the evidence gathered from the marked scales and the confidence they have in their understanding of the text to that point. The character's predicted actions must be in keeping with the character's personality and behaviors, as presented in the story; none should be allowed to assume new personality traits in the predictions. In completing this activity, students will ask themselves, "Will a character respond with courage or timidity to the situation that he/she must face?" among other relevant questions. Following the example above, for instance, students might decide that Henry Fleming is a failure as a soldier, and predict that he will be killed in battle. They should file their predictions until they have completed the novel, and repeat the activity at several points during the study of the novel.

Once they have completed the reading, students can again get into their groups in order to compare and contrast the predictions they had written, and to assess their predictions for accuracy (in this example, their descriptions of and predictions about Henry Fleming). You will be able to informally assess students' comprehension of the text and understanding of the characters while students are engaged in sharing their predictions. This activity provides a connection to Preview Activity One, in which they make predictions about the resolutions of actual events as reported in newspaper stories, and thus adds cohesion to the unit of study.

Mid-Unit Activity Two

This is an opportunity to have students become fully engaged in the theme of the unit. Ask students, during the unit of study, to collect songs that reflect the theme. Each student should write the lyrics of the song(s) he or she selects, and print a copy of the lyrics for each member of a four-five person group. (Lyrics are often printed on the cover of compact disc and cassette tape covers and in piano books that contain popular music.) The first step for students to complete, even before they have distributed copies of their songs to their group members, is to write a paragraph—or perhaps a poem or even an extra stanza—that expresses their reactions to the song, and the meaning they construct while listening to it.

In small groups, students can exchange lyrics and, if possible, play their songs for each other. Individuals can either discuss their reactions to their own songs, or may ask group members to first respond to each song before any discussion occurs. Each group should focus, at some time, on the relevance of each song to the heroes and courage theme. Depending on your particular instructional goals related to this activity, you might instruct students to further explore the songs with eyes and ears focusing on use of figurative language, the contributions of rhyme and rhythm, the intersection of form and theme, and so on. Each group might select from its members' songs a favorite to present to the class. With little extra effort, the group's favorite can be photocopied onto an overhead transparency so that when it is played, before it is discussed, students and you can follow the words with their eyes as well as with their ears. High school students typically enjoy hearing music; it is possible that this activity will teach them to really listen to lyrics, as a means of further enriching their responses. The activity adds a listening dimension to the "Courage File" idea introduced as Preview Activity Two, and thus also adds cohesion to the unit of study.

Occasionally, we have been dismayed with the choices of lyrics that students bring into the classes (and on a few occasions we have been shocked); a frank discussion of what is and what is not acceptable in your particular classroom is appropriate at this time. It shows respect for students to explain to them the boundaries that you wish to uphold; when they understand limits, they are less likely to try to go beyond those limits than when they are not given any explanation of acceptable boundaries. If you suspect that any student may not have access to cassette tapes or compact discs of current music, you might choose to make available to the entire class the copies of lyrics of several songs, including contemporary favorites as well as others, such as tunes from Broadway shows, folk songs, and so on. The school's music teacher might be a valuable resource to consult.

Another warning is perhaps also worth stating: Popular song titles change as rapidly as traffic lights. We cannot predict which ones will be right for your students. Instead of listing songs here that we would use if teaching this unit today, we would like to make a suggestion: demonstrate the first steps of this activity by bringing in one of your favorite songs, photocopying for the class, expressing your response to it in writing, and sharing your response with the class. Not only will this model the activity, but, perhaps more important, it will indicate to students that you believe that music has an important place in your classroom.

Completing the Unit—Activities to Use After Reading

A significant follow-up activity may be to have each student select a favorite piece from the class Courage File and write an original story, one that situates the person featured in the Courage File article as the protagonist. Alternately, a student might put a fictitious character in a situation that is depicted by an article in the class Courage File. For example, in Rodman Philbrick's *Freak the Mighty*, "Freak" is a character who defies his life-threatening condition in order to have many wild adventures, none of which takes him any further from home than his own neighborhood. In the meantime, he teaches his friend, "Mighty," to believe in himself (see book description, above). The student could create a story after asking herself, "How would Freak respond to a situation reported in a Courage File article, one that describes how a stranger jumped into a river to save a drowning child?" Another student might choose to reverse this possibility and take one of the heroes he finds in the Courage File and place that person within the context of a fictitious story; for example, the father who competes in triathlons with his nonverbal, quadriplegic son could be situated in the competitive world of Crutcher's *Stotan!* (see book description, above). Others might use the self-portrait of Melba Patillo Beals as presented in *Warriors Don't Cry* in order to create for their chosen person a role in which he or she will demonstrate great strength and grace in the face of overwhelming prejudice and violence (see book description, above). The possibilities for connections to be established between fiction and nonfiction are limited only by the students' imaginations.

Another option would be to ask students to identify a "hidden hero," someone who makes contributions to the world quietly and without fanfare, demonstrating the value of simple caring gestures. Students who chose this option should create an expressive work of literature about the hidden hero, using the genre of their choice. Cabrera's "Feeding the Birds," which opens this chapter, is an example of one teacher's effort to find heroic characteristics in one person whom society ignores or disparages.

If you feel that your students will benefit from a further connection to the preview and mid-reading activities, why not ask them to write a newspaper-style article in which they report the events of one of the stories read or viewed during the unit of study, with a focus on the courageous (or disappointing) acts of a particular character (or characters)? If students are grouped for this activity, they might assume different roles as news writers; one could write an editorial, one a biographical feature story, one a front page news account, and so on, all of which focus on the character(s) of the story they have read, and which incorporate the setting and other elements as they appear in the story. This activity might be completed as a response to any of the literary texts suggested within the chapter, or as a response to the films or other media suggested, as well.

While the best source of information about who today's teens look to as their heroes is the teens themselves, we, their teachers, can help them broaden their knowledge of heroic people and courageous acts by introducing to them many of the books, shorter literary works, television shows and movies, and Web resources mentioned within this chapter. Perhaps we do have the opportunity to make adolescence less a "perilous ordeal" and more a privileged passage when we offer them a variety of everyday heroes who face life's problems with courage.

Works Cited

Angelou, M. (1978). And still I rise. In *And still I rise*. New York: Random House.
Angelou, M. (1969). *I know why the caged bird sings*. New York: Random House.
Angelou, M. (1978). Life doesn't frighten me at all. In *And still I rise*. New York: Random House.
Angelou, M. (1993). Willie. In *Poems*. New York: Bantam, 141.
Anonymous. (1996). *Beowulf* (excerpts of The wrath of Grendel, The coming of Beowulf, and the Battle with Grendel, Burton Raffel, Trans. In *Literature: The British tradition*. Upper Saddle River, NJ: Prentice Hall, 20–30.
Anonymous. (1987). The bold Americans. In *American literature*. New York: Macmillan, 70.

Avildsen, J. G., Director. (1992). *The power of one* [video]. A. Michlan, Producer. Hollywood: Warner Home Videos.

Bambara, T. (1996). Raymond's run. In *The runner's literary companion*. New York: Penguin, 131–140.

Beals, M. P. (1996). *Warriors don't cry* (abridged version). New York: Archway.

Benetar, P. (1983). I need a hero. On *Footloose* soundtrack [cassette/CD]. RCA Records.

Brooks, G. (1991). The river. On *Ropin' the wind* [cassette/CD]. New York: Capitol.

Carey, M. (1993). Hero. On *Music box* [cassette/CD]. New York: Sony.

Carter, T., Director. (1993). *Swing kids*. F. Marshall & F. Melenandri, Producers. Hollywood: Hollywood Pictures.

Chesnut, M. B. (1996). From *Mary Chesnut's civil war*. In *Literature: The American exprience*. Upper Saddle River, NJ: Prentice Hall, 371–374.

Comer, J. P. (1988). *Maggie's American dream*. New York: New American Library, Plume .

Connick, H., Jr. (1991) With imagination (I'll get there). On *Blue light*. New York: Sony.

Crane, S. (1976). *The red badge of courage*. New York: W. W. Norton.

Crutcher, C. (1986). *Stotan!* New York: Dell.

Demme, J.. Director. 1993). *Philadelphia* [film]. Huetzman, G., Utt, K., and Bozman, R., Producers, Hollywood: Tri Star Pictures.

Douglass, F. (1960). *Narrative of the life of Frederick Douglass, an American slave*. B. Quarles (Ed.). Cambridge, MA: Harvard University Press.

Ebert, A. (1996). Season's greetings from the heart. *McCall's*, December, 64–66.

Edelman, B. (Ed.). (1985). *Dear America: Letters home from Vietnam*. New York: Simon & Schuster.

Estafan, E. & Dremer, L. (1996). Reach [Performed by Gloria Estafan]. On *Rhythm of the games* [cassette/CD]. New York: Sony.

Farm, The. (1991). How long. On *Spartacus* [cassette/CD]. Sire Records.

Gibson, W. (1960). *The miracle worker*. New York: Atheneum.

Giovanni, N. (1997). A journey. In *Spotlight on literature* (silver edition). New York: Macmillan/McGraw Hill, 641.

Haley, A. (1976). *Roots*. Garden City, NJ: Doubleday.

Haley, A. (1993). *Alex Haley's Queen: The story of an American family*. New York: Morrow.

Hansberry, L. (1959). *A raisin in the sun.* New York: Random House.

Hemingway, E. (1952). *The old man and the sea.* New York: Scribner.

Henley, L. & J. Silbar (1988). Wind beneath my wings. [Recorded by Bette Midler]. On *Beaches* [cassette]. New York: Atlantic.

Herek, S., Director. (1995). *Mr. Holland's Opus* [film]. T. Field, M. Nolin & R. W. Cort, Producers. Hollywood: Hollywood Pictures.

Hesse, K. (1992). *Letters from Rifka.* New York: Henry Holt.

Homer. (1997). *The odyssey.* Robert Fitzgerald (Trans.). Excerpts in *The Language of Literature:* 9. Evanston, IL: McDougal Littell, 544–566.

Howard, R., Director. (1995). *Apollo 13* [film]. R. Howard & B. Glazer, Producers. Hollywood: Universal.

Hughes, L. (1987). Mother to son. In *Selected poems of Langston Hughes.* New York: Vintage, 187.

Hughes, L. (1958). Thank you, M'am. In *Something in common.* New York: Harold Ober and Associates.

Hurston, Z. N. (1937). *Their eyes were watching God.* New York: Harper and Row.

Ibsen, H. (1965). *A doll's house.* In *Four major plays,* volume I. New York: Signet.

Lamme, R. (1996). The employer. *Sky.* December, 124–129.

Lee, R. E. (1996). Letter to his son. In *Literature: The American experience.* Upper Saddle River, NJ: Prentice Hall, 378–379.

Lincoln, A. (1996). The Gettysburg address. In *Literature: The American experience.* Upper Saddle River, NJ: Prentice Hall, 380.

Lowry, L. (1993). *The giver.* New York: Houghton Mifflin.

Mallory, T. (1996). *Morte d'Arthur.* Excerpt in *Literature: The British tradition.* Upper Saddle River, NJ: Prentice Hall, 170–175.

Marchant, G. (1996). He ain't heavy, he's my son. *FootNotes,* Winter, 2–13.

McIntire, R. (1990). Climb that mountain high. On *Rumor has it* [cassette/CD]. MCA Records.

Meyer, C. (1993). *White lilacs.* San Diego: Harcourt.

Myers, W. D. (1988). *Fallen angels.* New York: Scholastic.

Newton, M. (1995). *Adolescence: Guiding youth through the perilous ordeal.* New York: W. W. Norton.

Painter, K. (1996). The ability to tackle Harvard. *USA today,* November 25, Section D, 1–2.

Petty, T. (1989). I won't back down. On *Full moon fever* [cassette/CD]. New York: MCA.

Philbrick, R. (1993). *Freak the mighty*. New York: Scholastic Point.

Robinson, J. G., Director. (1991). *Robin Hood: Prince of thieves*. M. Creek, Producer. Hollywood: Warner Brothers.

Sherburne, Z. (1986). From Mother with love. In J. S. Simmons and M. Stern (Eds.), *The short story and you*. New York: National Textbook, 205–214.

Shilts, R. (1987). *And the band played on: Politics, people, and the AIDS epidemic*. New York: St. Martin's Press.

Sophocles. (1974). Antigone. In *The Theban plays*. New York: Penguin.

Taylor, J. (1991). Shed a little light. On *New moonshine*. New York: Sony.

Taylor, M. (1981). *Let the circle be unbroken*. New York: Dial.

Taylor, M. (1976). *Roll of thunder, hear my cry*. New York: Dial.

Tennyson, A. (1996). Ulysses. In *Literature: The British tradition*. Upper Saddle River, NJ: Prentice Hall, 718–720.

Thomas, D. (1987). Do not go gentle into that good night. In *Sound an sense: An introduction to poetry*, 7th edition. San Diego: Harcourt Brace, 300.

Ulibarri, S. R. (1997). My wonder horse/ Mi caballo mago [Translated by Thelma C. Nason.] In *The Language of Literature:* 9. Evanston, IL: McDougal Littell, 818–827.

United States Marine Corp (1985). Good enough for me. On *Run to cadence with the U. S. Marines*, volume 2. Documentary Recordings.

Walker, A. (1997). Women. In *Spotlight on literature* (silver edition). New York: Macmillan/McGraw Hill, 531.

White, T. H. (1958). *The once and future king*. New York: Ace.

Whitman, W. (1991). I hear America singing. In *Prentice Hall Literature* (gold edition). Englewood Cliffs, NJ: Prentice Hall, 647.

Yeager, C. & Janos, L. (1985). *Yeager: An autobiography*. New York: Bantam.

Zemeckis, R., Director. (1994). *Forrest Gump*. S. Tisch & W. Finerman, Producers. Hollywood: Paramount Pictures.

Zwick, E., Director. (1990). *Glory* [film]. F. Fields, Producer. Hollywood: Tri Star.

Television Series

60 Minutes (currently on CBS)
Dangerous Minds (currently on ABC)
Dateline (currently on NBC)
ER (currently on NBC)

JAG (currently on CBS)
Law and Order (currently on NBC)
Rescue 911 (currently on the Family channel)
Their Eyes on the Prize (PBS special Home Video presentation)
Touched by an Angel (currently on CBS)

Web Sites

African-American Heroes
    http://www.kaiwan.com/~mcivr/pioneer.html
    http://www.mecca.org/~crights/nc2.html
    http://www.seattletimes.com/mlk/index.html

Greek Mythology
    http://www.intergate.net/uhtml/.jhunt/greek-myth.html

Library of Congress
    http://lcweb.loc.gov

NASA
    http://quest.arc.nasa.gov/interactive.html
    http://spacelink.msfc.nasa.gov/

Sports Heroes
    http://www.studentpubs.runet.edu/tartan/spring96/April 12/sports#tragic

War Letters
    http://www.ucsc.edu/civil-war-letters/home.html

Supplemental Resources

Poetry (frequently anthologized selections)

Angelou, M. (1978). And still I rise, *And still I rise*. New York: Random House.
    Students and adults often read this poem as an affirmation that, despite difficulties and even mistreatment by others, each person can become what he or she wants to become.

Angelou, M. (1978). Life doesn't frighten me at all, *And still I rise*. New York: Random House.

> This poem presents a catalogue of things that a child or adolescent might fear, but the speaker triumphantly declares, "Life doesn't frighten me at all." This is an upbeat poem; its rhyme, repetition, metaphors and similes may appeal to students who have previously experienced frustration when reading poetry.

Angelou, M. (1993). Willie, *Poems*. New York: Bantam, 141.

> Willie is lonely, with no family or friends, and with a noticeable limp. Yet Willie's spirits are as light as the games and songs of children; he provides a courageous example for adolescents who sometimes feel like hiding from life because they feel imperfect.

Anonymous. (1996). *Beowulf* (excerpts of The wrath of Grendel, The coming of Beowulf, and The battle with Grendel, translated by Burton Raffel). In *Literature: The British tradition*. Upper Saddle River, NJ: Prentice Hall, 20–30.

> In this classic, first century A.D. story, Beowulf comes to battle the fierce monster, Grendel, who is terrorizing the Danish king's court.

Anonymous. (1987). The bold Americans, *American literature*. New York: Macmillan, 70.

> This poem originated in colonial America; its purpose appears to be one of stirring patriots to heroic action. It would be especially appropriate in a unit that focuses attention on the courage of soldiers.

Giovanni, N. (1997). A Journey, *Spotlight on literature* (silver edition). New York: Macmillan/McGraw Hill, 641.

> In a poem that serves as a perfect complement to Angelou's Life Doesn't Frighten Me at All, and Hughes' Mother to Son, Giovanni's speaker offers the brave message, "I am not afraid . . . of rough spots . . . or lonely times."

Homer. (1997). *The odyssey* (R. Fitzgerald trans.). In *The language of literature: 9*. Evanston, IL: McDougal Littell, 544–566.

> In these excerpts, the hero Odysseus has returned home to Ithaca; he takes the advice of the goddess Athena and spies on those in his court who would take from him Penelope. He and the son with whom he is reunited, Telemachus, plan to restore honor to the family.

Hughes, L. (1959/1987). Mother to Son, *Selected poems of Langston Hughes*. New York: Vintage, 187.

In this poem, a mother speaks to her son, explaining that although, "Life for me ain't been no crystal stair," she has continued to climb, sometimes through tacks and darkness. She encourages him to follow her courageous example and continue through struggles, too.

Tennyson, A. (1996). Ulysses, *Literature: The British tradition.* Upper Saddle River. NJ: Prentice Hall, 718-720.

A poem that brings attention to the restlessness of Ulysses after he has fought the Trojan war and experienced myriad adventures on his return to Ithaca, and his valorous desire to complete, "Some work of noble note.../ Not unbecoming men that strove with Gods" and even as an old man, "To strive, to seek, to find, and not to yield."

Thomas, D. (1987). Do not go gentle into that good night. In *Sound and sense: An introduction to poetry* (7th ed.) San Diego: Harcourt Brace, 300.

Thomas' speaker implores a dying person (often interpreted as the speaker and poet's father) to "rage, rage against the dying of the light," to fight against death as if death is a visible opponent and courage can disarm it.

Walker, A. (1997). Women. In *Spotlight on literature* (silver edition). New York: Macmillan/McGraw Hill, 531.

This poem is an extended metaphor that looks at the war fought for civil rights by "headragged generals" who have courageously fought discrimination for the sake of their children.

Whitman, W. (1991). I hear America singing. In *Prentice Hall literature* (gold edition). Engelwood Cliffs, NJ: Prentice Hall, 47.

Whitman celebrates common heroes such as carpenters, shoemakers, and mothers, using free verse.

Popular Songs

Benetar, P. (1983). I need a hero. On *Footloose* soundtrack [cassette]. On RCA Records.

The singer discusses the need for a hero figure that we all have.

Brooks, G. (1991). The river. On *Ropin' the wind* [cassette/CD]. Capitol.

This country music song focuses on the need for people to face hard times with courage and determination, and challenges all to take risks. It also offers opportunities for the exploration of similes through lines such as "a dream is like a river. . . ."

Connick, H., Jr. (1991). With Imagination (I'll Get There). On *Blue Light* [casette/CD]. Sony.

    Connick croons, "I started with a dream, but came to a decision . . . I've got to be strong . . . When weary is your world, go and spin another." His attention to the act of making a conscious choice to be strong may be worth consideration.

Farm, The. (1991). How Long. On *Spartacus* [cassette/CD]. Sire Records.

    This song begins by reminding the listener that the Berlin Wall fell because people had the courage to work for changes, then suggests that changes need to continue, and that a hero needs to emerge or the people need to become more courageous.

McIntire, R. (1990). Climb that Mountain High. On *Rumor has it* [cassette/CD]. MCA Records.

    The song implores listeners to face challenges, large or small, in order to reach their dreams, and seems to imply that courage and determination will lead to success.

Petty, T. (1989). I won't back down. On *Full moon fever* [cassette/CD]. MCA.

    In a complement to Dylan Thomas's "Do Not Go Gentle into That Good Night," this song indicates that courage requires determination to transcend obstacles.

Taylor, J. (1991). Shed a little light. On *New moonshine* [cassette/CD]. Sony.

    A song that would complement study of civil rights heroes, this one speaks of the ties that bind all humans as we travel the "passage through the darkness and mist" to our goals, and implies that only those who are courageous will succeed in the journey.

United States Marine Corp (1985). Good enough for me. On *Run to cadence with the U.S. Marines*, volume 2. Documentary Recordings.

    This chant reminds listeners of the bravery displayed by American soldiers in a variety of famous battles, and of the ultimate sacrifices many soldiers have made for the country.

Short Stories and Drama (often anthologized)

Bambara, T. (1996). Raymond's run. In *The Runner's literary companion*. New York: Penguin, 131–140.

    In this short story, Squeaky is a young girl whose talent is for running, but whose duty is to care for her retarded brother, Raymond. She is confident that she can protect him from others' taunts, and must forfeit her chance to gain glory by winning a race in order to pay attention to Raymond. She is heroic in that she defends her brother and is willing to critically examine her own motives and actions. This story often appears in textbooks that are intended for middle school readers; however, we believe that it is appropriate for serious study by high school readers. We list this particular collection of stories and other literature that are collected for runners, because we have found that our students accept stories for their reading much more readily when the stories are drawn from a nonschool textbook than when they see that it comes from a middle school textbook.

Hansberry, L. (1959). *A raisin in the sun*. New York: Random House.

The issue of a woman's right to make a decision for abortion is paramount in this play; the play depicts the courage of a woman who believes she has the right to choose, and fights for that right.

Hughes, L. (1958). Thank you, M'am. In *Something in common*. New York: Harold Ober and Associates.

This is a quick short story in which an old woman turns the tables on a young boy who tries to snatch her purse. She befriends him and takes time to teach him right and wrong. Students might discuss whether or not her kind of courage is possible in the violent, late twentieth century.

Ibsen, H. (1965). *A doll's house*. In *Four major plays*, volume I. New York: Signet.

The courage displayed by a woman who willingly leaves her marriage shocked early audiences of this play; the play continues to raise questions about the ways women are expected to behave.

Sherburne, Z. (1980). From Mother with love. In J. S. Simmons and M. Stern, Eds. *The short story and you*. New York: National Textbook, 205–214.

As a young girl's mother struggles with a terminal illness, the mother and daughter find the courage to make the most of their time together. Both demonstrate bravery: the mother, in dying, and the daughter, in living.

Sophocles. (1974). *Antigone*. In *The Theban plays*. New York: Penguin.

This is the classic play about a sister who fights a law that she considers to be unjust, so that she can honor the death of her brothers. Might be taught with other plays of the Theban cycle, including *Oedipus Rex* and *Oedipus at Collonnus*.

Ulibarri, S. R. (1997). My wonder horse/Mi caballo mago (Thelma C. Nason trans.). In *The language of literature: 9*, Evanston, IL: McDougal Littell 818–827.

This is the mystical story of a white horse that lives in the West, a horse that is the subject of Native American legends and Western folk tales, a courageous horse that does not know how to surrender.

Novels

Hesse, K. (1992). *Letters from Rifka*. New York: Henry Holt.

This epistolary novel describes thirteen-year-old Rifka's flight, in 1919, from Russia to the United States in an effort to avoid persecution of the Jews. The remarkably brave girl manages to be kind to others even while enduring separation from her family, disease, and other hardships.

Mallory, T. (1996). *Morte d'Arthur*. Excerpts in *Literature: The British tradition*. Upper Saddle River, NJ: Prentice Hall, 170–175.

Mallory's is often cited as the finest prose account of the story of legendary King Arthur. The story is exciting and intriguing, as King Arthur must fight his enemies and is betrayed by his own knight, Lancelot, who has an affair with the Queen, Guenevere. A wonderful book to pair, in excerpt, perhaps, with T. H. White's *The Once and Future King*, also the story of Arthur, and with a movie version of the 1960 Lerner and Lowe musical, *Camelot*.

Meyer, C. (1993). *White lilacs*. San Diego: Harcourt.

A young black girl learns of the plans of city leaders to take over the black community and turn the area into a park for themselves and their families. While some black adults fight the decision and others acquiesce, she fights to preserve the memory of her neighborhood the best way she can, by painting each of the homes and buildings.

Taylor, M. (1981). *Let the circle be unbroken*. New York: Dial.

The first of three sequels to *Roll of Thunder, Hear My Cry* (1976), this book continues the story of the Logan family's courageous and determined quest for respect, as well as survival, in the Depression-era South.

White, T. H. (1958). *The once and future king*. New York: Ace.

Another telling of the King Arthur legend. The chivalry of King Arthur and his beloved yet deceitful knight, Sir Lancelot, pervade the text. (See Mallory, *Morte d'Arthur*, above.)

Nonfiction

Angelou, M. (1969). *I know why the caged bird sings*. New York: Random House.

    In this autobiography of the author's childhood and teenage years, there are loving references to Angelou's loving grandmother and brother, poignant memories of the family's struggle against poverty, the painful revelations of the young girl's rape and its lasting effects.

Chesnut, M. B. (1996). Excerpts from *Mary Chesnut's civil war*. In *Literature: The American experience*. Upper Saddle River, NJ: Prentice Hall, 371–374.

    These excerpts reveal the thoughts of a Southern daughter and wife during the battles of the Civil War. Her words chronicle the presumptions and confusion of those who believed their side was right and would therefore prevail.

Douglass, F. (1960). *Narrative of the life of Frederick Douglass, An American slave*. B. Quarles, Ed. Cambridge, MA: Harvard University Press.

    Douglass writes, graphically in parts, about his struggles to achieve freedom from slavery and to become an educated man.

Edelman, B. (Ed.). (1985). *Dear America: Letters home from Vietnam*. New York: Simon & Schuster.

    This troubling and powerful collection of soldiers' letters is likely to make the war of the 1960s become "real" for today's teens. This is a powerful complement to Crane's *The Red Badge of Courage* and Myers' *Fallen Angels* (see above).

Haley, A. (1976). *Roots*. Garden City, NJ: Doubleday.

    The author traces his ancestry through its history of slavery; the people of Haley's story defy odds to survive and thrive. Also a motion picture and video.

Haley, A. (1993). *Alex Haley's Queen: The story of an American family*. New York: Morrow.

    The continuation of *Roots*, with a focus on Haley's mother, who epitomizes strength, courage, and wisdom. Also a motion picture.

Lee, R. E. (1996). Letter to his Son. In *Literature: The American experience*. Upper Saddle River, NJ: Prentice Hall, 378–379.

    In this poignant letter, the Southern general explains his fears that secession will bring revolution and anarchy, and he vows that if the union dissolves, he will return home and "save in defense, draw my sword on none."

Lincoln, A. (1996). The Gettysburg address. In *Literature: The American experience*. Upper Saddle River, NJ: Prentice Hall, 380.

> The full text of this eloquent speech gives modern readers a sense of the courage of Lincoln, a president who had to maintain the courage to look to the future of a united nation, from the midst of the Civil War.

Yeager, C., and Janos, L. (1985). *Yeager: An autobiography*. New York: Bantam.

> This is the story of one of America's premier air and space explorers, and of the courage and strength he drew from his wife and family.

Movies (Videos)

And the band played on. (1993). Directed by Roger Spottiswood. Starring Matthew Modine and Alan Alda; produced by Aaron Spelling and E. Duke Vincent. Hollywood: HBO Pictures.

> Based on the book of the same title, this is the documentary-style movie that focuses on homosexuality, sexual promiscuity, AIDS, AIDS research, and the politics of a stigmatizing disease.

Dangerous minds. (1995). Directed by John Smith. Starring Michelle Pfeiffer; produced by Don Simpson and Jerry Bruckheimer. Hollywood: Hollywood Pictures.

> An ex-marine becomes an English teacher and a compassionate hero for a group of inner-city students whose lives are riddled with violence, gangs, drugs, pregnancies, and despair. Most teachers will need to seek parental and administrative consent before showing this movie. A current television series of the same title, starring Annie Potts, is based on the movie.

Glory. (1990). Directed by Edward Zwick. Starring Matthew Broderick, Morgan Freeman, Denzel Washington, and Cary Elwes; produced by Freddie Fields. Hollywood: Tri Star.

> This is the story of the 54th regiment, first Black regiment to fight for the North in the Civil War. (Interestingly, Frederick Douglass, a former slave and author of the often-taught autobiography, had a role in forming the regiment.) The soldiers are underpaid and given few provisions; nevertheless, they endure and earn dignity and respect. Teachers should get parental and administrative consent before showing.

Philadelphia (1993). Directed by Jonathan Demme. Starring Tom Hanks and Denzel Washington; produced by Gary Huetzman, Kenneth Utt, and Ron Bozman. Hollywood: Tri Star Pictures.

The story of an attorney whose rise to the top is halted when he contracts AIDS through sexual involvement in a gay relationship, and of the attorney and his representative's courageous fight for fair, unbiased treatment. Most teachers will need to seek parental and administrative consent before showing this movie. Available on video.

The power of one. (1992). Directed by John G. Avildsen. Starring Morgan Freeman, Stephen Dorff, and John Gielgud; produced by Arnon Michlan. Hollywood: Warner Home Videos.

This is the story of a young white boy who is persecuted for his political beliefs. He is befriended by a kind, wise, black prisoner who teaches him to box, and to face his problems with bravery. But realistic torture scenes may cause trouble for some high school viewers.

Robin Hood: Prince of thieves. (1991). Directed by James G. Robinson. Starring Kevin Costner and Morgan Freeman; produced by Morgan Creek. Hollywood: Warner Brothers.

Robin Hood is a popular tale of an outlaw who steals from the rich to give to the poor; he is thus a rogue-hero. He bravely faces his enemies and battles for what he believes is right. (Available on video.)

Swing kids. (1993). Directed by Thomas Carter. Starring Robert Sean Leonard, Christian Bale, and Barbara Hershey; produced by Frank Marshall and Christopher Melenandri. Hollywood: Hollywood Pictures.

Set in Nazi Germany in 1939, this is the story of a group of adolescents who defy the Nazis by defining themselves according to "swing era" music. Two young heroes dare to stand up against the power of the Nazis for their ideals.

Please note: For many audiences, Westerns, war movies, and superhero movies may also be suitable choices for a focus on heroes and courage.

Television Series

(We recommend that you record several episodes of any of the following and then review them for relevancy during the study of heroes and courage; like songs, though, the popularity of television shows often shifts, and therefore we also suggest that you enlist the help of students in finding shows that would be appropriate to study as a means of furthering understanding of the heroes and courage theme.)

60 Minutes (currently on CBS)—an investigative news program.
Dangerous minds (currently on ABC)—a drama about a Marine-turned English teacher in an inner-city school.
Dateline (currently on NBC)—an investigative news program.
ER (currently on NBC)—a doctor and hospital drama in which patients and their physicians are often forced to be brave and in which doctors are often, but not always, heroes.
JAG (currently on CBS)—a military adventure/crime drama featuring Naval Judge Advocate Generals.
Law and order (currently on NBC)—a detective/courtroom drama in which law enforcement offices are often in situations that demand courage, and attorneys have to face serious choices and consequences as they try to convict criminals.
Rescue 911 (currently on the Family channel)—a docudrama in which life-threatening situations are reenacted to demonstrate how people risk lives to help others.
Their eyes on the prize (aired on PBS at various times; check with your school or county media specialist to see if there are copies available for your use in the classroom)—documentaries in a series, each segment of which focuses on an aspect and/or leader in the Civil Rights Movement, including topics such as Rosa Parks, the integration of Central High School in Arkansas, the Student Non-Violent Coordinating Committee (SNCC), and Medgar Evers.
Touched by an angel (currently on CBS)—a drama featuring an angel who, in human form, intervenes to save people from self-destruction. This may be offensive to some in the class who do not believe in heavenly powers; it does not promote a particular religion, but because of its premise that an angel is operating in the lives of people on earth, it is Christian in its orientation.

World Wide Web Sites (a sampling of possibilities)

We encourage teachers and students to set aside an hour or so to explore for themselves the Web; links emerge and, almost serendipitously, lead to information that is useful and interesting. Below are examples that we hope will demonstrate a small part of the range of Web possibilities.

African-American Heroes
http://www.kaiwan.com/~mcivr/pioneer.html
> Brief summaries of "African American Pioneer" heroes including Maya Angelou, Martin Luther King, Jr., and Rosa Parks are presented.

http://www.mecca.org/~crights/nc2.html
> This site provides information on several aspects of the Civil Rights movement and its heroes, including links to a virtual tour of the Civil Rights Museum and descriptions of historic events.

http://www.seattletimes.com/mlk/index.html
> This site is devoted to Martin Luther King, Jr., with links to information on "The Man," "The Movement," "The Legacy," an electronic classroom, and more.

Library of Congress
http://lcweb.loc.gov
> This Web site of the Library of Congress offers collections including, for example, the Gettysburg Address Exhibit, and many others that can enhance the study of American heroes and courage.

Mythological Heroes
http://www.intergate.net/uhtml/.jhunt/greek-myth.html
> This is a site that focuses on Greek mythology.

NASA
http://quest.arc.nasa.gov/interactive.html
> This NASA site allows students to engage in exciting explorations of NASA projects, such as robotics, and allows teachers to sign up for the NASA Internet Projects that can become part of the classroom curriculum.

http://spacelink.msfc.nasa.gov/
> Another NASA location, this site includes documents such as lesson plans, historical information related to NASA and the American space program, and information on the NASA educational programs.

Please note: Be sure that students use the .gov suffix with the NASA sites; if they use the ".com" suffix they will find themselves in a pornographic site—an example of at least one person's idea of a joke in cyberspace.

Sports Heroes

http://www.student pubs.runet.edu/tartan/spring 96/April 12/sports#tragic

>   This page is an article written by a university student who is inspired by the story of the beloved college basketball coach, cancer-victim, and founder of the "V-Foundation," Jimmy Valvano. In addition to providing interesting information, this site might encourage students to explore other "student-produced" sites.
>   (Please note, though: It may be less permanent than other sites listed herein.)

War Letters

http://www.ucsc.edu/civil-war-letters/home.html

>   This site contains the texts of letters written during the Civil War by Private Robert Scott, Company A of the 36th Infantry, Iowa Volunteers.

CHAPTER THREE

A Teenage Crisis: Gangs and Violence

Gail P. Gregg

Did You Know the Boy?
Belkis L. Cabrera

Did you know the boy
He wore oversized jeans and
Combed his hair with Vaseline
Collar up, eating pudding filled *churros*
Smelling like baked pork, and cigarette
And cheap cologne
Wore gold chains and Shango colored beads
Played pool on weekdays; Smoked weed
Raced tinted-window Mustangs
Tagged street signs and bus stops
And made his rounds
By *el barrio* with a piece
Spent last night in the alleyway
Bleeding from metal dumpsters into gutters
Saw it in the morning news
In the gun-downed stats
My brother
Sixteen
Did you know
The boy?

Why Study Violence and Gang Activities in the Language Arts Classroom?

Any reflection on the short history of American education would reveal that it was not such an uncommon occurrence for isolated incidents of male students engaging in fisticuffs on the playground or female students involved in hair pulling contests to settle disagreements or feuds. In those early years, feuding adolescents were usually separated by adults or their peers without the threat of violent repercussions. Sometime in the mid to late 1980s, the nature of youth violence changed. Adolescents who once would have expressed their anger and aggression with words or fists began reaching for knives and guns. Split lips and black eyes are being replaced by bullet and knife wounds. Unlike in years past, adolescents who disagree today, more often than not, wind up in emergency rooms bleeding from gun and knife wounds, or confined to wheelchairs paralyzed by a bullet, or in graveyards.

In an atmosphere of deteriorating social conditions, overcrowded housing, unemployment, weakened family structure, lack of opportunity, and absence of hope, adolescent acts of violence are multiplying at an alarming rate. The breakdown of the family unit, coupled with no reasonable hope of attaining by acceptable means the "good life" as portrayed in the media, teenagers are becoming increasingly more violent, turning to gangs and deadly weapons to attain their most basic human needs of respect, acceptance, and security. Recent statistics reflect that the number of fifteen-year-olds arrested for murder soared 217 percent between 1986 and 1994 (Wormser, 1994); more teenagers are killed by firearms than by all natural causes combined; three times as many African-American adolescent males die in homicides as in auto accidents; and more and more adolescents in rural as well as urban areas are now carrying handguns (Carey-Webb, 1995). In addition, not only are street gangs increasing in numbers, they are also becoming more violent, committing crimes ranging from vandalism to armed robbery and finally to murder.

Today's students live in a violent world and are exposed to images of violence everywhere—in the media, in their neighborhoods, their schools, and perhaps even in their homes. Our students are also the victims of violence, oftentimes in such a pervasive sense that it is hard for them to remain unscathed; it threatens not only their physical well being, but their emotional health as well, making them feel frightened, unsafe, and insecure. At times, violence is so pervasive in their lives that they cannot help but think that it is the normal result of conflict and that using weapons and resorting to violent action are acceptable ways to behave. As more and more teen-aged students are affected by violence and show interest in the supposed "glory" of gang life through the clothing they wear, the language they use, and the companions they keep, it becomes increasingly important that teachers discuss violence and gangs in high school classrooms. Exploring what creates violence in addition to studying what fuels it and defuses it may best be tackled through the study of relevant literature (both fiction and nonfiction) and other media, including film, video, drama, and musical lyrics. Through a variety of genres relevant to the theme of violence and gangs, the language arts classroom can become a laboratory for the debasement of the "glamour" of engaging in violent behavior by focusing on the short- and long-term causes and consequences of violence perpetuated by gangs and other random acts.

Exploring the Many Causes of Violence

Please note: The subject matter of violence, especially when violence involves young victims and young criminals, is one that sparks controversy in many high schools and communities. Some teachers have told us that they do not address gangs and violence because they do not want to support or condone either. We respectfully contend, however, that teachers will better understand students if we look carefully and honestly at our students' worlds. Often, those worlds include gangs that both entice and terrorize teens. We are aware that in the high schools of some communities, depictions of violence, in written or visual form, are inappropriate and unacceptable. However, we have chosen to address the issue of teen violence perpetrated and suffered by adolescents in a way that does not ignore the ugly realities.

High school students often don't realize or understand that there are reasons and conditions beyond their control that create situations that spark violent behavior. Thus, it is important that ample time be devoted to exploring the many conditions that could give rise to violent acts. A picture book, *Life in the Ghetto* (Thomas, 1991) and a brief scene from the video *Menace II Society* will enhance student discussion and understanding of personal choices versus societal conditions as causes for violence. Both works serve as an introduction to societal conditions that enhance the prevalence of violence. In the picture book, a twelve-year-old girl describes the violence of her daily life in a poor neighborhood. While viewing the photos in the book, students can write and share their own explanations as to what might have caused the violence depicted by each picture. The scene from the video depicts a robbery that leads to a murder, and should be used in classrooms only after you have discussed with students your purposes for incorporating it into the unit of study. In it, two older teenage boys are purchasing alcohol from a convenience store in an impoverished neighborhood. One of the boys, O'Dawg, is angry at the wife of the owner, who is following him around the store to ensure that he doesn't shoplift. As the boys are paying for the alcohol, the owner makes a comment about how sorry he feels for their mother. Responding to the remark, O'Dawg shoots the owner of the store, beats and shoots the owner's wife, empties the cash register and the pockets of the dead man. The scene finishes with O'Dawg kicking and beating the dead owner before exiting the store. While the class watches the video, students who do not wish to see a violent action scene could continue working with the still photographs, or they could search local newspapers for photographic and written evidence of juvenile crime and violence in or near their own communities. Whole-class discussion can revolve around societal ills that could be the cause of the violence in the film clip and in the photographs and local news. We suggest beginning the discussion with a direct question: "What was the cause of the violence?" and following with questions about the role of poverty, racism, and individual responsibility for behavior. The purpose of beginning the unit with photographs and a video before any textual literary offerings is to lure students visually to investigate the idea of violence. This will help remind them that literature treats the theme as a verbal representation of what photo/video journalists capture visually every day. The idea here is that students have become so accustomed to images of violence provided by the media that they may become desensitized and, therefore, speechless (not in the sense of awe, but of boredom to the commonplace). Asking students to focus on concrete images and what those images represent should get them to think about what they see—in other words, to provide an opportunity for students to observe and reflect on what they think caused the violence in both the picture book and the video.

A follow-up to the pictorial display of violence is Francisco Alarcon's poem, "L.A. Prayer," and the short story, "Then They'd Watch Comedies" (Rios, 1984). At first glance, the poem seems simple—two columns of words divided into four stanzas each, with four two-word lines. The speaker in this poem reveals, from a citizen's perspective, the fear and insecurity of living in a violence-plagued community, specifically Los Angeles, immediately after the Rodney King verdict. The poem begins with the sense that something is wrong, then moves to how these conditions affect the speaker and fellow inhabitants, and ends with a hope or wish. Following a reading of the poem and discussion of its organizational pattern, students can compose their own poems relative to violence in a setting of their own choosing, using "L. A. Prayer" as a model. Another activity can be centered around associating the politically and socially charged abstractions in the poem with the concrete images of *Life in the Ghetto* and *Menace to Society*.

The short story tells of a teenage Mexican boy who has just arrived home, disheveled from another fight at school with a boy who insists on calling him Leo rather than by his given name of Leocadio. The boy's father encourages and praises his son, telling him how good it was that he beat up the other boy and made him bleed. The father focuses on Leocadio's fighting abilities and only wants to hear details of the fight and how badly the other boy was hurt. Students can work in groups, discussing questions about the relationship between father and son, whether the characters remind them of someone they know, and whether they have ever experienced anything similar to what was depicted in this story. Students can also write a letter to the father addressing the issue of violence and how they feel that the father's encouragement of such could affect his son in the future.

Poems and rap music can be used as fodder for discussion of societal or institutional conditions that could provide a predilection for violent behavior. "Virginia Pilgrim," "Tamara Jackson," and "Mr. Mack Pilgrim," three poems from *My Friend's Got This Problem, Mr. Chandler* (Glenn, 1991), discuss issues of violence. The first two poems discuss two teenage girls wanting to fight each other over reasons neither can determine when questioned by their school counselor. The third recounts a meeting between the counselor and one of the girls' (Virginia's) father. In this meeting, Mr. Pilgrim explains how he wants his daughter to defend herself, even if it means fighting because he has taught her not to allow anyone to walk all over her. Students can be asked to compare and contrast Mr. Pilgrim with Leocadio's father in the previous short story. The rap song "Trapped" by the group 2PAC tells about a young man who desires to leave the ghetto but cannot escape the violence prevalent in his life. Whole-class discussion on issues of gender and violence, and socio-economic status and violence can take place in conjunction with these works.

Three short works to conclude discussion on the causes of violence are "The Code of the Streets" (Anderson, 1994), "The Woman Who Loved Worms" (Inez, 1972), and "38 Who Saw Murder Didn't Call the Police" (Gansberg, 1964). Anderson discusses how an inner-city environment creates a need for respect and identity based on violent acts. After reading this article, students can write their own definitions of violence, followed by a whole-class attempt to categorize each student's definition into violence that is caused by personal choices versus violence that is spawned by social conditions. The purpose for this activity is to help students understand that despite societal ills that at times increase the opportunity for violence, ultimately it is individuals who are responsible for choosing to engage in violent acts, such as reacting to racism or name calling with violent anger. When we lead students to explore causes for violence, and ask them to consider an individual's responsibility to choose violent or nonviolent means for dealing with problems, we may help them understand that they have an obligation to discontinue participating in choices that lead to violence.

Exploring the individual's role in violence can also include discussion of the individual's responsibility for stopping or preventing violence. Inez's poem mixes the act of watching television with the imagery of violence. It also juxtaposes the passivity of watching television safely at home while gang members and others are fighting their wars outside on the streets and in empty lots. This piece would serve well for a discussion on the responsibilities of individuals who are aware of what's going on in society and choose to play a passive role. Gansberg's widely reprinted and frequently anthologized article is an account of a woman, Kitty Genovese, who is stabbed in three different attacks over a lengthy course of time, while witnesses did nothing. The account is an argument, in story form and in simple terms, for people to take notice of what is happening in their neighborhoods and to take appropriate action if a fellow citizen is in trouble and needs help. The article appeared two weeks after the murder it recounts and is based on an incident that is still cited today, more than thirty years after the fact, as an example of public indifference to violence.

A longer work to consider in a unit on violence is Richard Wright's, *Native Son*. This powerful and graphic novel depicts how the societal ills of economic and racial inequality are oftentimes tied to violence. An excellent contrast to the use of violence as an answer to oppression in Wright's novel is Martin Luther King, Jr.'s frequently anthologized "Letter from Birmingham Jail" (1964), which speaks to the use of nonviolence in the Civil Rights era.

After students have read and discussed a variety of materials depicting the various causes of violence, the teacher might lead a discussion of the consequences of committing violent acts. "Y," a short story about a young man who killed someone over a drug deal and is now in jail, is found in *Ask Me if I Care* (Rubin, 1994). In a letter written to his former teacher, a young man tells about his experiences growing up surrounded by violence and frankly acknowledges the power of violence to ruin a young person's future. We have found this story to be an excellent vehicle for prompting student discussion about the victim, the perpetrator of violent acts, and family members of both the victim and the perpetrator of violence. The song, "Ain't No Sunshine," performed by Kid Frost (1991), is another vehicle to use in a discussion of the repercussions from living a life of violence. This song dwells on the consequences of getting caught for a crime—in this case, murder. The speaker tells the story of his life of violence, as well as the stories of his cell mates. The regretful tone of the speaker serves well to depict cases where, if given another chance, perpetrators would not have taken a violent path to resolving their problems. Students are also likely to read this song as one that destroys the glamorized Hollywood notion that life in jail is as comfortable and pleasant as a long-term membership in a health spa.

Gary Soto's poem "After Tonight" (1988) is another effective segue toward the issue of gangs. In this poem, the reader is reminded of both the unexpectedness and unpredictability of living in a world filled with violence. We use the poem to help students reflect on how one's indifference, dislike, or hatred for someone else, if acted upon irrationally, can end a life, and to lead them to think about the precarious nature and value of human life.

A Bridge from Violence to the Topic of Gangs

A good way to move from the general topic of violence into the more specific topic of gangs is through the use of excerpts from three works of nonfiction including *Voices from the Future* (Goodwillie, 1993), *Makes me Wanna Holler* (McCall, 1994), and *Crews* (Hinojosa, 1995). *Voices* contains a series of interviews of teens by teens and is subtitled "our children tell us about violence in America." Excerpts from this powerful and shocking work should include those interviews detailing violence in the home and those speaking of gangs. Student discussion can involve comparing and contrasting their own experiences with those of the interviewed teenagers. Among excerpts to use from McCall's work should be his chapter on respect and how important this is to some adolescents. A good activity to accompany this chapter is to ask students to write a paper on what kinds of things teenagers are willing to do to gain respect. You could also ask students to write about an incident when they were disrespected ("dissed") by another student and how they handled it. Hinojosa's introduction to *Crews* and the chapter "To Go Dancing" should be included as a bridge between violence and gangs. The introduction discusses what prompted the book—a random incident of violence. A group of adolescents attempted to mug a family from out of town who were in New York City in order to watch the United States Open Tennis Championships. In an attempt to defend his mother, a teenager was stabbed and killed. The newspaper later reported that the mugging and resultant killing were the horrifying consequence of some teenagers who wanted money to go dancing. Hinojosa, an acclaimed correspondent for National Public Radio, interviews street kids who are members of gangs or "Crews" (as they call them) in an effort to find out what makes it so easy for an adolescent to stab and kill someone. The interviews give readers an excellent look at violence and gangs from the "inside" or from an adolescent perspective. The issue of respect comes to the forefront with each of the teenagers interviewed. A worthwhile activity is to have the readers compare their experiences with the issues of respect and disrespect to those of the teenagers interviewed in the book. Other activities can include a comparison of the neighborhoods where gang members live versus where readers live. Students could also write letters or columns of advice to those interviewed in Hinojosa's or Goodwillie's book.

Gang Members: Who Are They? Why Do They Join?

Two scenes from Edward James Olmos' video, *American Me* are excellent vehicles for initiating students into the topic of gangs. The first scene begins the video as the main characters are forming their gang. In this segment, three boys in their early teens secretly meet to initiate each other into their newly formed gang, La Primera (The First). This scene takes place in the mid-1950s and serves as a reminder of the long existence of gangs, which date back to the mid or late 1800s when Mexican communities in California formed gangs as a means of protecting their neighborhoods from outsiders. Olmos authentically and objectively portrays the ritual, speaking in a mixture of English and Spanish or Chicano slang and showing the members binding themselves to the gang "por vida" (for life). The video even focuses on one of the boys' flinching while being tattooed with the gang's mark between his thumb and index finger. In the second scene, towards the end of the video, one of the gang members must kill his younger brother, who is anxious to leave the gang after he has betrayed one of its members.

Although the entire video is highly informative in showing students the dynamics and politics within and between gangs of different ethnic backgrounds (Mexican, Anglo, and African-American), the many instances of strong language and sexual violence should be previewed and perhaps edited for appropriateness.

Before showing excerpts from Olmos' video, a good activity is to ask students to describe the job they might consider doing for the rest of their lives. Reiterate that for the purposes of this activity, they can never part from their pledge to the occupation they choose except by death. Ask the students to explain how they can be so sure to commit themselves to any job for the rest of their lives. After discussion, show the students the clip of Olmos' gang initiation ritual. Remind the students that the characters in the video have committed themselves to the gang for life and can only depart by death.

Another way to emphasize the permanence of choosing to join a gang is by reading to the students an untitled poem found in the work *Street Gangs in America* (Gardner, 1992). This anonymous poet describes the inescapable cycle of gang life. He knows that he is slowly killing himself by remaining in the gang, yet he is forever unable to leave it. Showing the murder scene of the brothers—one wanting to leave the gang and dying as a consequence, the other so blindly committed to the gang that he would kill his own brother—reinforces the permanence of choosing to join a gang. Using excerpts from Olmos' shocking and brutally portrayed video also immediately centers students into the motivating factor of allegiance or the need to belong beyond a rational point, a characteristic common to those who belong to gangs.

Allegiance or need to belong can also be highlighted via examining the clothing styles of gang members. The chapter "Adirondack Iron" from *Rule of the Bone* (Banks, 1996) is an excellent literary vehicle to enhance class discussion in this area. The narrator in this novel is a fourteen-year-old drop-out and runaway who shares an apartment with members of a motorcycle gang in a white lower-class neighborhood. In this chapter, he describes the gang members and their activities from a very youthful perspective, which includes both adulation and repulsion. Overall, the gang is depicted as looking tough in appearance despite the fact that they are "losers" who function without any direction. Students can compare and contrast the wardrobe of the members of Adirondack Iron to that of the gangs in Olmos's video clip, the dress of gang members in their own community, and the clothing of the young boy portrayed in Cabrera's poem, "Did You Know the Boy," featured at the beginning of this chapter. Artistically inclined students can provide sketches or collages of the gang wear described in "Adirondack Iron." Asking the students if gang members are as conscious of their clothing as non-gang members, or if they think that gang members have a need for a certain wardrobe, should once again point to an irrational need for allegiance or belonging as a common denominator for gang members. Additional discussion can center around identification needs of gang members, including the role of dress in gangs, why external appearance is important to gang members, and whether or not clothes affect behavior.

In the rap song, "Colors," (Ice-T) the speaker, a gang member, uses a hardened street persona to try to persuade others to join a gang. Students can evaluate the strength of his contentions and argue whether or not the lyrics provide valid justification for entering a gang and engaging in violent activities.

Some Classic Options

Two classic pieces of literature in which gangs play a key role are *The Odyssey* and *Romeo and Juliet*. Another, suited to adolescent audiences and/or unskilled readers in high school, is S. E. Hinton's young adult classic, *The Outsiders*.

Hinton's book demonstrates that gangs are by no means confined to minority youth and is useful for thinking about the development in the recent history of gang life since it takes place thirty years ago. The novel might also be helpful in enticing lower-level readers, since there is a film adaptation of it starring Matt Dillon, Patrick Swayze, and Ralph Macchio. It lends itself to cross-cultural examination, as well, since it deals with white kids and can be easily juxtaposed to African-American and/or Hispanic films such as *Boyz N the Hood* and *Mi Vida Loca*.

In Homer's centuries-old epic, the world of Odysseus is a harsh place—a world in which violence is all too commonplace and not unlike our society today. In a sense, Odysseus and his men act like gang members, unconcerned about entering a town (read "home invasion" or "car jacking") and carrying off all of the town's possessions (see Book 9 and the raid on Cicones). Also, violence motivated by revenge plays a prominent role, particularly in Books 22 and 24. Athena's speech at the very end of this work can be easily tied to the poem and activity previously mentioned in the discussion of Alarcon's "L.A. Prayer."

Asking students to read, dramatize (after practice), or view and evaluate Act I, scene 1, and Act III, scene 1 of Shakespeare's *Romeo and Juliet* is an excellent way to engage students in consideration of the topics of gang allegiance and revenge. The first scene begins with an encounter between the clans of the Montagues and the Capulets. Particular focus should be made of this encounter in light of the discussion previously made on gang allegiance. Ask students whether Sampson and/or Abram have acted irrationally, fueled on by the idea of allegiance to their clan—Montague or Capulet. In Act III, scene 1, there is a clash between the Capulets and Montagues as Romeo seeks revenge on Tybalt for the death of his best friend, Mercutio. Ask students to draw parallels between this scene and current-day revenge killings so prevalent in gang life. Questions to pose include: Are the weapons as deadly? Is human life just as trivial? Is revenge ever an excuse for violence? Reenactment by students of both these scenes using modern day language, props, and costumes, is useful for comparing the characteristics and violence of gangs in the sixteenth century versus those of the current day.

Suggested Young Adult Novels

Although Hinton's *The Outsiders* is a worthy adolescent work to use when examining the topic of gangs, there are certainly others that fit the bill as well. *A Nation of Amor* (McConnell, 1996) is a violent glimpse of the reality of gang life and how its violence can involve and affect families. The story begins in the 1960s when three brothers form the "Latin Kings," a Puerto Rican gang on Chicago's west side. Tracing the lives of the three brothers into adulthood and one of the brother's children, the author vividly depicts the tough situations these Latin teens face, including teen pregnancy, drug use, gang wars, crime, and jail. This novel lends itself in particular to many role-playing situations, specifically those where conflicts within the families are portrayed. Student portrayals can include solving the various conflicts in a nonviolent way.

Way Past Cool (Mowry, 1992) is a novel about the urban reality of street gangs in Oakland, California. Gordon, age thirteen, is the leader of the "Friends," a gang of African-American boys in their early teens who struggle to hold on to their turf against the "Crew" who are fiercely loyal to one another and live by a strict unwritten code of honor and rules. Though they are enemies, the "Friends" and the "Crew" share many problems, such as the protection of their turf, intimidation, violence, and death by other gangs. The teens in this novel live in a world surrounded by death, police brutality, and hatred—a world filled with violence. While reading, students can be asked to discuss alternate or nonviolent ways that the gangs could have handled their problems. The thrust here is to point out that kids in gangs get hurt—lots of them even get killed—because gangs solve their problems through violence. A culminating activity that should be considered is to ask students to compare and contrast the gangs' code of conduct and rules to those held in traditional society.

The narrator in *Soul Fire* (Hewett, 1996) is Todd, a fourteen-year-old boy, living with his brother and two stepsisters. His brother, sixteen-year-old Marcus, is the leader of a gang. Todd's cousin, Zeke, becomes furious when another cousin, Tommy, and other teens, join Marcus' criminal gang. Tommy's initiation into the gang involves brutal beatings by the other members of the gang. When Zeke confronts Marcus, he is seriously wounded by a bullet believed to have been fired by one of Marcus' gang members. Tommy is killed by a bullet that had also been meant for Zeke. This novel speaks to students who have friends or even family members in a gang, and to those who have idealized visions that gangs serve well as surrogate families. Many activities can be used with this novel revolving around family issues. One activity involves asking students to develop a script for a scene in which various family members are notified of Tommy's death. Another activity can involve students writing a eulogy for Tommy, to be delivered by Marcus or by Zeke, at Tommy's funeral. An alternative is to have students rewrite the ending of the story to include a nonviolent settlement of the confrontation between Marcus, Zeke, and Tommy. As they read, ask students to look for ways to turn each violent act into one of nonviolence.

To effectively begin to bring closure to this unit, consider discussing the poem "Do Not Go Gentle Into That Good Night" (Thomas,

1952) followed by Coolio's hit song from the *Dangerous Minds* soundtrack, "Gangsta's Paradise" (1995). In Thomas' poem, the speaker urges a dying man to use all of his remaining strength and will to resist death. Coolio's "Gangsta's Paradise" describes the supposed glory of gang life with a background vocal suggesting that gang members are just too blind to see that they are really only hurting themselves. Ask students to discuss how life would be different for the gang member in Coolio's song if he had heeded Thomas' pleas. This same question could also be asked relative to any of the characters in *A Nation of Amor, Soul Fire* or *Way Past Cool*.

A worthwhile final activity for this unit should be one in which students can gain an awareness that they are at a crossroads in forming lifetime attitudes and building the basis for making critical personal decisions. In so doing, there should be a clear understanding that their attitudes and ideas are shaped each day by an array of messages, not the least of which is one that comes from their own knowledge and experiences. Thus, students can compose a children's book loosely based on a character from one of their readings and demonstrate their ability to make better choices for the character given the same set of circumstances. The book should be written in language appropriate to children between the ages of eight and ten years old and must contain a similar plot or storyline to the one in the original work. The major difference in the original works and the student works would be the refusal of the main character to participate in a gang and the peaceful resolution of conflicts via nonviolent choices by the character. If logistically possible, the children's books could be shared with an elementary school nearby, which would help teach younger children about the evils of becoming a gang member and/or how to resolve conflicts peaceably.

Works Cited

Alarcon, F. X. (1995). L.A. prayer. In V. Cruz, L. Quintana & V. Suarez (Eds.), *Paper dance: 55 latino poets*. New York: Percy Books, 4.
Anderson, E. (1994, May). Code of the streets. *The Atlantic Monthly*: 81–94.
Banks, R. (1996). Adirondack iron. In *Rule of the bone*. New York: Harper Perennial, 42–57.
Carey-Webb, A. (1995). Youth violence and the language arts: A topic for the classroom. *English Journal*, September, 29–37.

Coolio (Performer). (1995). Gangsta's paradise. On *Gangsta's paradise* [CD]. New York: Columbia.

Frost, K. (Performer). (1991). Ain't no sunshine. In *Eastside story* [CD]. Priority Records.

Gansberg, M. (1964, March 27). 38 who saw murder didn't call the police. *New York Times*.

Gardner, S. (1992). *Street gangs in America*. New York: Watts.

Glenn, M. (1991). *My friend's got this problem, Mr. Chandler*. New York: Clarion Books.

Goodwillie, S. (1993). *Voices from the future*. New York: Crown Publishers.

Hewett, L. (1996). *Soul fire*. New York: Dutton Children's Book.

Hinojosa, M. (1995). *Crews*. San Diego: Harcourt Brace Jovanovich.

Hinton, S. E. (1971). *The outsiders*. New York: Dell Publishing.

Homer. (1986). *The odyssey*. New York: Penguin Books.

Ice-T. (Performer). (1988). Colors. In *Colors:* The motion picture soundtrack [CD]. Warner Bros.

Inez, C. (1972). Slumnight. In *The woman who loved worms*. New York: Doubleday.

McCall, N. (1994). *Makes me wanna holler*. New York: Random House.

McConnell, C. (1996). *A nation of amor*. New York: HarperCollins.

Mowry, J. (1992). *Way past cool*. New York: Farrar Straus Giroux.

Olmos, E. (Director). (1992). *American me* [Video]. Universal Pictures.

Rios. A. (1984). Then they'd watch comedies. In *The iguana killer: 12 stories of the heart*. New York: Blue Moon & Confluence Press, 74.

Rubin, N. (1994). *Ask me if I care*. Los Angeles: Ten Speed Press, 304–311.

Scott, D. (Producer). *Menace II society* [Video]. Los Angeles: New Line Cinema.

Shakespeare, W. (1986). *Romeo and Juliet*. New York: Penguin.

Soto, G. (1988). After tonight. In R. Ellmann & R. O'Clair (Eds.), *The Norton anthology of modern poetry*. New York: W. W. Norton, 1683–1684.

Thomas, A. (1991). *Life in the ghetto*. Kansas City: Landmark Editions.

Thomas, D. (1952). Do not go gentle into that good night. In X. J. Kennedy & D. Gioia (Eds.), *Literature: An introduction to fiction, poetry, and drama*. New York: Harper Collins, 771.

Wormser, R. (1994). *Juveniles in trouble*. New York: Simon & Shuster.

Supplementary Resources

Poetry

Clifton, L. (1971). Those boys. In *Poetry brief: An anthology of short, short, short poems.* New York: The Macmillan Company, 119.
A short powerful poem relating the anguish felt by people whose loved ones decide to join a gang and participate in violent activities.

Glenn, M. (1982). Orlando Martinez. In *Class dismissed.* New York: Clarion Books.
A student is randomly stabbed right in front of the school where he used to skip classes. He is saved by school employees and wonders if they even found "the guy who stabbed me?"

Justice, D. (1988). The tourist from Syracuse. In R. Ellmann & R. O'Clair (Eds.), *The Norton anthology of modern poetry.* New York: W. W. Norton,1152.
Written from the point of view of a stalker waiting out his victim, the speaker dwells on his anonymous appearance and how he could be mistaken for anyone because he is a stranger to his victim. This idea, coupled with the stalker not knowing his victim, emphasizes the randomness of violent crimes of opportunity—robbery, rape, serial homicide. The poem ends with a very ominous warning from the speaker: "You turn/To approach that place where now/ You must not hope to arrive."

Soto, G. (1985). The morning they shot Tony Lopez, barber and pusher who went too far, 1958. In D. Bottoms & D. Smith (Eds.), *The Morrow anthology of younger American poets.* New York: Quill, 638.
A barber's life flashes by as he collapses from a fatal gunshot wound. The language in the poem is concrete and filled with poignant imagery.

Short Stories and Drama

Geiogamah, H. (1980). Body indian. In *New Native American drama: Three plays.* Norman: University of Oklahoma Press.

Laurents, Arthur (1956). *West side story.* New York: Random House.
A modern day version of Shakespeare's Romeo and Juliet,

depicting conflicts between the Anglo Sharks and the Puerto Rican Jets. The fighting intensifies when Tony, a member of the Sharks, falls in love with Maria, the sister of a Jet.

Mowry, J. (1990). Fire. In *Rats in the trees: Stories.* New York: Penguin, 79–124.

A runaway, Robby, is introduced to a gang called The Animals just in time to get involved in a war with another gang. Words are exchanged, a fire is started, and Robby kills one of the other gang members.

O'Connor, F. (1977). Masculine protest. In C. E. Redman (Ed.), *Introduction to the short story.* New York: Litton Educational Publishing, 205–206.

The story of a twelve-year-old child who, lacking love and attention at home turns to a life on the streets. As a result, he becomes a member of a "classy" gang that aims to keep "slummy" kids from their neighborhood.

Stern, S. (1996). Rebel without a cause. In S. Thomas (Ed.), *Best American screen plays first series: Complete screen plays.* New York: Crown Publishers.

A young man gets involved in a gang conflict while struggling to come to terms with the reality that he cannot hide behind his parents' social and economic status. This work is also available in a video version starring the late James Dean.

Novels (Fiction)

Bonham, F. (1965). *Durango Street.* New York: E. P. Dutton.

This novel depicts the violent world of Rufus Henry, gangs, and the people who try to help teenagers who get involve in violence.

Brown, M. (1974). *The second stone.* New York: Putnam.

Fright and loyalty keep a fifteen-year-old youth from turning in his best friend who he suspects is part of a gang that is terrorizing the neighborhood.

Butterworth, W. (1980). *Leroy and the old man.* New York: Four Winds Press.

A young man witnesses gang members mugging an old lady and is faced with the moral dilemma of testifying against the gang members or remaining in hiding with his grandfather. Though not involved with a gang, Leroy is impacted by the violence of gang life.

Cormier, R. (1991). *We all fall down*. New York: Delacorte Press.
> Teenagers from middle-class families participate in random acts of violence because of lack of guidance and love from their families. This novel explores the motivating forces behind teenagers who inflict violence on innocent victims.

Dean, W. (1988). *Scorpions*. New York: HarperCollins.
> Jamal, an adolescent boy, is appointed the leader of the Scorpions and is given a gun as a symbol of his new position. Both the gun and his new position change Jamal's life forever.

Garland, S. (1993). *Shadow of the dragon*. San Diego: Harcourt Brace.
> This novel is about a sixteen-year-old Asian-American boy who feels caught between the two worlds of American and Vietnamese gang life when he becomes a silent witness to the actions of his gangster cousin.

Katz, S. (1987). *Florry of Washington Heights*. LA: Sun & Moon.
> The main character, Swanny, a nice boy who is more interested in baseball than being in a gang is forced into a violent situation when a member of his baseball team falls in love with Florry, the sister of a gang leader.

Lopez, S. (1994). *Third and Indiana*. New York: Penguin Group.
> Gabriel, who began his life of violence and crime at twelve, is now the youngest member of the Black Cap gang and deals drugs on the most dangerous corner in downtown Philadelphia. Although he would like to escape the gang life, he is trapped by Diablo, a gang leader and drug dealer who kills for fun. Readers can see how gang life is filled with crime and violence and difficult to outrun.

Platt, K. (1975). *Headman*. New York: Greenwillow Books.
> This novel features a teenage boy who tries to find some way of surviving a neighborhood that is filled with violence and gangs.

Wright, R. (1994). *Rite of passage*. New York: HarperCollins.
> This novel focuses on Johnny Gibbs, a good student and well behaved teenager who finds out that he is a foster child. When told he is going to be moved elsewhere by welfare authorities, Johnny runs away and joins a gang. To gain respect, Johnny wins a vicious fight with the gang leader and participates in a mugging. Readers can see how societal conditions and institutions sometimes set up conditions that can create violent reactions.

Nonfiction Works and Essays

Atkin, S. (1996). *Voices from the street: Young former gang members tell their stories.* New York: Little, Brown & Company.
> The book is filled with photographs, poems, and interviews with former gang members who speak of their lives and experiences.

Bing, L. (1991). *Do or die.* New York: HarperCollins.
> Bing enters the dangerous world of the notorious gangs, the Crips and the Bloods, and succeeds in capturing what life is really like on the streets.

Gale, W. (1977). *The compound.* New York: Rawson Associates.
> Using the voices and experiences of gang members and their women, Gale relates the story of how gangs virtually ruled a high school and extorted money from local businesses. This is a true story that deals with teens without families who faced racism and poverty, and turned to gangs for support and a sense of belonging.

Rodriguez, L. (1993). *Always running: La vida loca: Gang Days in LA.* New York: Touchstone.
> An insider's view of Hispanic gangs in California. The author addresses this book to his son in an effort to keep him out of gang violence.

Welch, J. (1986). *Fools crow.* New York: Viking.
> A historical novel, set in Montana during the nineteenth century, which tells the story of retaliatory gangs formed by Native Americans to respond to White encroachment.

Movies and Videos

Mi vida loca [Video]. HBO. (1994). Directed by A. Anders.
> This film portays the female perspective of gang life. Anders brings the reality of the violent life of Latina gang members who share their innermost thoughts and emotions. Beware of occasional foul language, however.

That was then, this is now [movie]. (1985). Directed by C. Cain. Hollywood, CA: Paramount.
> This movie is based on S. E. Hinton's book of the same name and tells the story of Byron, a teenager who wants to end the violence and crime in his neighborhood. His desire is complicated by the

fact that his child-hoodfriend, Mark, is actively involved in pushing drugs to young kids.

Boyz n the hood [Video]. (1991). Directed by J. Singleton. Columbia Pictures.

This movie can be easily juxtaposed with *Romeo and Juliet* because it has the elements of revenge and violence that threaten the relationship of the two characters who are in love.

South central [Video]. (1992). Produced by O. Stone. Burbank, CA: Warner Home Video.

A former gang member comes home after being incarcerated to find his son is now a member of his former gang. He must face members of his former gang and gain the respect of his son in order to take his son away to a new and better life. This movie is violent, but is useful in helping viewers understand how joining a gang is a lifelong commitment that is difficult to leave.

CHAPTER FOUR

GROWING STRONG FAMILY TREES

Pamela S. Carroll

Morning Noon and Night
Belkis L. Cabrera

The mango pokes through fences
Scraping kitchen windows
As language falls like leaves.
He crosses the newspaper
Over his chest
And leans to cup
Hot coffee
The warm white smoke
Settling on his mustache
And his blue-black frames
The paper crumbles into half-folds
And she makes pancakes
And he says butter
With the sizzle of bacon
On the side
She lays the some-brand corn flakes
Centerpieced on the table
And cracks eggs along
Stove corners
Pouring into non-stick pans
And he calls over
Easy

And she wipes her hands
On the blue-white bathrobe
Tossing rags in the sink.
I drink my milk
In salad bowls
Reading between the columns
And her sandals
And the bald spot on his head
And there is nothing said.
Outside
The mango moans in a heavy breeze
Like the house
Settling
Its limbs bruised brown
As noon comes
With the lightning
With the flicker of the tube
That rapes silence
In blurs of action and sound
As she pushes my chair
And molds my back with her hands
We dine
In with home-cooked TV dinners
And remote company.
The mango grows quietly
Branch by branch.
At night
He checks the locks
She tucks me in
And I motion a prayer
Into curtained windows.

Selecting a Family-Oriented Topic and Literary Texts for Your Students

Despite differences in their racial, ethnic, economic, and educational backgrounds, our students have one thing in common: All have some experiences with families. Some of our students have experiences that are predominantly positive, ones that gently yet firmly support the adolescents' growth toward adulthood. Other students have family experiences that are devastating and destructive, ones that create barriers that interfere with their ability to develop into trusting, loving, and contributing adults. It seems that no matter how different today's families are from yesterday's, or one community's are from another's, students need to be offered the opportunity to discover that healthy family relationships require communication and understanding. However, students are not likely to appreciate or understand others in their homes if they do not see themselves connected to the family. By focusing on families and family relationships in a media-enhanced literary unit, students will have the opportunity to think about themselves, their families, and others' families as they expand their definition of "family." Regardless of where their personal experiences fall on the continuum of definitions of the modern American family, a continuum that ranges from traditional (two parents, two children structures) to modern (one parent, one child or more) to controversial (single-sex parents with one child or more), students are likely to benefit from a concentrated look at their families as they compare and contrast the roles of family members as presented in literature and portrayed in popular media.

Our topic choice is "Growing Strong Family Trees." In the following pages, we offer suggestions for an introductory activity that sets the stage for a culminating one, and mid-unit activities that incorporate contemporary music, movies and videos, and printed texts, and which engage students as folklore researchers, actors, writers, and informed television viewers. We encourage teacher-readers to select the activities that develop the specific family-focused topic they have chosen, those that fit the needs and interests of their students, and those that best support their own teaching and learning goals. We hope that the list of suggested texts and other materials for the unit will help you begin to think of the novels, stories, songs, movies, and other media that you could include in your family-focused unit; we especially hope that our list will suggest to you a text or movie that you have not taught regularly, or which you have never found a place for in your curriculum. We believe that planning and implementing lessons should be an adventure for teachers, just as the results should allow for adventure among students.

We recommend reading and studying one or more of the following as core pieces of literature during the "Growing Strong Family Trees" or similar units. Clyde Edgerton's hilarious *Walking Across Egypt* would be our top choice if we were limited to only one novel to teach in a heterogeneously-grouped whole-class setting, and we wanted a light text that would be likely to cause students to laugh during reading. If our focus was on a more serious note, we would select Achebe's modern classic, *Things Fall Apart*, for its literary quality and its social implications. Small groups could read works from each category of texts, and view different movies or videos, and so on. Then each group could, periodically throughout the duration of the unit, report to the entire class on the family issues within the texts. Because family issues will be a part of each text, students should be able to engage in meaningful conversations about the modern family, despite the fact that no one will have read and studied every text that will be mentioned during class discussions.

Suggestions for Whole-Class or Small-Group Reading

These books are recommended for whole-class or small-group instruction, depending on your purposes and on the blend of students in your classes. Some are traditional choices; others are contemporary adult books; a few, as noted, are young adult books that will be especially appropriate for reluctant or unskilled readers. The suggestions include books that we hope will offer special appeal to readers with wide-ranging interests and reasons for reading; each book will promote discussion of family relationships. Please also see other recommendations at the end of the chapter.

Chinua Achebe. (1959). *Things Fall Apart*. New York: Doubleday. In this novel, the world of the Ibo, a Nigerian tribe, is brought to life. Rich with cultural elements, the story begins with the introduction of Okonkwo, the protagonist; his relationships with his family and tribe members are revealed. American readers are allowed a glimpse of a different culture's family life and rituals, including child-rearing practices, polygamy, and the role of women. Readers also may see that there are similarities in family relationships that transcend cultural differences.

Alden Carter. (1989). *Up Country*. New York: G. P. Putnam's Sons. In this engrossing young adult novel, Carl Stagger's love for his alcoholic mother causes him to continue to support her even after she has run-ins with the law. It is not until Carl has to move "up country" to live with his uncle's family, that he begins to understand what a supportive, close family can provide. Carl is left to decide whether he will return to his mother after her trial, or stay with his uncle's family, the kind of family he has always dreamed of having. Carter speaks clearly and eloquently to teenage readers. This is a fine novel for reluctant readers; its fast action and realistic presentation of a kid with serious problems make it rewarding for students who do not normally like to read fiction.

Clyde Edgerton. (1987). *Walking Across Egypt*. New York: Ballantine. This delightfully funny and poignant book, presents a quirky seventy-eight-year-old protagonist, Mrs. Mattie Rigsbee, and the two strays she adopts: a dog and Wesley Benfield, a juvenile delinquent. Her grown son objects to her actions, usually between bites of her famous apple pie. Mrs. Rigsbee, whose favorite hymn is the title of the novel, will be instantly familiar to readers who have eccentric characters in their families, and will represent a new way of looking at the world for those who do not instantly recognize her. The family relationships in this book are unusual; Mattie grows to be more dependent on delinquent Wesley Benfield than on her own son; nevertheless, the extended "family" works in its unique way. Important questions about love and loyalties, right and wrong treatment of others, are raised in this entertaining novel.

Connie Mae Fowler. (1992). *Sugar Cage*. New York: Washington Square. This is the remarkable story of adolescent Emory Looney's family—his father and he fight, his mother tries to hold them together but is unable to—and the people whose lives touch theirs. The characters include the wise African-American maid, Inez Temple, who transcends the racial prejudices of those around her in the southern United States of the mid-twentieth century, and the mysterious Haitian woman, Soleil Marie Beauvoir, who is a blend of other-worldliness and innocence. Each character tells his and her own story, and the reader is left with the pleasure of piecing the tales together.

Barbara Kingsolver. (1990). *Animal Dreams*. New York: HarperCollins. This novel, told in first person by Cosima (Codi) Noline, grown daughter of Dr. Homer Noline, the only doctor in tiny Grace, Arizona. Codi has returned home, after quitting medical school and failing, too, in relationships, because her father is growing senile. The presence of her twin sister, Hallie, who has gone to Central America to help farmers, is a strong one. Codi tries to make sense of her memories of a deeply troubled childhood, and to accept the now-manly affection of a one-time boyfriend who is part Apache, Navajo, and Pueblo Indian. She still feels like the outcast she was as a child and marvels that her sister is able to take actions to try to improve the world. Kingsolver's language is, in places, mesmerizing—this novel is likely to provide student writers with a bank of examples of figurative language to use as models. Once they become aware of the narrative structure of this book, in which speakers alternate chapters, this book becomes accessible to most average high school readers. Its length, 342 pages, however, will frighten some reluctant readers away.

Lee Smith. (1983). *Oral History*. New York: Ballantine. This novel represents the strength of family against outsiders. Jennifer Cantrell, a city cousin to the country Cantrell clan, wants to record their story for a family project. Several narrators share the duty of telling the stories that Jennifer gathers.

John Steinbeck. (1947). *The Pearl*. Toronto: Bantam. This modern classic features a fisherman, Kino, who finds a pearl of great value. With the pearl, Kino hopes to provide his wife and his son with happiness and prosperity. As it turns out, though, the pearl does more damage than good. Kino's struggles lead him to understand that the happiness he wants for his family can only come from love, not material possessions. This book, offered for years in English curricula, is appealing for reluctant readers because of its short length and its seemingly simple structure. Average high school students can read and makes sense of it, at least on the literal level, without intervention from teachers.

Alice Walker. (1982). *The Color Purple*. New York: Pocket. This novel, recommended for mature high school readers, those who are willing to wrestle with a complex text and sophisticated subject matter, depicts the bond between two sisters, Celie and Nettie, who struggle to survive despite being torn from each other and forced to live apart, and experiencing vitriolic racial prejudice, hatred, poverty, rape, and other horrors. Celie tries to make sense of her world, and finds hope in the attention she receives from Shug Avery, her husband's girlfriend. Violence and abuse, both physical and emotional, take on the significance of characters in this powerful novel.

Growing Strong Family Trees: Teaching and Learning Activities

In the pages that follow, we have attempted to describe instructional activities and the literary and media suggestions in such a way that teachers can easily transfer and adapt our ideas for their own specific units on the American family. Literature-based studies of the American family also might be developed and organized around topics similar to the ones included in this group of one dozen suggestions:

- Families of the Past and Families of the Present
- Parents and their Children: Learning to See the World with the Other's Eyes
- Family Folklore
- Skipping a Generation: Grandparents and their Grandchildren
- Siblings: Rivals and Friends
- Families Across Cultures
- Smooth and Bumpy Rides: The Family as a Lifelong Adventure
- Family Strength and Family Frailty
- Appreciating our Families
- Fictitious Families: Comedy, Tragedy, Irony, and Satire
- Families in the Media: Values Affirmed, Values Tested
- Single Parent, Same-Sex Parents, and other American Families Structures

It might be interesting for the teacher to ask different classes to study the American family from slightly different perspectives, such as those implied in the list above. Another option is to have small groups of students within a single class select a family-related subtopic for investigation; each group could, as a culminating activity, develop a presentation in which the subtopic is discussed in terms of literature and other media, and in which students' original written and visual compositions are highlighted.

Planting and Nourishing the Tree with an Oral History Project

As a complement to their reading both required and self-selected literature about families, viewing films and videos that feature families, and developing expanded definitions for what constitutes a "modern family," students may be particularly interested in investigating their own families more closely. One activity that we recommend for the "Growing Strong Family Trees" unit is a modified oral history project. The primary job for students during the modified oral history project will be to conduct interviews and record the information they gather. The project serves as both an introductory and, ultimately, a concluding activity, and complements the reading and/or viewing of any of the core novels (listed above). Students will develop oral histories throughout the duration of the unit, and will present their oral histories as a culmination (as described in more detail, below).

Ideally, teachers will introduce the oral history assignment on the first or second day of the families unit. The time during which they will work, outside of class, on the oral histories should correspond with the time they engage in the in-class literature and media studies of the unit. The teacher may choose to require students to turn in, at regular intervals, keep a "project log" for the duration of the families unit. The project log will be a place in which students record a realistic plan for conducting oral history interviews, and then report, on a weekly basis, the progress they are making on their projects.

After students have gathered and transcribed oral histories, they might be given several class periods in order to compose, peer edit, revise, and polish their final products. Several days may need to be reserved for the presentation of oral histories, depending on class size and the types of presentations that students choose. Presentations may take many forms, with evaluations based on the quality of research and presentations, as appropriate for individual classes. Please see the section, "Concluding the Unit," below, for specific suggestions regarding the culminating activity.

Guidelines for Beginning the Oral History Project

Informed by Steven J. Zeitlin's "How to Collect Your Own Family Folklore" in *A Celebration of American Family Folklore* (Pantheon, 1982) students may benefit by receiving and discussing the following hints about conducting interviews with a goal of compiling an oral history of the family:

1. Talk to as many family members as possible, and remember that "family" has many definitions; even if the adults who are raising you, for example, did not give birth to you, they are filling the role of parents, and are thus members of your family. (See the list of possible interview

questions below.) Include everyone whom you identify as a member of your family, regardless of whether or not you are actually related by blood.

2. Record every detail you can, using a tape recorder if possible, since it is difficult to maintain a conversation if you are trying to write down your informant's words. Test the microphone and volume level before you begin interviewing an informant, to be sure that both of your voices are audible. Try to make the surroundings as quiet as possible to reduce interference with your voices on tape. Soon after the interview, transcribe the conversation, adding notes about facial expressions and gestures that were particularly effective in conveying the speaker's intended meanings, since those will not be captured on an audio cassette tape.

3. Start by interviewing yourself as a member of your family. What do you know about the history and unique characteristics of your family? Some specific questions that might prompt your thoughts in several directions are these: How do you celebrate birthdays? Are family dinners a part of your daily routine, or reserved for special occasions? Are any items passed from father to son, or mother to daughter? Are the names of children in your family part of a tradition? How are nicknames bestowed upon members of your family? Where have you lived during your lifetime? How many of your relatives do you know? Whom do you visit, as a family? Do you take time off from work/school together?

4. Next, interview someone with whom you feel quite comfortable. In a traditional family, one's siblings or grandparents are a likely choice. If you have a non-traditional family structure, you can choose anyone who is a part of your group with whom you feel at ease talking, even if he or she is not related "by blood" to you.

5. Remember that your family's history is ongoing. Include attention to traditions, habits, expressions, and rituals that are part of your family in the present as well as those that were associated with your family in the past. Ask everyone who gives you information for the names of others who might also know about your family's events, traditions, expressions, rituals, and talk with those people to get their own personal perspectives, too. This cross-referencing of ideas will add depth and thus enrich your family history. When you write about events that happen in the present and that happened in the past, be sure to give details about the times and settings, so that the stories you have to tell speak clearly of your family as it exists or existed in a particular time and place.

Conducting Oral History Interviews

Students can use a list of questions, such as the one that follows, as a way to begin asking questions of themselves and then of family members, if they wish. The teacher might remind students that the list of questions can and should be modified to fit the informant and the student).

Gathering Oral Histories: Possible Interview Questions

A. Stories

What stories do you know about your parents and grandparents or guardians? Do other adults fulfill "family roles" for you, such as an "aunt" who is not related by blood but who is such a close friend of the family that she has been "adopted" as a relative? Have any of these significant adults described their childhood to you? What have they told you about themselves as school children and as adolescents? What do your parents and grandparents like to do for recreation? Do they worship, and if so, how? Is the past a time that is pleasant to recall, or a time that is better forgotten, from your parents' and grandparents' perspectives? Are there certain pieces of your family's history that you have heard references to, but which no one has explained to you? How do your parents, grandparents, aunts, uncles, stepparents, siblings, step-and half-siblings, and so on tell stories about the same events in your family's recent history? What do the differences in their tellings say about them? Are there family heirlooms that are passed from one generation to the next, with stories attached? What are the stories, and how have they changed over time?

B. Characters

Are there any members of your family (in the past) who are notorious or infamous characters? Have stories about those characters grown more exaggerated as they have been passed down through the family's generations? Who is the most flamboyant member of your family today? What makes him or her so? Do other family members agree with your choice? Why or why not? Are there any stories of a family member making a great fortune (and perhaps losing it, too)? Do family members recall incidents related to that fortune with laughter or regret?

C. Love

Are there any family stories of lost loves, jilted brides, unusual courtships, arranged marriages, elopements, runaway lovers, and so on? How do the men and women in your family show their love for each other? Do you (and other family members) get along with your siblings and cousins? Are there members of your family whom you just cannot seem to appreciate, no matter how hard you try? If so, what is it about them—and you—that creates a clash? Who has been included in your family who was not born into it (is there a friend of your brother who came to live with the family, for example)? Have housekeepers or cooks been included in the family by any of your generations? What were their roles like? Where did they eat and sleep? How were they paid? What privileges did they enjoy?

D. Historical Events

Have any historical events affected your family in a direct way? For example, are there survivors of World War II concentration camps in your family? Have members survived a hurricane, flood, tornado, earthquake, volcanic eruption, or other natural event? Have conflicts within the family over national events, such as the Viet Nam war, caused a serious break in family relations? Where have your family members lived, during your lifetime and in previous generations? Have the moves affected the family?

E. Language

What expressions do members of your family use that are unique to your family? What are the origins of those expressions? Which dialects have had an influence on the kind of language your family members use? Are there generational differences in the ways some common items, such as refrigerators and lunch, are referred to by members of your family? How are nicknames established in your family? Are there any with unusual histories? Are there any that are too embarrassing to be used outside of the family? Is any particular member of your family especially adept at assigning nicknames? Do your family members use any unusual or special titles to refer to each other? Is anyone called "Uncle" or "Aunt," and so on, who is not related by blood to any member of your family? If so, why?

F. Food

Have any recipes been preserved in your family from past generations? What were their origins? How have they been passed from one generation to the next? Are they still in use? When and by whom? Does Great-Grandma's special pie recipe taste as good when it is baked by Uncle Charles as when Great-Grandma used to bake it?

G. Artifacts

Does your family have photograph albums, scrapbooks, boxes of memorabilia, home movies or videos, or slides? Who created them? Who keeps the collection? Is the collection still growing? What do the photos, scrapbook entries, and so on say about the family members that they reflect? What could a stranger learn about your family by looking through the collection of memorabilia?

H. Other questions

(Sometimes, you will need to develop questions that make sense only for your family. Often, these questions will emerge after you have begun talking with family members to whom you feel close. Be sure to add your questions so that you will not forget to ask them when the time and informant is right.)

Culminating Activity: Presenting Oral Family Histories

A few of our favorite modes for presentation of the information that students gather while conducting interviews and compiling oral histories of their families include these:

1. Family scrapbooks, in which photographs and other artifacts are accompanied by excerpts from transcribed oral histories, and shared orally, then put on display for the class.
2. Edited audio-scrapbook, in which the student carefully selects and edits excerpts from the tape-recorded oral histories, compiles them into one history, then adds a narrative strand in which he or she connects and comments of the recorded voices and stories.

3. A videotape or slide presentation, in which the student videotapes people and places that are important in the family's present and or past, and adds a narrative that comments on the visual images and their significance to the family. Where it is impossible to use family members' faces or footage of actual locations (images of those who are deceased or living too far away for access, and places that have been destroyed, for example) students might choose to include abstractions that represent those people and places.

4. A family web site, in which the student designs a web page with links to information about the family's history in several categories, such as "stories," "language," "artifacts," and so on.

In each instance, students could present their products to their peers and answer questions about the contents or methods of presenting information. (Before using classroom technology as a part of a presentation, be sure that each student conducts a "run through" using the school's equipment, to test for glitches in the equipment, or other possible problems, such as classroom lighting, availability of equipment, and so on.) Specific presentation dates for each student should be arranged at least one week ahead of time, so that each can invite family members, if possible, to attend the presentations.

Other Activities to Include During the Growing Strong Family Trees Unit

Popular Music

One of our favorite activities for enhancing the families unit involves the use of recorded popular music of the recent past and present. Since one of our instructional goals is to help students develop several legitimate definitions of the family, we recommend using contemporary music as a vehicle in which the family is presented in a variety of ways. We refer briefly to the following songs, each of which has been popular with our students, but we encourage you to select songs with which your own students may already be familiar and to which they are likely to respond.

John Lennon's "Beautiful Boy (Darling Boy)" (*Double Fantasy*, Capitol, 1980) speaks lovingly of a father's affection for his adored son, with a refrain that affirms the father's love and desire to protect and soothe his child. Our students have enjoyed studying it and imitating its words with their own.

In contrast, Suzanne Vega's "Luka" (A&M Records, 1984) presents a sad and abusive family. Its lyrics include troublesome lines that hint not only at the ugliness of the family's fights, but also at the hopeless despair felt by a young victim of the family violence. Most of our students are deeply bothered by this song; it has provided an impetus, in a few cases, for students who were previously uninvolved in the issues studies in class, to begin to conduct research on abuse within families.

You may wish to give students a full or partial copy of the lyrics of each song and then play the songs while students listen. Students should write or draw their responses to each song before any discussion of the songs ensues. With these two songs, or another pairing that presents opposing views of family relationships, students can be asked to react by brain storming to two word-pair prompts: healthy family/dysfunctional family. You might ask them to respond further to some leading statements about functional and dysfunctional families that are drawn from portrayals of the family relationships presented in the songs. For instance, in association with "Beautiful Boy (Darling Boy)," you might ask students to consider these statements:

- It is vital that fathers act as the protector of the family.
- Children are more secure when their fathers openly demonstrate affection toward them.
- A father's love is always strong enough to drive away children's monsters.

Students should not feel obliged to agree with these statements. The statements should be written and presented as a means of opening conversation about the issues underlying them; discussion that ensues is likely to explore the assumptions upon which the statements are based. Benefits of this activity do not stop with the insights about family relationships that students will be able to articulate and consider. As a teacher, you will grow to understand your students' stances and feelings regarding family relationships better during this brainstorming activity if you pay close attention to students' remarks; students' comments are also likely to reveal some of the sources that influence their thoughts about today's families during the brainstorm.

Another provocative pairing is Carly Simon's "Like a River," (*Letters Never Sent*, Arista, 1994), and Harry Chapin's "Cat's in the

Cradle" (*Greatest Stories: Live*, Elektra, 1976). In Simon's song, the daughter's voice explains, in a moving chorus, that her relationship with her mother has evolved; she will not think of herself in the role of daughter any longer, but instead will be an eternal, life-filled and life-giving river for her mother. The mother's voice assures, in a dramatic flourish, that she will never abandon her daughter, because she will live always in her child's memory. Students might be encouraged to respond, perhaps by writing a poem, to symbols sprinkled throughout the song (such as the river, a candle, or stars), to the family scene on the occasion of the mother's death that is presented in the first stanza, to the kinds of questions the child had asked her mother as recalled in the second stanza, or other aspects of the song that catch their attention. The simple questions that ask students to think about how someone might be a river, or mountain, or glacier, or beach, and so on, for another person, may also prompt thoughtful discussion and student writing.

In Chapin's song, a father admits that he was often not available to his son when the boy was growing up; he laments that the son, now grown, has no time for his father. There is no evidence of abuse in the relationship, merely the strain on a father whose priority seems to be making money for his family rather than spending time with them, contrasted with the son's simple requests for time to play with his dad. Early in the song, the refrain is the son's hopeful promise that he will grow up to be just like his father. Later in the song, the refrain twists to the father's melancholy realization that his son has, indeed, grown up to be like him, driven by money and a career, and with few strong connections to the people who have loved him most. Students can explore the irony of the father's actions being repeated by the son; they might also explore the symbolic power of the silver spoon that is referred to in the refrain, and of other symbols in the song. Provocative assumption statements that could be derived from these songs include these:

- Daughters and mothers get along better after the daughter has grown up and appreciates her mother as a woman.
- Mothers should spend more time trying answer their daughters' questions about life.
- Fathers push sons into adult roles too quickly.
- The strongest influence on the kind of person a boy will become is his father.

Students might also compare and contrast, and then rate the effectiveness of the figurative language used in two or more of the songs, and prepare a chart or compose an essay in which they compare and contrast two songs in terms of similarities and differences in purpose and tone. Some may even choose to write an additional verse or refrain for one or more of the songs, perhaps adopting the perspective of the son ("Beautiful Boy"), either parent ("Luka"), the mother ("Like a River") or the grandson ("Cat's in the Cradle"). Of course, popular songs that address the issue of family relationships will continue to emerge; if we keep our ears and minds open, we will continually hear possibilities for instruction when we tune in to the music of the day.

One of the benefits of these activities is that they begin with a focus on the texts of the songs, but move immediately toward the ways in which the students connect with the songs through their own experiences and understandings. It may be necessary to explain to students that they do not have to feel that the song describes their family exactly in order for them to "connect" with it in some way. While, for some, one or both of the songs may evoke a direct memory, for others it may cause a memory of someone else's family to emerge. It may even cause them to remember a fictitious family from literature, television, or a movie; in each of these cases, students' prior experiences can be brought to bear on the song(s), so that when the students engage in a literary event that focuses on the song texts, they grow as thinkers.

After studying the songs, students are likely to begin understanding that the family can be described and defined in many ways, some of which are pleasant and comfortable, and others that are threatening and oppressive. They might be asked to create a graph of where they see themselves, and their families, along the continuum of family relationships that emerges as they react to the songs.

Tableaux as Response for Literature, Songs, Television, Movies/Videos

Another activity that we have found interesting for students and teachers is the creation of a tableau as a response to a part of a literary text, television show, or movie. A tableau, as described by Purves, Rogers, and Soter in *How Porcupines Make Love, III: Readers, Texts, Cultures in the Response-Based Literature Classroom* (1995), is simply a type of still-life pantomime. Classroom actors depict a particular scene or moment from the text, then, on the count of three, freeze the scene by being absolutely motionless and silent. The audience looks on to try to make sense of actors' facial and bodily expressions, their relationships in space to the other actors in the scene, and so on. Students can simply be asked to select a passage, line, or even phrase that arrests their attention. Next, they work in small groups to create a "tableau" for one or more of the images evoked for them, as readers, listeners, or viewers.

This activity requires students to collaborate to identify the scene they wish to freeze and to determine whether the tableau will reflect the text exactly, or if changes in chronology, and so on, may be necessary. For example, a group of students recently created a tableau response to Virginia Euwer Wolff's *Make Lemonade* (1994). In the fixed scene, teen-mom Jill is with her two young children when the daughter begins to choke. The boy reaches the telephone and points to "9" in an attempt to do what he vaguely knows is proper, to dial 911, but he is unable to actually dial the number. For the tableau, though, the students took artistic license; they portrayed the little boy as if he were talking on the telephone to the 911 operator, the distressed operator, and, to the side, the desperate mother with the choking child.

Students who choose to respond to literature or other media using a tableau will find that they have several decisions to make, few of which are obvious at the outset of the project. For example, imagine that those who read Eudora Welty's "Why I Live at the P.O." (1979) as part of the instructional unit of families decide to freeze the scene in which Sister is arguing with her Mama and her sister, Stella Rondo, about Stella Rondo's odd daughter. Mama asks Stella Rondo, at Sister's urging, if the child can talk. A moment later, the child, unseen, begins to sing like the theme of the *Popeye the Sailor Man* cartoon, and to tap dance. Students would have to decide which of the characters to show in the tableau, and whether or not (or how) to show the mother and sisters arguing at the same time that the child begins to sing and dance. They would also need to give special care to spatial relationships between the characters, and to each character's facial expressions in order to reflect the attitudes toward each other that are implied in the literary text. Students in the audience, if they too have read the short story, could guess which scene is being presented in tableau, then discuss its significance in the story.

Purves, Rogers, and Sotor suggest that tableaux allow students to concentrate their efforts on a specific part of a text and to respond to it physically and visually, two response modes that we often forget to offer in high school classrooms. We find that this kind of response is particularly effective for students who are reluctant to spend time writing. It is also fun and a nonthreatening way to encourage the full participation of students whose native language is not English. As an additional benefit, teachers are able to see what attracts students' attention in texts by asking them to present tableaux; students in the audience quickly realize that different readers, listeners, viewers, are affected by different parts of texts.

Tune in to See Yourself: A Television Family Project

A fourth activity that we have found popular among students involves a critical look at the family as it is portrayed on television. Teachers might begin this activity by asking themselves and their students this question: Why is the television an important source of information for teenagers as they try to define the modern American family? Answers might lead to a consideration of ideas such as the mixed messages that teens absorb as they try to identify with characters and situations on television:

- Some of our students see their families reflected in the pleasant and sometimes silly situations of the mother, father, and two children of the Cunningham family, on Nickelodeon's reruns of *Happy Days*; others see this 1950s family as a dated and humorous reminder of a past era in America's social history.
- Some feel the angst of the daughters of the cutting and sometimes crude parents on CBS's *Roseanne*. Others identify with the rebellious, introverted daughter of the overly involved, divorced mother, Cybill, of the CBS show that bears her name.
- Some see themselves like the often rejected Steve Erkel of CBS's *Family Matters*, or the ever-embarrassed Bart Simpson, son of Homer on Fox's cartoon *The Simpsons*.
- A few have lived through experiences similar to the revolving doors of romance, marriage, and family destruction of television's Fox's *Melrose Place*.
- Some have single parents who, like the eponymous character of *Grace Under Fire*, cannot seem to get ahead no matter how hard they try; and despite those parents' efforts to keep a positive attitude, life at home sometimes seems gloomy.
- Some feel as if their family relationships are fit for television talk

shows, with topics such as "My Dad Drinks Too Much," "Caught in the Middle When My Parents Got Divorced," "My Mom Doesn't Know My Dad's Name," or "Dad is Dating My Best Friend."

We recommend that teachers allow students to talk, with the whole class or in small groups, about how their families remind them of particular television shows. Next, a fun and challenging activity for high school students can be developed around the families that are portrayed on television. Here is how it works:

1. Students work in small groups (three to five per group works well). Each group lists three television series that members will watch, videotape, and analyze. Each show needs to feature family members who interact often with each other—ideally in each episode. Students need to see at least two episodes of each selected series, in order to get an idea of how the characters interact in a variety of situations; therefore, they should be allowed two weeks to view, videotape, and analyze the selected shows.

The viewing and analyzing sessions in which members of the groups engage can be done, in many cases, in conjunction with the other reading and studying activities that are part of the families-oriented unit. However, if students need to use school-owned equipment for recording then reviewing and analyzing videotapes of the recorded television shows, they will need to be allowed some class time to meet in groups and do their work. The teacher may also need to arrange to have the media specialist record the student-selected television programs in the event that no group member has access to a video recorder at home.

2. While viewing the shows and the recorded tapes, students in the groups will complete comment sheets (see example below). The sheets require that students pay close attention to the specific mannerisms, including speech, attitude, posture, facial expressions, use of language, and any other observable aspects, of all key characters in the episodes. They will chart the characters' interactions with their television family members and friends. Students will also record information about the plot, temporal and geographic setting, and mood of each episode. This sheet becomes the group's reference tool; the more filled with information it is, the more useful it will be during the next stage of the project.

3. Students in the group will select one memorable literary passage—one that features a family—from the literature studied by the entire class during the unit. The excerpt may portray a family in conflict or in crisis; on the other hand, it may show them helping one another or celebrating a holiday or enjoying an average day. The only requirement is that the family-focused literary passage be one that appeals to the group.

4. Students will rewrite the passage to include the characters from one or more of the television shows that they have watched critically. The revised version should be true to the characters from the television series, but also true to the setting and basic plot of the literary passage. The tone of the literary passage may have to be changed in order to accommodate the inclusion of the television characters. This kind of change should actually be encouraged, since it helps students to understand the connection between situation, characters, and tone by demonstrating first hand how one change has a ripple effect. The addition of comic characters, for example, to a serious scene, may change the nature of the scene, even if the setting remains constant. Such would be the case in the following situation: Suppose a group chooses to view *Home Improvement* (CBS) and they record an episode in which the two older brothers are trying to convince the youngest brother that he was the child of a space creature, only to be discovered by their father. The group will have to pay particular attention to the ways the three boys act and interact. The information will be recorded on the comment sheet. The group will then select a passage of literature into which the three brothers will be added, in a revised (and possibly updated) version. If they particularly enjoyed reading *Death of a Salesman* (Miller, 1949) as a part of the unit that focuses on the family, they might select a scene that involves Willie Loman with his sons Biff and Happy as the passage they will revise. The three boys from *Home Improvement* will be added into the scene, at the discretion of the group members, who have now assumed roles not only as readers, but as a collaborative writing team.

5. Groups will engage in peer editing to polish their rewritten excerpt, and turn in one copy to be evaluated for consistency in characters, setting, and plot. They will then revisit their adaptation and convert it into a play. Some teachers may choose to present a series of mini-lessons to provide students with hints for play writing or screen writing, with attention to how to add notes on action, setting, stage directions, and so on. Others may prefer to let students determine what they will need to

include in the written, dramatic versions in order to make the script a useful one for actors to follow.

6. Students will act out live, or videotape and then show, the revised versions of their creative writing. They have accomplished several things by this point: they have decided on which shows to watch, and which characters they feel are particularly interesting or entertaining in those shows; they have collaborated to select a literary passage that all agree upon, then to rewrite the literature to include characters from the television show. Finally, they have added a dramatic version of the rewritten literature. The final step will be for the group to perform the revised, expanded excerpt.

An alternative version of the television activity will change steps three and four, above; in the modified version, students will be required to add their own families into the television shows that the group chooses to analyze. Each group member, in this case, would write a different script, in order to include his and her family, after collaborating on the analysis of the television shows. Peer editing would be necessary, as described in number five above, and the presentation modes described in number six above0 would be options that could be available to students who complete the television-family project, just as they are for students who complete the television-literature project. This alternative activity does not promote students to make direct connections between the literature and the television shows included in the unit; instead, it emphasizes the connection between television fiction and family reality for the teenage viewers/writers.

Other Suggested Resources to Use When Presenting a Unit of Family Relationships

(Like the list at the chapter's opening, this list includes books that will appeal to students with wide ranges of reading interests and abilities. Young adult literature is noted.)

Books

Allende, Isabelle (translated by M. S. Penden). (1995). *Paula.* New York: HarperPerennial.
    This book is the autobiography of writer Isabelle Allende, author of *The House of Spirits* (New York: Bantam, 1992). It was written

for her daughter, Paula, after Paula fell ill and lapsed into a coma. In it, Allende embraces the stories of her childhood and adolescence, and her family's history; it is a family tree brought to life. Paula's death is tragic and moving; through writing about it, Allende allows herself and her family to come to terms with their grief.

Alvarez, Julia. (1991). *How the Garcia girls lost their accents*. New York: Penguin.

This novel is a compilation of fifteen different stories that tell the tale of the four Garcia sisters, Carla, Sandra, Yolanda, and Sofia, who arrive in New York City from the Dominican Republic in 1960. It shows us how the girls try to "Americanize" themselves and distance themselves from their native culture. They refuse to use Spanish, iron their hair, and date boys without chaperones. This book gives high school readers a glimpse into a family that is culturally different from the mainstream.

Blacker, Terrence. (1993). *Homebird*. New York: Macmillan/Bradbury.

Nicky Morrison is a thirteen-year-old in his first year of boarding school. But he hates school and his classmates, and he has a hard time coping with a family that is breaking up. He runs away from school only to find himself in a dangerous situation on the streets. Possible controversial elements in this young adult novel include running away and life in the streets.

Bridgers, Sue Ellen. (1993). *Keeping Christina*. New York: HarperCollins.

This young adult novel offers few reading challenges for high school students, but its themes are provocative and may lead students to consider the hidden messages that parents send their children about expectations, behavior, loyalty, and obligations. In it, Bridgers presents a solid family whose harmony and ability to communicate are at first enhanced, then threatened by, Christina, a teen who imposes on teenaged, well-meaning Annie. Christina is not the person she pretends to be.

Collier, James Lincoln. (1987). *Outside looking in*. New York: MacMillan.

The protagonist is a fourteen-year-old boy named Fergy; he is tired of living in a van with his parents and younger sister. Fergy's father is a thief, and Fergy is disgusted with him and with the lifestyle of the family. He is determined to take his sister and run away to make a better life. With help from his grandparents, Fergy is able to come to grips with his family relationships and his expectations. Though appropriate also for middle school readers, this book, because of its portrayal of a contemporary teen who has many questions and problems, is likely to appeal to high school students who are reluctant readers.

Conroy, Pat. (1986). *The Prince of Tides*. New York: Bantam.

This touching novel, recommended only for mature high school students, details the life and memories of Tom Wingo. As an adult, Tom is a troubled man; his marriage is shaky and his relationship with his family is strained at best. When he leaves South Carolina to visit his sister in New York City, Tom meets psychiatrist Susan Lowenstein. She helps him uncover long-buried secrets from his childhood, including sexual abuse, but also awakens his previously-sleepy passion. Students could follow reading with viewing the movie of the same title, produced in 1991 by C. Carmen and J. Roe for Columbia Pictures.

Devito, Cara. (1993). *Where I want to be*. New York: Houghton Mifflin.

Last summer, Kristie was stuck in Show Low, Arizona, because of the death of her father. She questions who she really is, why her mother left her when she was two, and what secret it seems her well-meaning brothers are protecting her from. Possible controversial elements in this young adult novel include parental death and abandonment, and the presence of mixed families.

Fleischman, Paul. (1986). *Rear-View mirrors*. New York: Harper Row/Charlotte Zoltow Books.

This is the story of sixteen-year-old Olivia, who goes from her home in California to visit a father, in New Hampshire, whom she has not seen in fifteen years. It is the delicate story of how she and her father develop a close bond, only to be shattered one year later by his tragic death. Olivia fights to claim her heritage and a different way of life after being touched by her father's.

Giovanni, Nikki (Ed.). (1994). *Grand mothers: Poems, reminiscences, and short stories about the keepers of our traditions*. New York: Henry Holt.

This is a collection that offers a wealth of teaching possibilities; in it, poet Giovanni presents pieces by famous writerly friends including Gloria Naylor and Gwendolyn Brooks, and by women who are not known as creative writers, such as Giovanni's own mother, residents of old folks homes, and college professors. It is a fine addition for the teacher's collection of texts that can be used on the spur of the moment, with assurance that it will provoke thought among student readers.

Guest, Judith. (1976). *Ordinary people*. New York: Viking.

This novel tells the story of seventeen-year-old Conrad Jarrett, who has just returned home after spending eight months in a mental institution following a suicide attempt. His suicidal tendency is fueled by the accidental death of his older brother, his father's overly anxious questions, and his mother's emotional barriers.

Mazer, Norma Fox. (1986). *Three sisters*. New York: Scholastic.

It seems to fifteen-year-old Karen that all of her problems stem from her rank as the youngest of three sisters. The pressures she feels to please everyone, and to rise to her grandmother's expectations, are complicated by her attraction to her sister's fiancé. This young adult novel is easy to read for most high school students and may attract the attention of readers who are usually resistant to the idea of completing an entire novel.

Namioka, Lensey. (1994). *April and the dragon lady*. San Diego: Browndeer.

This young adult novel depicts an female Chinese-American teen as she struggles to bridge the gap between the conservative Chinese customs of her family and heritage, and the more liberal American customs of her boyfriend and other school friends. Because her mother has died, April is responsible for her diabetic, demanding, and often dramatic grandmother. Yet April is also actively trying to be accepted to college and to be an ordinary American adolescent. Despite tense times with a brother who thinks she should serve him, a distant father and unfamiliar stepmother, April finds her place in her family and in the world.

Paulsen, Gary. (1993). *Sisters/Hermanas*. New York: Harcourt Brace.

Written in both English and in Spanish, this beautifully crafted novella presents in parallel vignettes the lives of two teen girls who, though the same age, have very different lives. Traci is a spoiled and popular high school student. Traci's mother insists that Traci's life might be ruined if she does not make the school's cheerleading squad. In contrast, Rosa is the child of an illegal immigrant. Her only dream is to be glamorous—like the models she sees on advertisements. Paulsen skillfully brings the two girls to the same place, at the same time, for a brief yet powerful moment. The questions each has about the life of the other, both spoken and unspoken, can provoke many sessions of classroom discussion.

Peck, Richard. (1992). *Don't look and it won't hurt*. New York: Dell/Laurel-Leaf.

Carol has lived her entire life in a rundown house with her mother and two sisters. She serves as protector of her younger sister and mediator between her mother and older sister. She gains new perspective when her long-missing father reappears, her older sister becomes pregnant, and her mother loses faith in Carol. Possible controversial elements in this young adult novel include attention to poverty, an absent father, and unwed teen pregnancy.

Potok, Chiam. (1972). *My name is Asher Lev*. New York: Random House.

This is a powerful family-centered novel based on the strict Hasidic Jewish culture. The story tells of a troubled Jewish boy who is kicked out of his religious sect.

Roy, Jacqueline. (1992). *Soul daddy*. New York: Harcourt Brace Jovanovich/Gulliver.

In this young adult book, Hannah Curren is confused about who she really is, and where she comes from. She and her twin sister live in a white London suburb with their white mother. One day, their father, a black reggae musician, returns home with their half sister, Nicola. Hannah soon learns what it really means to be black. Possible controversial elements, in some communities, include the focus on interracial families, and on race as an issue itself.

Shusterman, Neal. (1991). *What daddy did*. New York: Little, Brown.

Preston Scott's father murdered his mother and now, released from prison, has returned home to live with Preston and his grandparents. Preston is torn between his emotions for his father. Possible controversial elements include murder, violence/abuse, a parent in prison, and the loss of a parent.

Tan, Amy. (1989). *The joy luck club*. New York: Vintage.

This amazing story, which is currently excerpted in many high school literature textbooks, centers around two generations of Asian women who, after settling in the United States, must deal with familial misunderstandings and fight to hold onto their culture. Its narrative structure offers reading challenges that will intrigue experienced high school readers.

Wolff, Virginia Euwer. (1994). *Make lemonade*. New York: Scholastic.
Fourteen-year-old LaVaughn accepts a job baby-sitting the two children of seventeen-year-old Jolly. Jolly, a single mother who lives in poverty, is almost out of hope when LaVaughn begins to show her some alternatives, including an education. This poetic novel presents realistically a family situation which, though far from the norm, is growing more common.

Songs

Boublil, A. and Schonberg, C.-M. (1988). Fantine's death. *Highlights from the complete symphonic international cast recording of Les Miserables*. Lyrics by Herbert Kretzmer. Wembley: CTS Studios; Nashville: Studio Eleven Eleven; Sydney: Rhinoceros Studio. (Musical based on the novel by Victor Hugo.)
Fantine's death is sung by Gary Morris, who plays Jean Valjean, and Debbie Byrne, who plays Fantine. This is the dying Fantine's song to her baby daughter, Cossette. Fantine sings of the love and happiness that she wishes for her Cossette, then turns over the baby to the care of kind Valjean. The song is a poignant portrayal of a mother's love for her child.

Boublil, A. and Schonberg, C.-M. (1988). Epilogue/Finale. *Highlights from the complete symphonic international cast recording of Les Miserables*. Lyrics by Herbert Kretzmer. Wembley: CTS Studios; Nashville: Studio Eleven Eleven; Sydney: Rhinoceros Studio. (Musical based on the novel by Victor Hugo.)
Epilogue/Finale, sung by characters who play Fantine, Valjean, Cossette, Epione, and the entire musical cast, this piece focuses on the dying Valjean, and his wishes for Cossette's happiness. He warns her of the dangers she will face in the world, but balances the warning with praise for God's love and providence. This song suggests the depth of a bond established between a daughter and the father who has adopted her.

Baby mine (track 8) from the compact disc *Beaches original soundtrack recording*, sung by Bette Midler, produced by Arif Mardin for Atlantic Recording Corporation: A Time Warner Communications Company: 1988. Easy listening.
Originally from the Disney movie, *Dumbo*, this song portrays a

mother singing to her baby about accepting differences and knowing that no matter what anyone says, the baby is special and loved.

U2. (1987). Mothers of the disappeared (track 11), on the compact disc *The Joshua tree*. Produced by Daniel Lanois and Brian Eno. New York: Island Records Limited: 1987. Pop/rock.

This is a touching song about a mother's sadness at the disappearance of her child, and even deeper, about the difficulty of letting go of a child who has grown, especially when the child's innocence has been lost to drugs, sexual activity, and so on . The song reinforces the idea that, despite how children interpret their actions, parents act out of love and concern for their children's sakes, and that parents miss their children when they are gone.

Leigh, R. and Martin, L., Jr. (1993). "The greatest man I never knew" (track 10), on the compact disc, *Reba greatest hits, volume 2*, sung by Reba McIntire. Produced by Tommie Brown and Reba McIntire. Nashville: Reba McIntire Productions, 1993.

A girl sings about the love of a father whom she never really had the chance to know, on the occasion of his recent death. One of the song's messages seems to be, "Don't wait until it is too late to tell someone that you love him or her."

Morisette, A. (1995). Perfect (track 3) on the compact disc *Jagged little pill*. Sung by Alanis Morisette. Music composed by Morisette and Glen Ballard. Produced by Glen Ballard. New York: Maverick Recording Company for Reprise Records of Time Warner.

This is a somewhat angry song which focuses on the high and always unfulfilled expectations that parents place on their children. It presents a bitter struggle between the parents' demands and the children's desires and actions.

Movie Suggestions

Parenthood. (1989). Universal City Studios. Ganz, L., Mandel, B. and Howard, R., Producers. Ron Howard, Director. Hollywood. Starring Steve Martin, Rick Moranis, Martha Plimpton. Length: 124 minutes. Comedy.

The Buckmans are a modern family with the age-old problem of trying to raise children the "right" way. The parents strive to maintain successful careers while being loving spouses and respected parents. The Buckmans must learn that children—especially the grown ones, need to be allowed to make some decisions for themselves.

Sense and Sensibility. (1995). Columbia Tristar. (Based on the novel by Jane Austen). Thompson, E., Producer and Screenwriter. Hollywood. Ang Lee, Director. Starring Hugh Grant, Emma Thompson, Alan Rickman, and Kate Winslet. 135 minutes.

This movie, set in early nineteenth-century England, features a newly widowed mother and her three daughters, a family who suddenly finds itself poor and alone in England's high society. With the charity of family, they find a humble house. Together, the mother and daughters feel the joys of love, the despair of broken hearts and unkept promises, and the mysteries of the human heart. Thompson won an Academy Award as Best Actress for her role as the eldest daughter.

Add your own titles to this beginning list of other movies worth consideration for implementing during a unit on families:

Mrs. Doubtfire (1993) Blue Wolf/Twentieth Century Fox (comedy)
The little mermaid (1989) Walt Disney (animation)
Mr. Holland's opus (1996) Buena Vista (drama)
The prince of tides (1992) Columbia Pictures (drama)
Father of the bride (1991) Touchstone Pictures (comedy)
The sound of music (1965) Twentieth Century Fox (musical)
Steel magnolias (1993) TriStar Pictures (drama)
Meet me in St. Louis (1944) MGM/United Artists (musical)
The sea gypsies (1978) Warner Brothers (adventure)

Resources on the Web

(Add sites that you find, when exploring the Web using search engines like Yahoo! and Alta Vista, to this list, too. We realize that Web sites are fluid entities, and apologize if one that you find listed below is no longer in existence, or if it has fallen into a condition of untidiness, contains unreliable information, or is no longer helpful as a resource for teachers. Be sure to check the site for yourself before sending students to it.)

Interracial Families
http://www.commonlink.com/-chiron_rising/race/inter.html
>   This site offers links with others that support interracial and interethnic marriages and families. It offers visitors a chance to read everything from reports of incidents that involved interracial pairs to articles—written by members of interracial families—that discuss the prejudices and hardships they seek to overcome.

Divorce and Family Structure Changes (Site of the Stepfamily Association of Illinois)
http://www.parentsplace.com/readroom/stepfamily/index.html
>   This site offers support and understanding for children who are in families that are experiencing, or have experienced, a divorce. Advice for parents on how to talk with children is offered, and a section in which children are told that they should not blame themselves for their parents' divorces is included.

Home and Family
http://www.homeandfamily.com
>   This on-line version of the television show offers information and articles on topics such as self-esteem, resolving mother/daughter conflicts, family holiday planning, and so on. A link to previous issues is offered.

Counseling (Site of Advanced Counseling and Psychological Services)
http://www.response-net.com/ya-acp.htm
>   This site allows family members to interact with expert counselors about relationships, family issues, parenting, drugs, sexuality, addictions, depression, anxiety, and so on. This is an award-winning site that offers help for families.

Home and Family
http://www.dailyparent.com
>   This site is an on-line version of the magazine, *The Daily Parent*; it offers a wide variety of articles on topics such as parenting, education, health, family, childbearing, and so on. It includes many articles on how to deal with the everyday kinds of problems that parents and children experience. The site includes a chat and discussion

room where families can "sit" and communicate with each other over the Internet.

http://www.findout.com/famlib.htm

This site is an on-line library that offers direct information for parents and teens. It covers topics such as parenting, education, and substance abuse, and offers suggestions for many more reference sources, including books, journals, pamphlets, and videos.

Works Cited

Print Resources

Achebe, C. (1959). *Things fall apart*. New York: Doubleday.
Allende, I. (translated by M. S. Penden). (1995). *Paula*. New York: HarperPerennial.
Alvarez, J. (1991). *How the Garcia girls lost their accents*. New York: Penguin.
Blacker, T. (1993). *Homebird*. New York: Macmillan/Bradbury.
Bridgers, S. E. (1993). *Keeping Christina*. New York: HarperCollins.
Carter, A. (1989). *Up country*. New York: G. P. Putnam's Sons.
Collier, J. L. (1987). *Outside looking in*. New York: MacMillan.
Conroy, P. (1986). *The prince of tides*. New York: Bantam.
Devito, C. (1993). *Where I want to be*. New York: Houghton Mifflin.
Edgerton, C. (1987). *Walking across Egypt*. New York: Ballantine.
Fleischman, P. (1986). *Rear-view mirrors*. New York: Harper Row/Charlotte Zoltow Books.
Fowler, C. M. (1992). *Sugar cage*. New York: Washington Square.
Giovanni, N. (Ed.). (1994). *Grand mothers: Poems, reminiscences, and short stories about the keepers of our traditions*. New York: Henry Holt.
Guest, J. (1976). *Ordinary people*. New York: Viking.
Kingsolver, B. (1990). *Animal dreams*. New York: HarperCollins.
Mazer, N. F. (1986). *Three sisters*. New York: Scholastic.
Namioka, L. (1994). *April and the dragon lady*. San Diego: Browndeer.
Paulsen, G. (1993). *Sisters/Hermanas*. New York: Harcourt Brace.
Peck, R. (1992). *Don't look and it won't hurt*. New York: Dell/Laurel-Leaf.
Potok, C. (1972). *My name is Asher Lev*. New York: Random House.

Purves, A., Rogers, T., & Soter, A. (1995). *How porcupines make love, III: Readers, texts, cultures in the response-based literature classroom.* White Plains, NY: Longman.
Roy, J. (1992). *Soul daddy.* New York: Harcourt Brace Jovanovich/Gulliver.
Shusterman, N. (1991). *What Daddy did.* New York: Little, Brown.
Smith, L. (1983). *Oral history.* New York: Ballantine.
Steinbeck, J. *The pearl.* (1947). Toronto: Bantam.
Tan, A. (1989). *The joy luck club.* New York: Vintage.
Walker, A. (1982). *The color purple.* New York: Pocket.
Zeitlin, S. J. (1982). How to collect your own family folklore. *A celebration of American family folklore.* New York: Pantheon.

Songs

Leigh, R. & Martin, L., Jr. (1993). The greatest man I never knew (track 10), on the compact disc, *Reba Greatest Hits, volume 2,* sung by Reba McIntire. Produced by Tommie Brown and Reba McIntire. Nashville: Reba McIntire Productions, 1993.
Midler, B. (1988). Baby mine (track 8), on the compact disc *Beaches original soundtrack recording,* Produced by Arif Mardin for Atlantic Recording Corporation: A Time Warner Communications Company: 1988. Easy listening.
Morisette, A. (1995). Perfect (track 3), on the compact disc *Jagged little pill.* Sung by Alanis Morisette. Music composed by Morisette and Glen Ballard. Produced by Glen Ballard. New York: Maverick Recording Company for Reprise Records of Time Warner.

Movies

Ganz, L., Mandel, B., & Howard, R. (1989). *Parenthood.* (PG-13) Universal Studios. Ron Howard, Director. Hollywood: Universal City Studios. Starring Steve Martin, Rick Moranis, Martha Plimpton. Length: 124 minutes. Comedy.
Thompson, E. Screenwriter and Producer. (Based on novel by Jane Austen). (1995). (PG). Columbia Tristar. *Sense and sensibility.* Hollywood. Ang Lee, Director. Starring Hugh Grant, Emma Thompson, Alan Rickman, and Kate Winslet. 135 minutes.

Sites on the World Wide Web

http://www.commonlink.com/-chiron_rising/race/inter.html
http://www.dailyparent.com
http://www.findout.com/famlib.htm
http://www.homeandfamily.com
http://www.parentsplace.com/readroom/stepfamily/index.html
http://www.response-net.com/ya-acp.htm

CHAPTER FIVE

Homelessness in Literature, the Media, and in Our Minds

Gail Gregg and Michelle Tollentino-Davidson

Lola in a Cardboard Box
Belkis L. Cabrera

By Day

Lola bends her back above ash-trays
To scrub lipsticked rims from plastic cups.
Beside her
Mr. Coffee flashes his red hot ready
And the stains of last night's blue collared lunches
Settle
Along bottoms of glass pots
Hanging heavy
Like grill grease
And dried paste chewing gum
And melted cheese
And Lola's sweat.

She spreads over vinyl
And table tops
A net of thread crowning her head
The white apron and stockings
Clinging to her thighs
Like chains.

By Night

Between a bus stop and a cigarette
The streets are littered by a crumbled burlapped body
Under the downtown bridge
At the expressway edge
It coils onto a stone mattress
Blistered with wind
Stirring sins in a bottle
The alcohol like milk
Soothing chapped lips
And as a child into Eve's garden
It slithers.

In the shadows
Behind the dumpster
An orchard of pretends
It waits
Twisting in its emptiness
Rocking little Lola
In a cardboard box

Do Our Students See this Problem? Homelessness as a Topic and Theme: Goals and Rationale

Adolescence is an integral developmental stage in the transition from childhood to adulthood. It is during this time that teenagers begin to examine and question their own identities and thoughts as they begin to evaluate society through the eyes of pending adulthood. As many of the misperceptions of youth dissipate, literature and other nonprint vehicles can serve as a lens through which adolescents can explore aspects of reality both inside and outside the realm of their own personal experience. By examining real-life issues through prose and poetry, through nonprint vehicles such as film and music, and through hands-on experiences followed by discussion (both oral and written), adolescents will perhaps begin to think about their existence from a more global perspective.

One such real-life issue that can be explored in the high school classroom is homelessness. The topic of homelessness can be enriched by a concentration on the theme of students' attitudes toward the homeless. Between two and three million people per year in the United States find themselves living without homes or constant shelter (Kozol, 1988); the stories of the homeless are as varied and distinct as the fingerprints of the people that write or film their stories. Amid this diversity exists an opportunity for every student to find a way to connect as a maturing person with the issues that are central to this theme. Furthermore, an examination of this particular theme through discussions and activities relative to various literary selections, films, and music will afford adolescent students an opportunity to come to a greater understanding of the homeless individual in today's society while simultaneously gaining a greater understanding of themselves and the community of humanity in which they live. In addition, an examination of homelessness will perhaps break down barriers between social classes and create an awareness of the need for more caring, helping, and understanding attitudes among adolescents.

We have selected multicultural works and multiple genres, both print and nonprint, for study in this unit, in order to give students information on the topic and opportunities to explore the theme of their perceptions from a variety of perspectives and experiences. As a teacher who is interested in building instruction on a reader-response base, you will be able to have students use oral discussion, journal writing, expressive writing, and formal essays to elicit and articulate their personal responses to questions raised by a new understanding of the reality of this issue.

Into Our Consciousness: Developing the Theme

We recommend beginning the initial thrust into the theme of students' personal responses to homelessness by asking students to answer a survey that focuses attention on their opinions about the homeless. The survey can be completed by individuals anonymously, or, if you and the students are comfortable with each other, by small groups. Questions such as the following provide students with a preview to the literature and non-print media to follow, and lay the foundation for future class discussions in which students' personal responses are considered within the context of literary and other texts:

- Who are the homeless?
- Are people homeless because they are lazy and won't work?
- Are many of the homeless mentally ill?
- Do the homeless choose to be that way?
- Should society help the homeless? Should the government help?
- Are most of those who are homeless adults?
- What would be the fate of a homeless child?
- Is one race or ethnic group more likely to have large numbers of homeless people than other races or ethnic groups? If so, why?

After the surveys have been completed, results should be tabulated and reported to the students. The results might be displayed on a chart, and kept on display throughout the duration of the unit, so that students can monitor any changes in their original attitudes, and to evaluate progress that is made towards understanding more about the homeless—who they are as human beings, how the class members feel about them, and what can be done to solve the problems of homelessness and of uninformed ideas about the homeless.

From the Eyes of the Homeless: Introducing the Topic and Theme with Music, Videos, and Photography

Our teenage students have reported that they oftentimes see, but seldom think about, homeless people. When we ask them about their attitudes toward the homeless, they admit that they often are so preoccupied with their own lives and that of their peers, that they spend little time thinking about those outside of their immediate and limited realm, much less those who are apart from the mainstream, people such as the homeless.

Our Eyes on the Homeless—Introducing the Unit

A potent resource that can be used to encourage students to think about this theme is Hubbard's book, *Shooting Back: A Photographic View of Life by Homeless Children* (1991). This text is filled with photographs taken by homeless children from across the nation. The photographs speak eloquently about the world as seen from the children's eyes. Because the book uses pictures instead of words, it is especially appropriate both as a means of engaging the interest of reluctant readers and as a vehicle to promote expressive written responses of many types, from describing what is shown in a particular photograph, to writing a story about the people in the photo, to creating a poetic response after considering one's response to a particularly poignant or compelling photograph. See Cabrera's poem, "Lola in a Cardboard Box," p. 113, at the beginning of this chapter, for an example of a teacher's response to a photograph of a homeless woman. You may use it as an example, if you wish.

We found another attention-arresting resource after our students brought to our attention *But Seriously...The Video* (1988) by Phil Collins. We have begun using an entire class period for showing students this music video. When they watch it, students often begin to think of homelessness from the perspective of their own responses to the problem. The photographic essay introduces students very quickly to the realities of the homeless in a medium to which they are willing to listen; it is realistic without being didactic or condescending to students. It does present disturbing pictures, and thus when we bring it into classrooms, we show students that we take them seriously, that we respect their ability to face some of the ugly realities of our world.

There are several other aspects of this easily-implemented video introduction that make it valuable for students in high school classrooms. First, most teens "read" it as evidence that homelessness is not necessarily the result of laziness, drug or alcohol abuse, or mental instability. Second, the video depicts teenage runaways, and thus opens up classroom conversation about the possible causes and consequences of this problem. We all benefit from understanding each other's views about running away. In our classes, we have noticed that the respect for classmates' perspectives that is built during the beginning of the unit grows and supports our classes throughout the duration of this sometimes troubling unit. Third, the video may suggest to your students an important message that our students first brought to our attention: the video demonstrates that caring about the homeless, including runaway teens, is not only the concern for government agencies and distraught parents. Students reason that if Phil Collins, phenomenally popular recording artist and successful leader of the internationally celebrated group, Genesis, cares about the homeless enough to devote his talent and time to the issue, it must be an important concern.

Collins' ironic song, "Another Day in Paradise" (1988) can be played in the background as students watch the video. The lyrics of this song set the mood for the theme when it contrasts those who have money, resources, and support with those who are homeless, without material goods, and without human support; it asks the listener to consider whether or not there is anything that anyone can do, at this point.

One note is worth adding here: if you decide to prepare to teach a unit on homelessness that includes popular music, it is likely that your students will be listening to a new group of recording artists, instead of those our students have responded to in recent classes. We expect that, despite our success with it, we will need to find a replacement for Collins' video in a year or two, if Collins suffers the fate of many popular artists and falls from the graces of our students. It is important, in this introductory activity, to encourage students to become actively engaged in consideration of the issue of homelessness; you may not be able to accomplish this goal with music that is, in their opinion, out of date. The next time that we need to find a new music video that speaks in some way about homelessness, we will turn to the popular music experts among us—our students—to ask for help in identifying the artists who are interested in the issue.

After you have had students view the book of photographs and/or the video and listen to the song, you might ask them to rethink their understandings about who make up the homeless population. Further discussion should center on attempting to elicit how students feel about the homeless. Open-ended questions that might prompt discussion and probe their initial responses include these:

- What is your immediate reaction when you see a homeless person on the street?

- If you had the money and power to change the situation that homeless people find themselves in, would you step in to change their lives, or do many of them deserve their situation?
- Would you want to assist a teenager who came to school and confided in you that he or she did not have a permanent place to live? If you choose to help, what would you do?

Others' Perspectives on the Homeless

After discussing how the students feel about the homeless, time should be given to how other people view the homeless. In the challenging poems, "Street Musicians" (Ashbery, 1985), "The Old Lady Under the Freeway" (O'Hehir, 1984), and the song, "Man on the Corner" (Genesis, 1981) speakers are homeless people who are relating their plights. The first selection is a stirring poem told from a homeless street musician's point of view. He poignantly speaks of the world around him as winter approaches. The second is about a homeless old lady who lives under a freeway, and how she views the world from this perspective. "Man on the Corner" speaks about a lonely man who sits on a corner every day, waiting, but never coming into contact with someone who cares. The short length of these intense pieces makes them especially appropriate for study during a single class period. During the class period, attention can be given to the artistic elements as well as the topic and themes, with attention perhaps drawn to the effectiveness of the writer's choice to have a homeless person speak for him/herself.

The short story, "Homeless Woman Living in a Car" (Anonymous, 1986) could also be used to depict the perspective of a homeless person. Written in the first person, this story describes a few days in the life of an older homeless woman. It details the struggles she goes through to try and correct her situation. Despite the fact that she has a job, the speaker in this story is caught in the downward spiral that tugs strongly on her. Interesting discussion in a high school classroom could emerge if opened with the following set of questions: "Should adult children be responsible for the welfare of their parents? If they are not required to be financially responsible, should they be held morally responsible for them? Do the reasons that a person becomes homeless have any influence on your decisions; for instance, if someone's father became addicted to drugs then lost his job, his home, and his identity as a father, would your answers be the same as if he were the victim of a hurricane—one that destroyed his home and business, and suddenly found himself, through no fault of his own, penniless?" A natural extension is to ask your students what they would do if they discovered one of their friends or family members living in a car or on the street.

We recognize that questions such as this must be asked with great care, since some of your students or their families may be homeless, or may have been at some time in their short lives. We recommend at this point a focus on the strengths exhibited by those who live without the things that many of us consider to be basic to happiness. This discussion might begin with consideration of the nature of the things that today's teens believe are essential. When we ask our students to list the possessions that are essential for their daily lives, they usually compile lists that include hair dryers, CD players, and video games. It does not take long for them to realize that for homeless people, the list of basics is much different from the list compiled by the class. Direct yet compelling questions such as, "How would you prepare to look for a job if you could not wash, dry, and style your hair?" and "Do you think that your appearance would be a high priority if you did not know whether or not you would have any food during the day?" might help students begin to understand that for some of the homeless, developing physical and psychological strength is a means of survival.

Another short selection that could be used to give students another person's perspective is "Miss Rosie" (1985), a poem by Lucille Clifton in which an outside observer describes a homeless woman. The speaker alludes to the possibility that "Miss Rosie" once led a very different life as the most beautiful woman in Georgia. Miss Rosie, then, becomes an example, for some readers, of someone who was not necessarily destined to become homeless. If students construct a meaning that is built on this kind of reading of the poem, they may be compelled to question the assumptions they may have made about homeless people. At this point, some may return to their own list of "basics for happiness" and reconsider it. Other students may decide to focus on the poem as one individual's reaction to seeing a homeless person. This type of reading may lead them to reflect on the way they react when they see a homeless person on the street. You might ask them to consider specific reactions, using these simple questions as prompts:

- Do you look away from a homeless person if he or she approaches you?

- Do you avoid the side of the street on which a homeless person is sitting or standing?
- Would your immediate thoughts about the person best be classified as pity, contempt, or concern?
- Do you feel that you would like to report the homeless person to someone who will ask him or her to leave, or to someone who could help him or her find shelter?
- What do you think about the homeless people when they hold up signs like ones that declare, "Viet Nam Vet: Need food. Please Help. God Bless You"? Do you dismiss the signs as attempts to beg money that will be spent on drugs or alcohol?
- Would your attitude be the same if the homeless person were your age, or if you had known the homeless person before he or she became homeless?
- Do you wonder how the homeless person got that way, or what his/her life has been like in the past?
- Do you wonder if there is anything that a homeless person could teach you?

Again, we are sensitive to the fact that these questions may be difficult, emotionally, for some of your students; they have been painful for some of ours. We ask them only when our classroom environments have become filled with trust and mutual respect. Like us, you are likely to have students who themselves have been, or are, without a home. We need to be acutely aware of the fact that recent studies suggest that children comprise, as a group, the fastest growing homeless population. We also need to be aware of the fact that for some minority groups, homelessness is a more permanent condition than for other groups. Children in African-American families, for example, are likely to live in homeless conditions longer than their Caucasian classmates whose families are temporarily homeless (Holtz, 46).

Teenage Homelessness and the Runaways

To help students see connections between their own lives and contemporary society, we show the educational documentary film *Streetwise* (A. Selah, 1986). This film, which is often listed in school systems' film collections, presents a moving and somewhat shocking window into the painful lives of homeless teenagers struggling to survive in Seattle,

Washington. *Where the Day Takes You* (Hertzberg, 1992) is another educational documentary film, often available in school collections, that could be used to provide connections to the lives of adolescent students. This movie deals with teenage runaways and gives an inside look at what goes on in Hollywood's notorious underground. From the after-hours dance clubs, to the hidden drug dens, from pan handling to prostitution, this film is a no-holds-barred look at life on the streets.

After viewing either of these films, students could respond either orally or in written journals to the following questions:

- Do any of the teenagers in the films remind you of someone you know? If so, how do you feel about the connection?
- How and why did the teenagers in the films wind up living on the street?
- Are the teenagers responsible for their homelessness? What options, if any, did the teenagers in the films have?

Because of the shift to inquiries that focus on homeless teens, these questions may encourage high school students to reflect on the question of homelessness from a more personal stance than the perspective from which they previously viewed the issue. Following discussion, a short essay discussing the extent to which individuals are responsible for their fates might be a good way to help students make sense of the works in terms of their own lives. A re-viewing of excerpts that depict teen runaways in the Collins *But Seriously...The Video* may be a powerful tool for encouraging students to reflect on their attitudes before they begin to write. A brief return to the introductory lesson material would provide students with a sense of coherence and also with a means of monitoring changes in their perspectives at this mid-point in the unit.

There are several good young adult books, both fiction and nonfiction, that can be integrated into the study of either of these films. Swindels' *Stone Cold* (1993), set in London, tells the story of a homeless teenager as he tries to survive his first winter on the streets while being stalked by a serial killer. This book is full of suspense and is a very realistic portrayal of what it is like to be a homeless teenager in a big city. Nelson's *The Beggar's Ride* (1992), deals with a teenage girl who flees her unhappy home life and abusive stepfather only to wind up homeless, living under a boardwalk. She eventually joins a gang, and is coerced into a scam that would victimize an elderly man whom she has befriended.

Spinelli's *Maniac Magee* (1990), a young adult novel about a teenage boy who, as a result of becoming an orphan, is forced to live on the streets, is a good selection for unskilled and reluctant readers. This novel can be particularly pertinent to discussions that raise questions about whether or not the homeless deserve to be homeless, and whether the homeless really have a great deal of control over their fate. Attention to the protagonist Maniac Magee is likely to generate discussions about the similarities and differences in the accomplishments and predicaments of Maniac and those of the various teenagers in the documentaries, *Streetwise* or *Where the Day Takes You*.

Gordon Parks' autobiographical *A Choice of Weapons* (1966), particularly Chapter One, is especially appropriate for inclusion in this thematic unit when juxtaposed with either of the two films, *Streetwise* or *Where the Day Takes You*. It provides evidence that homeless people can overcome dire circumstances. *A Choice of Weapons* is the account of a black man who, despite poverty and homelessness, experiences success as a photographer for Life magazine, a composer, a film director, and finally, a writer. In Chapter One, a sixteen-year-old Parks is living on the streets and is very tempted to steal. Remembering his mother's values, he decides to struggle through his problems honestly. Discussion of this chapter could include how the teenaged Parks handles his homeless situation compared to how the teenagers in *Streetwise* or *Where the Day Takes You* handle theirs. Particular attention should be given to what guides the actions of Parks. Asking students to assume the persona of Parks and to write a letter advising any one of the teenagers in either film on how to survive his/her situation would be a worthwhile and thought-provoking activity that you might assign after discussion is completed.

Last, Berry's *Kids on the Run* (1978) is an excellent work that brings attention to teenage runaways and homelessness. This nonfiction work, which is comprised of seven memorable interviews of teenage runaways, allows the reader to explore the fears and frustrations of teenagers who left home and found themselves living on the streets. Once again, the teenagers in this selection can be compared and contrasted to any of the aforementioned fiction or nonfiction runaways.

Homelessness and Families: An Activity to Increase Empathy and Introduce a Classic American Film in an Academic Context

It is important that students realize that homelessness is not unique or specific to the many adults who live on the street, nor to the runaway teenagers who live in the shadows of society, but that homelessness can and does impact entire families as well.

The Films

An excellent way to create empathy among students for families who have had to give up treasured possessions when forced to leave their home and relocate into a shelter is to show them a clip from the film version of Steinbeck's American classic, *The Grapes of Wrath*, produced by D. Zanuck for 20th Century Fox in 1940. A particularly effective scene is the one in which Ma Joad is seen sorting through family memorabilia. Because there is little extra room in the truck, she is forced to discard many treasured items.

An alternative choice for this activity could be excerpts from *Gone with the Wind*; the scenes that would be particularly provocative in terms of this unit are the ones in which Scarlett O'Hara is pulling tiny carrots from her reclaimed but ruined garden, pledging to God and humankind that she will never suffer hunger again, or when she has the draperies—ones that graced the windows of her family's beloved homeplace, Tara, before the Civil War—made into a dress so that she can present herself as the lady she was before the war changed her fate.

Both films are likely to raise questions about pride; our students have been surprised to learn that even people who carry all of their material possessions around in a bag or on their bodies often defend their rights to possessions. We were riveted when colleague and book co-author Sissi Carroll told us this story of her experience with a homeless woman; we share it with our students, and welcome you to do so, as well:

> One steamy summer day, I was driving to work when I saw a pregnant homeless woman on the street corner where she'd stood for the past two days. She was dirty, dressed in a collage of ill-fitting, heavy clothes. I noticed that there was a puppy beside her. Something about the puppy tore at me; I had learned to ignore the eyes of homeless men and women when they beg for money, shoring up my emotions by telling myself that I would not really be helping them by giving them a single handout, that they need to go to a shelter for food and real help toward getting back on their feet. But the puppy, lying on the end of a string that the woman

held, suffering the heat and humidity of the north Florida morning, knew nothing about food banks and shelters. Its world was the street corner to which she'd tied it.

I surprised myself by stopping my car and walking to the woman. I asked her if she or the pup needed some water, and she said that she thought the pup was sick. I had had pet dogs all of my life; this one was lethargic and its swollen stomach suggested worms. She asked me to help her find a veterinarian. Had she asked for money, I may have said no, based on the force of a stereotype that all homeless people are drunks and addicts who squander all of the money they beg for on alcohol or drugs, but I could not deny help for the puppy. We got into my car and drove to the office of the veterinarian who'd cared for my pets for almost two decades. She told me that her name was Gloria, and that she'd left a boyfriend and the crack house where they'd lived in south Georgia three weeks earlier. She said she'd tried to get help through a government office, but that she had no identification cards, and therefore she couldn't receive any of their services. Whether the story about her lost identification was true or not, there was one fact that was evident: Gloria was expecting her baby soon. She told me that it was due in about one month, and that she hoped to find a hospital that would take her even though she had no insurance. I told her, lamely, that I was sure she'd be able to work something out for the baby's sake.

At the veterinarian's office, I entered the reception room and explained that I had a friend with a sick dog, signed a register, and sat with Gloria until my name was called and we went to the examination room with the puppy, which she'd named Scrappy, after a cartoon character she liked. I wonder if she realized the irony of the name. A technician, who knew only that Gloria was the owner of the puppy, asked her a series of typical questions, questions about Scrappy's eating habits: "Is he on dry puppy food or does he eat just canned food?" and about his behavior: "Has he chewed up any of your favorite shoes yet, or any of your furniture?" Each question stung me as I realized how programmed we are to expect that everyone lives in a home, with ample food and resources. Gloria merely answered politely, never mentioning that even she did not have regular meals, and that she had neither good shoes nor furniture.

The veterinarian found that Scrappy had worms and that he was dehydrated; he gave the pup a shot, and handed Gloria instructions to return with him in ten days. I asked the receptionist to put the bill on my account, and we left.

I took Gloria and Scrappy back to the spot where I'd picked them up, and promised Gloria that I would be there again, ten days later, for the return trip to the veterinarian. I felt sure that I would not see her again. I told her, suddenly, that I would be happy to take Scrappy home with me, to care for him, at least until after her baby was born, but Gloria refused, again with polite but weary words. She turned down the offer, an offer which I now realize was supremely arrogant, by telling me, "This little puppy is mine. I don't have much. I need to have something to take care of. Something that's mine."

I have not seen Gloria since that day; I returned to the corner in ten days and sat waiting, but eventually knew the wait was futile. My contact with Gloria was over. Yet the incident has troubled me ever since, forcing me to ask myself questions that I cannot yet answer: Why was I willing to turn away from Gloria, a pregnant woman who was begging on a street corner, until I saw that she had a puppy with her? Why did I not take her to my doctor's office after we left the veterinarian's office? Did she have a baby who was born addicted to cocaine after being conceived in a crack house? Has her cycle of homelessness ended, or is it reinforced daily? What more could I have done? What more should I have done? Why did I not try harder to help? What would I do if I found myself in her situation? What was it about Gloria that threatened me?

I am proud that I was able to help Scrappy the puppy, but am ashamed of myself for putting tight controls on the limits I was willing to go to help a human being. Now I am haunted by a glimpse of Gloria in every homeless person I see.

The Activity

After you show excerpts from either film, and perhaps share this incident with the class, divide the students into groups of four, give each group a shoe box and ask them to pretend that they have been forced to move from a house where they had their own bedroom, to a shelter where they will share one small room with other members of their group. The group is to decide what to include in their shoe box of memorabilia and then either draw a picture of each item or cut from a magazine pictures of items and place them in the shoe box. After deciding what to place in the shoe box, the group must write an explanation as to why each item was chosen and orally present their reasons to the rest of the class. To further sensitize students to the harsh reality of what life is like for the homeless, a reading of the chapter entitled "Rachel and Her Children," from the book of the same name (Kozol, 1988) will give students a brief glimpse into the life of a homeless family residing in a shelter in New York City. This particular chapter reads like a short story and shows the frustrations, trials and tribulations, and complexities that homeless families living in large cities must face on a daily basis. From the nonsensical ways of governmental bureaucracy, to the inhuman and totally squalid conditions they face every day, the chapter gives the reader a feel for the hopelessness of homeless families.

Reading and study of Kozol's chapter can be followed by reading excerpts of Berck's *No Place to Be: Voices of Homeless Children* (1992). This written documentary consists of "interviews with children of families who were living in or had recently moved from welfare hotels or shelters for homeless families in New York City. The children's words are interwoven with narrative and original poems, in an exposition of their circumstances, feelings, and opinions" (Berck, 1992). This resource, one with great potential for engaging high school students, uses the children's words to give readers a glimpse of what the homeless children endure, what they find most difficult, what they worry about, what they hope for, and so on; the voices that rise out of the text like dark clouds are clearly those of children who are adrift, wandering from place to place, or staying put in shelters while living at the margins of society. The poetry that is included may be particularly powerful for the readers who recognize the authentic voices of those who have been there. This book allows a return to consideration of the book of photographs taken by homeless children, *Shooting Back: A Photographic View of Life by Homeless Children* (1991), that was suggested previously as an introduction to the unit; this would be a fine place to ask students to reassess their knowledge and attitudes concerning the homeless, and to make revisions, if necessary, on the chart that resulted from the introductory survey of their attitudes.

Creating Lasting Impressions and Memories: Activities that Extend the Classroom Into the Community

Visiting

There are various ways to provide closure for this unit in a meaningful way. The most obvious is to schedule a class visit to spend time volunteering in a homeless shelter or soup kitchen, with the help of parents, teachers, and other school personnel who could serve as chaperones. As an alternative, invite people who are involved in the daily operations of a local food bank and shelter to come talk with your class, and have your class prepare a set of interview questions before the visit. Projects like these are suggested for teachers of English and other subjects who believe that their role is to help students to use language for specific purposes to discover where they fit within their own communities, and how they can contribute to those communities. (For a discussion of this teaching perspective, and specific teaching strategies, see Chapter 7, "Language as Social Construct," in the excellent text for teachers of secondary English, *Language and Reflection: An Integrated Approach to Teaching English* (1992), by Gere, Fairbanks, Howes, Roop, and Schaafsma.) Ideally, this unit might be completed just prior to Thanksgiving or Christmas; these holidays provide many opportunities for volunteers to assist in homeless food and shelter programs; participation in one or more of the community's services for feeding and/or housing the homeless is likely to be a memorable experience for adolescents.

Writing

Visiting activities can be followed by either formal or informal writing assignments. Our favorite follow-up is, admittedly, difficult to arrange, but we believe that the effort to move students out of the classroom into the community during at least one unit per year is well worth the extra time it requires of their teachers. We suggest that you find out how to arrange for students to interview a homeless person or family within your community. After students conduct interviews, ask them to write the interviews into short biographies. For students who choose not to interview a homeless person, we suggest that you find ways to arrange for an interview with an administrator or long-term volunteer at a local shelter or food program. The class might present a bound copy of the biographies, with additional segments from the administrators' and volunteers' points of view, to the shelter or food program where the clients were found and interviewed; they might also select one or more of the biographies to submit for publication in the local newspaper. Biographies of local homeless people are likely to increase newspaper readers' awareness that homelessness is not a disease that one catches, but a problem that cuts across many races, ethnic groups, age groups, and family situations, to reach people from a variety of backgrounds.

Students might also be asked to keep a journal on experiences that occur while working with or studying the local homeless; the class could compile the experiences into a written portrait of a portion of the community's homeless population and seek opportunities for publishing the compilation within the community, so that local awareness of the problems—and the realization that the homeless are human beings, too—might thereby be increased.

Visual Art: Billboard-Sized Murals

For students who like to use their creative talents, a class mural depicting images, ideas, and symbols that they gleaned from the literature, films, and music presented during the course of the unit is suggested. The article "Survival Kids Transform Classics to Murals" (Glueck, 1988) gives some excellent examples of how literature-inspired murals and collages can be designed by high school students, and is an excellent guide to beginning such projects. Another creative and thought-provoking activity involves asking students to create a visual essay addressing the theme of homelessness. In essence, a visual essay is a combination of carefully selected words and pictures (much like a billboard) that express a personal opinion or feeling; in this case, the expressions will be related to the theme of homelessness. This activity usually works best when students are allowed to work with partners or in small groups.

Last, the May 1988 issue of *Reader's Digest* (possibly available in your school's or city's media center collection, or in a pile in one of your student's homes) includes an abundance of selections that can connect high school readers with the theme of homelessness in many locations. Included in this issue is a story of an Afghan family that was forced to flee their home and live in a tent in Pakistan; another features Ali, a Sudanese adolescent who, because of famine caused by droughts, flees to Khartoum in search of food and shelter. A third feature is the story of Juan, a

Mexican adolescent whose only home is a shack without electricity or running water that he built with branches, cardboard, and scraps of metal. Other stories include those of the Kurtz family, who become homeless when the father loses his job, and of Michael, who is homeless because of mental and addiction problems.

Interdisciplinary Connections

Each of the selections that we have recommended, including books, stories, poems, songs, and movies, has the potential to make a lasting impression on students who engage in serious and focused study about the harsh reality of homelessness. They suggest many connections across the disciplines; if a team of high school teachers chooses to create an interdisciplinary unit on homelessness, the social studies teachers might have students conduct research to determine the known incidence of homelessness within the community. Students might also conduct research to discern the following: the factors that seem to contribute to homelessness in the area and/or within the state or nation; social problems, including difficulty in getting and keeping a job, that beset the homeless population; the educational outlook for children who are transients; the local government's policies for dealing with those who sleep in and occupy public places; other agencies' means of addressing the problem, and so on. Concurrently, the mathematics teacher might have students study statistics related to the local, state, and national homeless population, in terms of sex, age, race, ethnicity, addictions of homeless people, former positions in life, and so on. Meanwhile, the science teacher might have students engage in a study of topics such as these: the effects of malnutrition on children's and adult's brains and bodies, the reaction of the body to temperature extremes, the climate of the region and potential for homeless people to survive there, correlations of homelessness and disease, including alcoholism, and so on.

Units such as the one described here reach beyond the typical boundaries of a high school classroom; they address issues that students are not ignorant of, but about which many are uninformed, and from which others are often sheltered. Teachers who choose to go beyond the traditional school fare to present such a unit may find themselves explaining their rationale to parents, other teachers, and administrators. We are convinced that the rationale for a unit based on the ideas suggested above is defensible; students use language to examine and express themselves while studying a slice of their world. Through studying the suggested literary and multimedia works and engaging in a variety of the suggested activities, students will use language to explore and express their ideas about homelessness. They are likely to grow to understand that homelessness is an ongoing, universal problem, a problem that can strike almost anyone, at any time, and can bring with it pain and deprivation. Students might also learn that they can help their communities work to alleviate the problem through participation in short-term community projects, or eliminate the problem through involvement in more ambitious and demanding projects.

Works Cited

Anonymous. (1986). Homeless woman living in a car. In D. Laguardia & H. Guth (Eds.), *American voices: Multicultural literacy and critical thinking.* Mountainview, CA: Mayfield.

Ashbery, J. (1985). Street musicians. In A. Poulin (Ed.), *Contemporary American Poetry.* Boston: Houghton Mifflin, 18.

Berck, J. (1992). *No place to be: Voices of homeless children.* New York: Houghton Mifflin.

Berry, J. (1978). *Kids on the run.* New York: Four Winds Press.

Clifton, L. (1985). Miss Rosie. In *Contemporary American poetry.* Boston: Houghton Mifflin, 75–76.

Collins, P. (1988). Another day in paradise [Song]. On *But seriously.* [Cassette/CD] Atlantic Recording. Phillip Collins, Ltd.

Collins, P. (1988). *But seriously…The video* [Video]. A Vision Entertainment. Flattery Yukich, Inc.

Genesis. (1981). Man on the corner [Song]. On *Abacab* [Cassette]. Atlantic Recording Corp.

Gere, A. R., Fairbanks, C., Howes, A., Roop, L. & Schaafsma, D. (1992). *Language and reflection: An integrated approach to teaching English.* New York: Macmillan.

Hertzberg, P., Director. (1992). *Where the day takes you* [Film]. Magnus Films & Cinetel Films, Inc.

Hubbard, J. (1991). *Shooting back: A photographic view of life by homeless children.* San Francisco: Chronicle Books.

Johnston, L. (1988). Who are the homeless? *Reader's Digest.* May, 15–35.

Kozol, J. (1988). *Rachel and her children.* New York: Crown Publishers.

Nelson, T. (1992). *The beggar's ride.* New York: Orchard Press.

O'Hehir, D. (1984). The old lady under the freeway. In P. Dow (Ed.), *19 American poets of the Golden Gate*. San Francisco: Harcourt, Brace, Jovanovich, 35.

Parks, G. (1966). A choice of weapons. In *A choice of weapons*. New York: Harper & Row, 1–16.

Selah, A. (Producer). (1986). *Streetwise* [Film]. Angelika Films.

Spinelli, J. (1990). *Maniac Magee*. Boston: Little, Brown.

Swindels, R. (1993). *Stone cold*. London: Hamish Hamilton Ltd.

Zanuck, D. (Producer). (1940). *The grapes of wrath* [Film]. 20th Century Fox.

Supplemental Resources

Poetry and Popular Songs

Bukowski, C. (1968). Starting fast. In *Bukowski*. New York: Black Sparrow.

> This poem presents a reflection of a real life experience of being homeless.

Madonna. (1994). I'll remember [Song]. From the motion picture *With honors*. Maverick.

> A song about the many things a graduate student learned from a homeless man.

Rylant, C. (Ed.). (1994). *Something permanent*. Boston: Harcourt, Brace & Co.

> A book of poems by a popular writer for young adults dealing with the Great Depression and homelessness. Of particular quality are: "Hitchhiker" (p. 9), "Shoes" (p. 13), "Traveler" (p. 25), and "Mission" (p. 61).

Soul Asylum. (1994). Runaway train [Song]. Columbia Records.

> This song speaks to the severe problems encountered by runaways.

10,000 Maniacs. (1987). City of angels [Song]. On the compact disk, *In my tribe*. New York: Elektra.

> The singer in this song sings about seeing hungry people staggering in the "City of Angels" on earth and tells about how the average person reacts to such a sight.

Novels

Blacker, T. (1993). *Homebird*. New York: Macmillan.
> A boarding school student decides to run away from school rather than face his many problems. This is an excellent novel for high school students who are unskilled or inexperienced readers of novels.

Hahn, M. (1988). *December stillness*. New York: Clarion Books.
> A teenage girl attempts to befriend a homeless Vietnam veteran who spends his day in the library.

Jones, A. (1987). *Street family: A novel*. New York: Harper & Row.
> A group of street people come together as a family while sharing shelter beneath an LA freeway. This novel is also an excellent choice for reluctant readers.

Kennedy, W. (1984). *Ironweed*. New York: Penguin.
> An ex-ballplayer, part-time grave digger, and full-time drunk returns to his old home town with his hobo pal and tries to make peace with the ghosts of his past and present. A film by the same name is also available on videotape.

King, B. (1992). *Silicon songs*. Dell/Laurel Leaf Library.
> King tells the story of a homeless seventeen-year-old named Max, who has no home. Max works as a computer programmer and in a desperate attempt to make money to provide himself with a place to live, he decides to illegally sell computer time to South. The horror of a homeless life that serves as Max's motivation, also serves as a point of empathy for adolescent readers.

Nasaw, J. (1993). *Shakedown street*. New York: Delacorte.
> A teenager and his mother find a sense of community in a San Francisco shelter.

Swindells, R. (1995). *Stone cold*. London: Puffin Books.
> An excellent portrayal of the plight of the homeless, especially what it takes for adolescents to survive on the street.

Wright, R. (1996). *Rite of Passage*. New York: Harper Trophy.
> When a teenager suddenly finds out that he is a foster child and is being sent to a new foster home, he runs away. His secure world suddenly dissolves into a nightmare of subways, dark alleys, and the street warfare of the homeless.

Other Printed Material

Kosof, A. (1988). *Homeless in America.* New York: Franklin Watts.
   This book discusses the homeless problem specifically, homeless children and youth.
Laudau, E. (1987). *The homeless.* New York: Julian Messner.
   An examination of the background and experiences of the homeless. Giving special attention to the lives of homeless children, the author relates what it is like to spend nights in a shelter and days searching for food on the street.
Quindlen, A. (1991). *Homeless.* In *The Bedford reader* Boston: St. Martins Press, pp. 188–190.
   Quindlen is writing an article on the homeless and happens to meet Ann, a homeless woman. In this story, Quindlen juxtaposes her life with Ann's.

Films and Videos

Down and out in America [Documentary film] (1985). Joseph Feury Productions. J. Feury, Producer.
   An academy award winning movie on the homeless.
Inside life outside [Film]. (1988). The American Film Institute. S. Hamada & S. Sinkler, Producers
   This film centers around a group of homeless people living in a shantytown on New York's lower East side. It explores the realities of poverty and the homeless.

Suggested Additional Resources for the Classroom Library: Unit on Homelessness

10,000 Maniacs. (1987). City of Angels. On *In my tribe* [Compact Disk]. New York, NY: Elektra.
Barrio, R. (1984). *The plum pickers.* Phoenix, AZ: Bilingual Press.
Bassuk, E. L. & Rosenberg, L. (1988). Why does family homelessness occur? A case control study. *American Journal of Public Health,* 78 (7), 783–788.
Blacker, T. (1993). *Homebird.* New York: Macmillan.
Bland, B. (Director, Producer). (1991). *Home less home* [Film]. New York: Bill Bland Productions.

Bunting, E. (1991). *Fly away home*. Portland, OR: Clarion.
Carey-Webb, A. (1991). Homelessness and language arts: Contexts and connections. *English Journal*, 80 (7), 22–28.
Clifton, L. (1936). Miss Rosie. In B. Lawn (Ed.), *Literature: 150 masterpieces of fiction, poetry, and drama*. New York: St. Martin's Press, 461.
Collins, P. (1989). Another day in paradise. On *But seriously* [CD]. New York: Atlantic Records.
Crane, S. (1979). *Maggie: A girl of the streets*. New York: W. W. Norton.
Crystal, B. (1989). *The best of comic relief 3* [Compact Disk]. Los Angeles: Rhino Records.
Davis, R. C. (Ed.). (1982). *Twentieth century interpretations of "The Grapes of Wrath"*. Englewood Cliffs, NJ: Prentice Hall.
Deloria, E. C. (1989). Blue bird's offering. In P. G. Allen (Ed.), *Spiderwoman's granddaughter*. New York: Fawcett Columbine.
Dickens, C. (1982). *Oliver Twist*. New York: Bantam.
Eighner, L. (1986). My daily dives in the dumpster. In D. Laguardia & H. Guth (Eds.), *American voices: Multicultural literacy and critical thinking*. Mountainview, CA: Mayfield.
Gere, A. R., Fairbanks, C., Howes, A., Roop, L. & Schaafsma, D. (1992). *Language and reflection: An integrated approach to teaching English*. New York: Macmillan.
Hubbard, J. (1991). *American refugees*. Minneapolis: U. of Minnesota Press.
Hutchinson, L. (1993). Homelessness and reader-response: Writing with a social consciousness. *English Journal*, 82 (2), 366–369.
Johnson, S. (1992). *One of the boys*. New York: Atheneum.
King, B. (1992). *Silicon Songs*. New York: Dell.
Kismaric, C. (1989). *Forced out*. New York: Random House.
Kozol, J. (1988). *Rachel and her children*. New York: Crown.
Mathabane, M. (1989). *Kaffir boy in America*. New York: Charles Scribner & Sons.
Nelson, T. (1992). *The beggar's ride*. New York: Orchard Books.
Parks, G. (1966). *A choice of weapons*. New York: Harper & Row.
Selah, A. T. (Producer). (1986). *Streetwise* [film]. Angelika films.
Spinelli, J. (1990). *Maniac Magee*. Boston, MA: Little, Brown.
Walters, A. L. (1946). The warriors. In P. G. Allen (Ed.). *Spiderwoman's granddaughters*. New York: Fawcett Columbine, 111–128.
Wersba, B. (1992). *You'll never guess the end*. New York: Harper Collins.
Zanuck, D. (Producer). (1940). *The grapes of wrath* [film]. 20th Century Fox.

CHAPTER SIX

AMERICA: MOTHER OF EXILES

Gail Gregg, Melinda Miller, Nan Vollgracht

Big Green Lady
Belkis L. Cabrera

Two weeks in the Big Apple
With "I Love NY" still stapled on the door
And this yellow cabbed jungle with its
Steel Vines—Stirs into a rumble
As Mario, the driver, recites his "Where to"
Every hour on 'de hour
Through a goateed chin and a slight accent
The souvenir coffee mug on his dashboard reads
"New York, NY a Hellofa Town"
As we pulsate to potholes, he tells me things
Not on my Travel Guide, Like
How his grandmother slept on sewing machines
And how there was a living to be made
Canning food along the waterfront
Or so his father said.
As we pass the Dakota apartment where
John Lennon was shot, he signals at
Central Park and motions at flyers strung between
Tall Buildings, like Laundry
And for seven dollars, I take his advice and ride
The Ferry on the starboard side

To the Big Green Lady
A nice touch of democracy
And as she rises in copper waves
Crowned by spikes
She digs a hole in my head
To pour still frames of my mother's face and I
Remember for the first time
Piles like ants at her golden door
Muted by language and chicken pox
With chalk stains on shoulders
And newspaper bedding, bathtubs in kitchens
Twenty dollar pay checks and tattered clothes
Sand paper hands clasping books like visas
And I understand Mario and his grandmother
As I hear their cries shriek like pieces of
Metal
On metal.

A Bridge Across Early and Recent Arrivals

Many of the values that unite Americans as a nation are tied to the theme of exiles and immigration. Though some of us arrived earlier than others, and some of us came in bondage, this theme has framed our vision of our role in the world and has helped define our view of humanity. With the exception of Native Americans, we all have arrived here from other places and thus are all a part of a great continuum that seemingly has no end. Even though the doors to Ellis Island closed many years ago for all but tourists, immigrants continue to flood our borders by running, by swimming, by boat, plane, and makeshift rafts. Unfortunately, this constant influx of immigrants, both legal and illegal, has recently led to cultural clashes between those whose forefathers immigrated here many years ago, and recent arrivals. Measures such as Proposition 187 in California, which denies social services and free public education to non-documented aliens, demands by politicians and native-born citizens to close borders, and the cries for the passage of English-only legislation, are creating an anti-immigrant thrust that is now beginning to spill over into the classroom creating pockets of ethnocentrism featuring a "we" (ancestors of early arrivals) versus "them" (recent arrivals) mentality. Native-born students oftentimes blame recent immigrants for eroding their quality of life, while immigrant students argue that the native-born students don't understand the hardships they face and the isolation they feel. Despite being a country made up of exiles who came here from elsewhere, there doesn't seem to be a compelling humanitarian concern for the plight of the recent immigrant. A shelter, a haven, a home to all is quickly evaporating into a society filled with fear and misunderstanding of recent "others." A literary unit centered on early and recent immigrants and exiles, both forced and voluntary, will hopefully help to build a bridge across the chasm that separates the ancestors of early arrivals and the more recent newcomers while promoting ethical and fair treatment for all people.

The Harsh Journey

Focusing on the hardships of their journey to this country provides a dramatic way to link all immigrant groups in addition to providing an excellent structure to house beginning discussion of this important theme. A musical piece, "They're Coming to America," by Neil Diamond followed by reading "What is an American?" (DeCrevoceour, 1994), and

Russell Freedman's photo essay, *Immigrant Kids* (1980), can be used to sensitize students to the journey of the immigrant. Diamond's song tells about the many different groups anxiously traveling to this country while DeCrevoceour's short story describes the flight of European immigrants to America in the mid 1700s. Freedman's work is filled with period photographs depicting youngsters immigrating to this country on ships where they are stowed in steerage like baggage. An excellent docu-novel to use as a followup to Freedman's photo essay is *Wildflower Girl* (1992) by Marita Conlon-McKenna, which documents a thirteen-year-old girl's arduous five-week journey across the stormy Atlantic from Ireland to Boston during the nineteenth century. Excerpts from Brent and Melissa Ashabranner's *Into a Strange Land: Unaccompanied Refugee Youth in America* (1987) and *Journey of the Sparrows* (1991) by Fran Leeper Buss, will provide students with the journeys of more recent immigrants who are also close in age to the reader. The former recounts personal tales of the Asian boat people and their journey to America after the Viet Nam War. The first story in the Ashabranner's work is particularly poignant as it describes the journey of a youngster who has to leave Viet Nam without his family. *Journey of the Sparrows* tells the story of fifteen-year-old Maria, her sister and her brother, who make the journey from El Salvador nailed into a crate on the back of a truck.

Although there are other selections one might use, these selections are particularly relevant to introduce students to the theme of immigration, as they provide realistic accounts of the hardships encountered by adolescent youth who embark on risky life-changing journeys in order to seek a new "home" and better way of life. Discussion should center around the differences between the journey of the earlier immigrants and those of recent arrivals and whether the journey was worth it. A worthwhile activity to conduct with students is to ask them to list what personal effects they would take with them if they were to immigrate to a new country via steerage in a crowded ship, or in a crate loaded on a pickup truck, or on an open raft. A second activity would include asking students to write a letter to a friend explaining why they are moving to a new country and what they expect to find there upon arrival. Students should also keep an immigration chart that will help them organize what they read, see, and hear. The chart should list every immigrant group they are exposed to during this unit and should answer the following questions:

1. Who?
2. From Where?
3. To Where?
4. When?
5. Why?
6. Source?

Up to this point, discussion and literary pieces have centered on the general concept of voluntary or self-exile, which leaves some choice up to the individual as opposed to forced exile where there is no choice. A classic canonical text relative to forced exile is Milton's *Paradise Lost*. Excerpts of either Lucifer's expulsion from heaven or Adam and Eve's expulsion from Eden are excellent to use as examples of forced exile. Excerpts from *Exodus* (Uris, 1976), a historical novel about European Jews leaving Europe during World War II and their settlement in Israel will offer students a more modern approach to this topic. Using the video of the same name will work just as well. To stretch the global boundaries of exile, an excerpt from *One Day in the Life of Ivan Denisovich* (Solzhenitsyn, 1963), or the entire book (it is very short, but requires slow reading because of its depth) gives the reader a view of life as an exile in Siberia as it chronicles one day in a labor camp prisoner's life. This work can be explored with a biographical note on the author, who himself was a dissident and spent time in exile first in a Russian prison and later in the United States before moving back to Russia recently. Of course, it goes without saying that the Middle Passage was the source of one of the largest movements of forced immigration and exile. Because this is such an important and tragic event in the history of the United States, the Middle Passage will be covered separately in the next chapter.

An academic transition from a focus on the journey to a focus on the arrival in the new land can be accomplished through the use of the Chinese poem, "My Promised Land" by A. Apolinaro (1989). In this poem, the poet describes the "promised land" as a land in which caring and mercy replace hating and prejudice. After discussing the poem's explicit and possible implicit messages, students should write a similar poem based on the framework of the original. Each stanza in the student poems should begin with the original poem's first line of each of the four stanzas, followed by the students' words.

Their Arrival

The arrival of immigrants to a new "home" and a desire for a better life can be very vividly portrayed visually through the use of clips from the following videos:

- *The North* (1983) is the story of a Guatemalan family who travels through Mexico and finally arrives in Los Angeles. Show the scenes from entering the tunnel to when the family arrives at their new "dream home."
- *My family* (1995) celebrates three generations of Mexican-Americans in California as they grow and struggle to succeed. The scene where the grandfather finally reaches California after walking through Mexico will give the students a good sense of how it feels to immigrate to a totally foreign place.
- *Far and away* (1994) is the story of an Irish couple who flee Ireland, arrive in Boston Harbor, live in an Irish enclave, and eventually fight for land in Oklahoma. Show the scene of the couple's arrival in Boston Harbor and their move into their first apartment.
- *The godfather II* (1976) is about a Mafia crime family in New York City. The scene in which Don Corleone arrives at Ellis Island, has his name changed, and moves into an Italian neighborhood is an excellent one for students to view.
- *The Perez family* (1995), is the story of a Cuban man who spent twenty years in Castro's prisons and arrived in the United States during the Mariel boat lift. The film depicts the struggle of culture shock, the fight for freedom, and acceptance in bicultural Miami. We recommend that you make an excerpt of the scene of the Cuban man's arrival and life in a refugee camp near the Orange Bowl and allow students to view it during this thematic unit.

Each of these films contains diversified views of the immigration process and, if you have time, should be shown in their entirety. However, with the time constraints prevalent in today's high school classes, use of the excerpted clips, as noted, offers a mix of immigrant groups and different immigration processes in one class period and provides a focal point for comparing and contrasting the different arrival experiences of each immigrant group.

Life in Their New "Home"

The next section of this unit begins with exploring how various members of immigrant groups have adjusted to life in American. Start with a simple, yet artistic and an ongoing project, which begins with a bulletin board displaying a large picture of the Statue of Liberty. Students should use the remaining space on the bulletin board to place illustrations (drawing, photos, and cut-outs) and quotes from the material that is covered in this unit describing/depicting how various immigrant groups have adjusted to their new life in America. There are several sources you can use to provide background information relative to the Statue of Liberty. Chapter One of Mercer's, *The Statue of Liberty* (1979) gives a very thorough description of this famous monument. Students should also be exposed to "The New Colossus" (Lazarus, 1957), which is imprinted on the base of the Statue of Liberty and has come to symbolize America's open arms to the poor and tired immigrants who come into this country. There are also two marvelous articles in *National Geographic*, the July 1986 issue that can be used to provide background material, text, and photos, on the Statue of Liberty. One photograph in this issue (p. 16) depicts an immigrant family standing by the water looking out toward the Statue of Liberty. This photo is an effective prewriting prompt; after they view and discuss it, ask students to write a short descriptive story in which they explain who the people are, why they are there, what they are thinking, and where they are going. Another excellent writing activity is to have students compose their own inscriptions for the base of the Statue.

Ellis Island should also be included in this unit. Fisher's pictorial book, *Ellis Island: Gateway to the New World* (1986) is a short work filled with vivid images of the immigrant experience at Ellis Island. The book also takes the reader through the many phases of the construction of the buildings on Ellis Island, as well as the stories of many of the people who entered there. Ask students to select one of the photos in the book and write a brief essay from the perspective of the person whose picture has been selected, describing the person's feelings and thoughts upon entering their new "home."

The poem, "I Am an American," by Elias Lieberman (1957), provides a wonderful segue into immigration because through it students can begin to look at individual immigrant experiences in their new "home." In this poem, Lieberman contrasts two very different Americans. The ancestors of the first Americans participated in a revolution that won them independence, while the ancestors of the second Americans worked themselves to death in Siberian mines. The first American looks to the past with pride; the second American looks to the future with pride. Students should be asked to compare and contrast the two different immigrant experiences described in the poem and then asked to respond to why one is proud of the past and the other of the future. You may want to consider following Lieberman's poem with reading some excerpts from interviews in the book *New Kids in Town: Oral Histories of Immigrant Teens* by Jane Bode (1989). This work revolves around recent immigrant teenagers from countries such as China, India, Greece, and Afghanistan who share their experiences of what it is like to be an adolescent immigrant in today's society. High school students relate quite well to this particular work due to similarities in age and adolescent problems. *Aekyung's Dream* (Paek, 1988) and *Krik? Krak!* (Danticat, 1995), two young adult books, are quick reads that provide valuable insight into some of the terrors faced by immigrants who make crossings without any money or support, and of some of the adjustment problems faced by immigrant children. *Aekyung's Dream* is the story of a young Korean girl's first experiences and frustrations with adjusting to a new culture. It compares life in San Francisco to life in Seoul, South Korea. *Krik? Krak!* is a collection of short stories for mature adolescents; in it, Danicat draws attention to Haiti and Haitian immigrants during recent war-torn times.

To provide students with an outlet for creativity and an authentic writing activity, break them into groups and have each group write a short children's book. Each book should advise immigrant children from various cultures on how to deal with United States culture and traditions, including practices we often associate with holidays, family relationships, religious rituals, language, dialects, and so on. The books must be complete with text and illustrations, and when complete students will present them to the rest of the class. Of course, if feasible, this activity could include students reading their books to a group of elementary school children. A good teacher's resource to use in this book publishing activity is *Multicultural Books to Make and Share* (Gaylord, 1994), which offers creative ideas for making books from different materials such as tongue depressors and crepe paper. This assignment not only provides artistic and creative students with an outlet for their talents, but encourages each group to consider the perils and difficulties of adjusting to a new "home."

Two works that provide adult perspectives on adjustments that immigrants must go through when first they arrive into a new country are Studs Terkel's *American Dreams: Lost and Found* (1980) and Mark Mathabane's (1989) essay, "I Leave South Africa." "O Canaan Land," which is Chapter Two in Terkel's book, features interviews from a wide variety of immigrants, including Arnold Schwarzenegger, a teen favorite, who emigrated from Austria in 1968. A worthwhile activity is to ask students to compare the adjustment experiences of the earlier and older immigrants in Terkel's work to the recent and younger arrivals in Bode's book. Some of the questions that should be explored include:

- How were the adjustment experiences similar? Different?
- Does age create more/fewer adjustment problems?
- How would you react to moving to a country where the customs and language were different from your own?

Mathabane's first-person narrative relates his initial encounter with the culture of the United States after leaving the repressive regime (at the time of his departure) of his country. In his essay, Mathabane tells of having to adjust to a new country. He must also attempt to understand his new identity within a new culture and merge these two things into a coherent whole. Students should be asked to comment on Mathabane's first impressions of the United States and compare them to the first impressions related by the immigrants in Terkel's and Bode's works.

Disappointment, Disillusionment and Loss of Identity

Mathabane's essay serves well as a transition into an exploration by students of the painful emotional suffering that immigrants experience as they try to redefine themselves, and as they make sense of their lives in a still-foreign land. Oftentimes this process causes great disappointment and disillusionment with the immigrant winding up caught between two cultures, feeling at "home" in neither. Two poems by Adrienne Rich, "Prospective Immigrants Please Note" (1967) and "Can We Live in Two Cultures" (1967) can also serve to focus discussion of these issues. The first is a short poem that warns the prospective immigrants of the possibilities of losing their original identity and heritage when they choose to immigrate to another country. In the second, Rich touches on the topic of assimilation and the task of maintaining one's original cultural background while participating fully in the new culture. These two poems can lead to the topic of assimilation, and may prompt students to talk and write about the difference between seeing the United States as a "salad bowl," where immigrants blend into the culture while maintaining their own identity, and a "melting pot," where immigrants lose their original cultural identity.

Ryu's "Poem by a Yellow Woman" (1994) can be used to continue discussion on the issues of disappointment, disillusionment, and loss of identity. Beginning with a description that compares America to a huge snake-man, Ryu, a Chinese woman, goes on to describe the hardships that immigrants have to face, including the ironies, hypocrisy, and injustice she has found in this country, where the wealthy ignore the homeless, and the powerful ignore others' rights. It is apparent to most readers that Ryu is not only confused but is also disillusioned by her new "home." Though she always dreamed of coming to the United States, now that she is here, she doesn't understand a country where her brother, who earned a graduate degree in English literature, and who can fluently discuss the American Dream, must work in a restaurant and serve white neighbors day and night in order to make ends meet, and whose sister who likes Picasso has to spend her days behind a sewing machine, where her only chance to experiment with color is in her bleached hair. We recommend that you ask students to explain the ironies, and to find and delve into the examples of hypocrisy and injustice in Ryu's poem. Following discussion, students can read Neruda's "Goodbyes" (1994), which tells the story of an inveterate traveler who recommends living within one's own identity regardless of where one happens to be. We suggest that you ask students whether they agree or disagree with the poet's decision to never become identified with any particular place or culture.

Young Adult Novels Depicting Immigrant Life in America

Ideally, you will have the time and resources to assign a full-length adolescent novel that contains an immigration theme during the course of this unit. Although there are many to choose from, our selections represent a variety of reading levels and immigrant groups, and have been successfully used in our classrooms.

Three books that are appropriate for students who are unskilled or reluctant high school readers are these: *The House on Mango Street* by Sandra Cisneros (1994), *A Tree Grows in Brooklyn* by Betty Smith (1947), and *Children of the River* by Linda Crew (1989). It should be noted although these novels are "easy" reads, students who do have the ability and willingness to read and understand more sophisticated material will also probably enjoy them.

The House on Mango Street tells, through a series of vignettes, the story of a young Mexican-American girl growing up in a Mexican-American neighborhood in California. The author shares with her readers her frustrations with a new language, culture, and poverty. The reader sees Mango Street and the surrounding neighborhood through the eyes of a young girl. Discussion of this work is likely to center around how the protagonist's immigrant status and cultural differences affect her life. You might want to ask your students to write a short story about their own neighborhood, in which they address questions such as these:

- What are the sounds and smells of your neighborhood?
- What does it look like?
- What kinds of people live there, and what do they do?

A Tree Grows in Brooklyn shares the story of a young Irish girl growing up in Brooklyn, New York, during the early twentieth century. Francie, the protagonist, encounters many different cultural conflicts within her Irish neighborhood and in nearby Jewish and Italian enclaves. The chapters in this work are not titled, leaving fertile ground for students to interact with the text by giving each chapter a title. This activity can be completed by individual students via a journal entry and explanation as to why each particular chapter title was selected. The same activity can be completed by groups of students working together.

Crew's *Children of the River* is a fictional story centering on Sundara, who, at the age of thirteen, escapes the Khmer Rouge army in Cambodia and immigrates, with relatives, to the United States. She leaves behind her parents, her brother and sister, and the boy she has loved since she was a young child. Four years later, she is struggling to fit in at an Oregon high school while at the same time remaining faithful to her own culture and family. As she waits for her family to arrange her marriage to a Cambodian boy, she meets an American boy to whom she is powerfully drawn. The book vividly portrays Sundara's courage and devotion while experiencing generational conflict and clashes between the old and new cultures.

A successful way to connect all three of these works, which are all told through the eyes of a young girl, is to ask students to compare and contrast each narrator relative to their points of view and immigrant experiences. Another activity we suggest is to have students write descriptions of how the protagonist in each book viewed "home." Students might also write descriptions of customs and traditions celebrated in each of the protagonist's homes.

Four book-length works that we have found successful when used with more sophisticated readers are *My Name is Asher Lev* by Chaim Potok (1972), *The Joy Luck Club* by Amy Tan (1990), *How the Garcia Girls Lost Their Accent* by Julia Alvarez (1991), and the autobiographical *Kaffir Boy in America* by Mark Mathabane, 1989.

Asher Lev is the son of European Jewish immigrants who is pulled from his parents' traditional ways into the western world where he wants to be an artist. He is forced to make a choice between the two and chooses art over his family.

The Joy Luck Club illustrates the dilemmas of Chinese immigrant mothers and their daughters as they strive to be a part of two cultures. The book details the differences between the American and Chinese cultures, shows how family traditions can fall apart from one generation to the next, and explores the stereotypes and prejudices faced by Chinese-Americans.

How the Garcia Girls Lost Their Accent depicts the lives and challenges of four Puerto Rican sisters living in New York. The girls struggle to find a middle ground as they experience one culture in school and society, and another at home.

Kaffir Boy in America is a autobiographical work that recounts the author's coming of age as a black South African immigrant in a country that is overwhelming in its mixture of luxury, poverty, and despair. Beginning with his early college days, when he first discovers African-American writers, to the reconciling of his identity within the framework of his new home, *Kaffir Boy* reflects on America's racial and social injustices, and its strange and confusing ways. This work is a moving saga of hardship, inspiration, and determination that is basic in the lives of all immigrants.

Each of these works is an excellent example of the plight of immigrants who must adjust, understand, and attempt to reconcile the old versus the new in customs, traditions, oftentimes within the framework of a new language and in a new "home." Activities used with these works can be the same as those applicable to less sophisticated works mentioned previously.

A Final Activity or Two

We recommend giving students choices for a culminating activity. Those mentioned here have met with success in our classrooms. If logistically possible, ask students to interview an immigrant in their community and write a paper relating this immigrant's experiences to those of the different characters in the literature.

To bring the immigrant experience to a very personal level, students can complete a family history project. Ask students to research the following with a family member:

- When did their family come to this country?
- Who came?
- Where did they come from?
- Why did they come and to where?
- What emotions did they feel upon leaving their original homeland?
- What are some memories of the former home?
- What problems were encountered in the new "home"?

Students should present their research in presentations to the rest of the class, using visual aids gathered from the family member who is interviewed and graphics available on World Wide Web sites that deal with the times and places described by those who are interviewed.

Another possible concluding activity, one that is less time and energy-intensive, is the sharing of "Joy of an Immigrant, A Thanksgiving" by Emanuel Di Pasquale (1985). This short poem tells of a country that is no longer life-sustaining and where the immigrant, after his journey, longs for nothing more than a safe home where he can express himself.

Works Cited

Alvarez, J. (1991). *How the Garcia girls lost their accents*. Chapel Hill, NC: Algonquin Books.

Apolinaro, A. (1989). My promised land. In L. Knight (Ed.), *Butterflies on the wind: An anthology of poetry by Chinese and American writers.* Robbinsdale, MN: Guild Press, 54–55.

Ashabranner, B & A. (1987). The most vulnerable people. In *Into a strange land: Unaccompanied refugee youth in America.* New York: Putnam, 4–5.

Bode, J. (1989). *New kids in town: Oral histories of immigrant teens.* New York: Scholastic.

Buss, F. (1991). *Journey of the sparrows.* Dallas: Dutton/Lodestar.

Cisneros, S. (1994). *The house on Mango Street.* New York: Vintage Books.

Conlon-McKenna, M. (1992). *Wildflower girl.* New York: Holiday.

Coppola, F. (Director). (1976). *Godfather II.* [Video]. Los Angeles: Paramount Pictures.

Coppola, F. (Director). (1995). *My family.* [Video] Los Angeles: New Line Cinema.

Crew, L. (1989). *Children of the river.* New York: Delacorte.

Danticat, E. (1995). *Krik? krak!* New York: Soho Press.

DeCrevoceour, M. G. (1994). What is an American? In B. Bernstein (Ed.), *Literature and language.* New York: McDougal, Littell & Co, 24–26.

Diamond, N. (Singer). (1980). America. On *Jazz singer* [CD]. New York: Capitol Records.

DiPasquale, E. (1985). Joy of an immigrant, a Thanksgiving poem. In M. C. Livingston (Ed.), *Thanksgiving poems.* New York: Holiday House, 15.

Fisher, L. E. (1986). *Ellis island: Gateway to the new world.* New York: Holiday House.

Freedman, R. (1980). *Immigrant kids.* New York: Dutton.

Gaylord, S. K. (1994). *Multicultural books to make and share.* New York: Scholastic.

Howard, R. (Director), & Grazer, B. (Producer). (1992). *Far and away.* [Video]. Los Angeles: Universal City & Imagine Films.

Lazarus, E. (1957). The new colossus. In H. Ferris (Ed.), *Favorite poems old and new.* Garden City, NY: Doubleday, 448.

Lieberman, E. (1957). I am an American. In H. Ferris (Ed.), *Favorite poems: old and new.* Garden City, NY: Doubleday, 448–449.

Mathabane, M. (1994). In S. Hirschberg (Ed.), *The many worlds of literature.* New York: MacMillan, 786–791.

Mathabane, M. (1989). *Kaffir boy in America.* New York: MacMillan.

Mercer, C. (1979). Most famous monument. In *Statue of Liberty*. New York: Putnam, 7–9.
Milton, J. (1993). Paradise lost. In M. H. Abrams (Ed.), *The Norton anthology of English literature* (1474–1610). New York: W. W. Norton.
Nair, M. (Director). (1995). *The Perez family*. [Video]. Los Angeles: Goldwyn.
Nava, G. (Director). (1995). *The North* [movie]. Los Angeles: CBS-Fox.
Neruda, P. (1994). Goodbyes. In S. Hirschberg (Ed.), *The many worlds of literature*. New York: MacMillan, 883.
Paek, M. (1988). *Aekyung's dream*. Denver: Children's Book Press.
Potok, C. (1972). *My name is Asher Lev*. Greenwich, CT: Fawcett.
Rich, A. (1967). Prospective immigrants please note. In J. Beatty (Ed.), *Literature and language*. Evanston, IL: McDougal, Littell & Co, 467–469.
Rich, A. (1967). Can we live in two cultures. In J. Beatty (Ed.), *Literature and language*. Evanston, IL: McDougal, Littell & Co, 467–469.
Ryu, S. L. (1994). Poem by a yellow woman. In S. Gillespie, T. Fonseca & C. Sanger (Eds.), *Literature and language*. New York: Allyn and Bacon, 695–696.
Solzhenitsyn, A. (1963). *One day in the life of Ivan Denisovich*. New York: Signet.
Smith, B. (1947). *A tree grows in Brooklyn*. New York: Harper.
Tan, A. (1990). *The joy luck club*. NY: Ivy Books.
Terkel, S. (1980). O Canaan land. In S. Terkel, *American dreams: Lost and found*. New York: Ballantine, 86–162.
Uris, L. (1976). *Exodus*. Garden City, New York: Doubleday.

Supplemental Resources

Poetry

Gillian, M. M. (1994). Public school no. 18: Patterson, New Jersey. In S. Gillespie, T. Fonseca, & C. Sanger (Eds.), *Literature across the cultures*. New York: Allyn and Bacon, 696.
This poem tells of a child's struggle to be accepted by both her new society and within her family's heritage. A young Italian girl learns

to deny herself and her country as she tries to be accepted by mainstream classmates. In the end she learns to be proud of her heritage.

Hawkins, R. F. (1989). Proud upon an alien shore. In *Emerging voices* Fort Worth: Harcourt Brace, 35–38.

A poem describing three generations of Japanese people living in America. The first generation arrived in 1921. The second generation is the transitional generation caught between the old ways and new. The third generation is the author who talks about the previous generations.

McKay, C. (1987). The tropics in New York. In *The world's best poetry: Minority poetry of America: An anthology of Asian, Black, Hispanic and Native American poetry*. Great Neck, NY: Roth Publishing, 318.

The poet tells of a distant home and cries for the old and familiar ways.

Mora, P. (1994). Legal alien. In B. Bernstein (Ed.), *Literature and language*. New York: McDougall Littell, 1116.

The poet is caught between two cultures, and neither one is fully accepting. Although she speaks fluent English, Americans notice that she is different. Her Mexican relatives, on the other hand, treat her differently as well because she is American-born.

Morales, A. L. (1997). Ending poem. In A. Applebee (Ed.), *The language of literature*. Evanston, IL: McDougall Littell, 329–330.

The poet describes herself using a plethora of adjectives inferring several different races and ethnicities. She is asking people to look beyond her "race" and see her as an individual. She denies any label, simply calling herself "immigrant."

Songs

Bernstein, L. & Sondheim, S. (1957). America. In *West side story*. [Video or CD] New York: Chappell and Co. Ltd.

One of the many hits from the Academy Award winning musical. This song describes the different emotions, fears, and desires of two young Puerto Rican women immigrants living in New York City. One girl yearns to return to her homeland, remembering her family, neighborhood, and old lifestyle. The other only remembers the negative aspects of Puerto Rico and now loves the American way of life. This song deals with the challenges every immigrant must deal with, adjusting to their new setting and successfully separating from their homeland.

Simon, P. (Singer and Producer). (1988). Rene and Georgette Magritte with their dog after the war. On *Negotiations and love songs: 1971–1986* [CD]. New York: Warner Bros.
A song about immigrants and their new land.

Short Stories and Drama

Augenbraum, H. (Ed.). (1993). *Growing up Latino*. New York: HoughtonMifflin.
A compilation of short stories all related to the Latino experience. The short stories in this anthology all focus on growing up in American society as an Hispanic.

Cisneros, S. (1994). Never marry a Mexican. In *Women of Hollering Creek*. New York: Vintage Books, 68–83
In this short story Cisneros describes life in a Mexican immigrant neighborhood and the suffering one must endure trapped in a new land, married to a "macho" Mexican.

Miller, A. (1993). Grandpa and the statue. In M. L. McClouskey & L. Stack (Eds.), *Voices in literature*. Boston: Heinle & Heinle Publishing, 179–194.
A short play that details an excursion of a grandson and his grandfather to the Statue of Liberty. This play offers a description of the statue, its history and the impact of the statue on the grandfather. It also gives the reader insight into the emotional affects the statue has had on immigrants.

Virgil, S. (1991). *Welcome to the oasis and other stories*. Houston: Arte Publico.
A book of short stories about Cuban immigrants to this country during the Mariel boat lift. The stories deal with the clashing of American and Cuban culture and the changes in language.

Novels

Greenberg, J. E. (1996). *Newcomers to America*. New York: UPI/Bettmann.
Introduces the young faces and voices of some of America's most recent immigrants. Through interviews and conversations, they

share their difficulties and sometimes terrifying experiences of leaving their native lands and coming to a new culture.

Jake, J. (1993). *Homeland*. New York: Doubleday.

This novel, which is historical fiction, tells the story of German immigrants to the United States in the 1890s. Details the account of the Kroner family leaving Hamburg, their arrival at Ellis Island, and finally their settlement in Cincinnati. The family deals with the issues facing many contemporary immigrants such as finding jobs, old world traditions versus new ways of doing things, and language difficulty.

Michener, J. A. (1975). *Centennial*. New York: Ballatine, Fawcett.

This novel tells the tale of a city representative of all of the cities in the United States. It weaves a fictional account of the historic waves of immigration through this country exploring how they have affected society as we know it.

Nixon, J. L. (1994). *Land of promise*. New York: Delacorte Press.

A short novel about a teenage, Irish immigrant who moves to Chicago to live with her alcoholic father and radical brother. The book gives a clear view of life in the early twentieth century. Appropriate for less sophisticated readers and offers an historical account of immigrant issues relative to adolescents.

Ortiz, J. (1993). *Silent dancing: A partial remembrance of a Puerto Rican childhood*. Houston: Arte Publico.

A Puerto Rican family living in New Jersey experience discrimination while trying to find an apartment. They finally locate in the barrio listening to Latin music and eating their typical food until slowly they begin to assimilate, forsaking the old ways of doing things.

Ramirez, E. (1982). *Family installment: Memories of growing up Hispanic*. New York: Penguin.

The author chronicles the journey of a family from a small Puerto Rican village to New York City. He describes the confrontations with a new culture, the loss of his heritage, and the warmth of a family surviving on inner strength and love.

Takaki, R. (1995). *From exiles to immigration*. New York: Chelsea House Publishers.

A narrative describing the struggles of Southeast Asian refugees as they fled their war-infested countries and then struggled with the challenges of life as new immigrants in the United States. Included is the history of different immigration trends and personal accounts of various immigrant experiences. Students can relate to true stories of Asian immigrants while learning the history of their migration.

Uchida, Y. (1981). *A far dream*. New York: Vintage Books.
The story of a Japanese family who fight prejudice, poverty, and cultural conflicts during the depression era in California.

Movies and Videos

Avalon. (1991). RCA/Columbia Pictures. Written and directed by B. Levinson. Produced by B. Levinson & M. Johnson.
This video follows Sam Krichinsky, after his arrival in America in 1914, and his extended family as they seek a dream called America. From poverty through prosperity, and family separation, loss, and devotion, the Krichinsky family face their changing world as immigrants with enduring humor and abiding love.

The Frisco kid. (1979). Los Angeles: Warner Bros. Produced by M. Neuyfeld. Starring Gene Wilder and Harrison Ford, this movie takes the viewer on a journey from Poland to San Francisco during the California Gold Rush. Wilder plays an Orthodox Rabbi who has many encounters throughout his journey, including a stay with Amish families in Pennsylvania and working with Japanese immigrants on the railroad. The film reminds the viewer of the differences and similarities between cultures. It also reminds the viewer that what may be acceptable and routine in one culture is not always acceptable and routine for other cultures.

CHAPTER SEVEN

THE MIDDLE PASSAGE

Linda Spears-Bunton

Mamma Says—A Tribute to My African Forefathers: Peace and Prayers
Iman Bunton, age 14

Why shouldn't the caged bird sing?
It sings a song of hope. Faith that one day
It will be free, free at last.
But the bird has bestial hatred for its captors
Flabbergasted by their brutality.
Bobby Hutton, Dr. Martin Luther King, Jr., Malcom X, Medgar Evers
Shot, all of them.
Mamma says they'll get Jesse, too
But not Maya. She is too smart, too educated.
Maya is powerful.
How did the African nation survive?
How did we persevere through four hundred and more
years of captivity, through assassinations of our people?
How did we endure four hundred and more years of
being educationally, politically held back—being withdrawn from society?
Mamma says,
"I'll tell you how we did it.
We sang songs of hope and faith. We let our true
colors show without being ashamed.
We fought our fear.
We sang songs of faith and praise so that one day we would be free, free
at last."

Please note: Although this unit can be presented independently, we recommend that it be used as an extension of the previous chapter, "America: Mother of Exiles." This chapter deals with one portion of the story of America's immigrant population, the Africans who were brought to North America against their will, and forced into slavery.

**No One Can Forget the Road to Her House:
Goals and Rationale for a Unit on the Middle Passage**

Humanity has a difficult time conferring value upon a silenced people or seeing itself reflected in another's pain. The stories of the "silenced" that have for too long been dishonorably dismissed are critical; adolescents need to hear the stories, and experience them, at least vicariously, as they begin to follow the road that will lead them toward an understanding of their own histories, their homes. "The Middle Passage" refers to the middle of the African's journey to the Americas; this particular chapter suggests resources and activities that may be used during the study of the Middle Passage as a distinct historical episode. This unit is offered as a map of landmarks on the road home for teachers and students who are attempting to understand one stretch of the road, the Middle Passage, the reality of slavery and its lasting effects on the African and African-American people. It is designed to produce empathy among adolescents for those who have suffered, especially Africa's approximately twenty million kidnapped citizens (Franklin and Moss, 1994) and with those who continue to suffer. It is designed to allow adolescents the opportunity to hear the often-silenced voices of those who have suffered and do suffer.

It is important, too, for teachers and students to realize that slavery represents only a part of the history of many culturally distinctive people who trace their ancestry to the continent of Africa. Students need to understand that African societies flourished for centuries before the coming of Arab and European slave merchants and that Africans and African-Americans have a notable history aside from the dark era of transatlantic slavery. The Middle Passage—a one-way journey—began in 1451 and continued for over 350 years (Bennet, 1966). When the Middle Passage is the focus for study in a secondary classroom, the history that preceded slavery must not be ignored or trivialized. Adolescents should not be left with the impression that the African's entry into civilization began in bondage.

Slavery itself, as an institution, is certainly not a condition that is unique to those who were taken from their homes in Africa and brought to the Americas. Africans, Asians, Arabs, Aztecs, Mayans, and Europeans, among many others, have at some time in their histories practiced slavery. At the core of each instance of slavery is an assumption that one person or group has the right to own the body, mind, heart, and beliefs of another human being, and to use that human to satisfy one's economic needs, social whims, and physical lusts. When students critically examine this assumption and reveal flaws in the forces that have sustained it, they can then abandon it. Also at the core of each instance of slavery is the fact that the voices of the enslaved have been entrapped just as the bodies have been. It is time that curricula in American schools attended to the voices of those who have been traditionally been silenced by their position as slaves.

The primary academic goal of the thematic unit described in this chapter, therefore, is to provide learners with literary resources that will help them begin studying issues related to the Middle Passage and its lasting influence on American society. Equally important is the primary affective and social goal of the unit: to provide students with a foundation upon which they may build fundamentally different relationships with others, relationships that are based upon knowledge, respect, and compassion, rather than ignorance, guilt, and blame.

The Middle Passage: A Difficult Yet Essential Feature of the Secondary School Curriculum

It is difficult to teach the Middle Passage in secondary schools. The event itself was horrific; sensibilities are assaulted by images that suggest the magnitude and depth of human pain that was suffered when Africans were kidnapped and transported to the Americas and the islands of the Caribbean. As teachers we usually want our students to feel comfortable about themselves and their surroundings; to teach the Middle Passage means we must be willing to allow discomfort to exist temporarily. It is also difficult to teach the Middle Passage because the events are still close to home; the descendants of Middle Passage survivors and the descendants of their oppressors sit side-by-side in our classrooms. Despite their physical proximity to one another, and despite even the friendships that are treasured among many, members of both groups rarely comprehend the extent of the differences that have traditionally separated them.

Adolescents and their teachers rarely understand the magnitude of differences created by the historical, cultural, intellectual, and personal context that defines a group other than one's own. It is difficult to teach the Middle Passage because it is a story of humanity's shamefulness. Ignorance, however, contributes to the perpetuation of misunderstanding, fear, and hatred; therefore, the Middle Passage, although difficult, should be taught.

The Middle Passage: A Teacher's Beginning

We cannot teach that which we do not know. Many teachers have not had the opportunity to learn about the Middle Passage as part of their own education; therefore, they will benefit from studying resources that provide basic factual information about the time and events that define the Middle Passage. Several good resources might be used as a starting place for the teacher's research. One such resource is Franklin and Moss' *From Slavery to Freedom: A History of African Americans* (1994). This nonfiction book offers an historically sound portrait of African civilizations prior to the Middle Passage, the Middle Passage, colonial slavery, and the African Diaspora. The format of the text encourages teachers to use just the section they need for general background information for themselves and their students. Along with the first three chapters of this text, we recommend that teachers read the Introduction to Tom Feelings' poignant pictorial history, *The Middle Passage: White Ships/Black Cargo* (1995). The pictures in this history are likely to have an impact on both teachers and students who have previously been unable to imagine the conditions that Africans endured as they were brought to the Americas. Another excellent source of background information is *The Interesting Narrative of the Life of Olaudah Equiano or Gustavus the African* (Edwards, ed., 1985). This is an authentic, first-hand account of a captured boy's voyage to the Americas. The descriptions in this work have often been used to document historical fiction.

Teachers might also use resources available or described on the World Wide Web. A search using Yahoo and the topic word "slavery" recently led us to the following sites, each of which is potentially useful as a resource for teachers and students:

http://h-net2.msu.edu/~slavery/
> This site, which is still under construction at the present, currently includes documents presented at the UNESCO Slave Route Conference, held in Ouidah, Benin, September, 1994, and promises links to other sites that present information on the world history of slavery, abolition, and emancipation.

http://squash.la.psu.edu/~plarson/smuseum/homepage.html
> This site is the home page of the Museum of the History of Slavery. Though still under construction, at present it contains information under topics including, "What is Slavery?" "Who Owns History?" and "The Origins of Slavery."
>
> An article an the history of slavery in North America , written by Ralph Austen, Chair of African and African-American Studies at the University of Chicago, is available under the heading of "Never Again." Also under that heading are examples of "ironic Americana," such as an early newspaper advertisement that announces that tickets for the raffle of a black colt and a mulatto girl can be purchased for $1.00 each. Also included are photographs of black people who have been hung during lynching by white mobs.

These examples of "Americana" found in early newspapers stray from the topic of slavery per se, but may help teachers and students understand the impact of the discrimination that was fueled during the Middle Passage. There is no way to talk about the Middle Passage, or about slavery in America, without an honest and open discussion of race. Race mattered a great deal to slave merchants, slave owners, and their captives; unlike early European slaves and indentured servants (who were white), the dark-skinned slaves from Africa could not easily run away and blend into the general population. In the classroom, students' vocalization of ugly words such as "racism," and words used historically to refer to Black Americans can evoke passion and discomfort; teachers must be willing to set parameters for discussions on race, and ensure that students express their views in terms that are respectful of differences in race, ethnicity, and attitudes. Critical thinking can emerge as learners, including teachers, are called upon to examine their understandings about race and their assumptions about themselves and those they have defined as "others."

The Middle Passage: Opening Students' Eyes, Ears, and Minds

A powerful way to unlock the voices of the Middle Passage is to begin the unit with Tom Feelings' pictorial history, *The Middle Passage: White Ships/Black Cargo*. Teachers might provide pairs of students with selected pictures from the book and ask them to talk about what they see. Students could write responses in individual journals, following their discussion with a classmate, then work with their partners to write a collaborative narrative based on the picture. These narratives can be revised as students acquire knowledge of Africa's geography and culture, and the historical aspects of the Middle Passage. If students begin the unit with no background knowledge of the Middle Passage, the assignment that asks them to write a narrative can be delayed until students build a foundation for understanding the time and events of the Middle Passage. Students could also study a map of the primary trade routes from Europe, to Africa, and to the Americas and the Caribbean as a means of enriching their understanding of the global implications of the Middle Passage. While students write and study maps, whether early or later during the unit of study, teachers might softly play music of African Americans; jazz by performers such as John Coltrane, Miles Davis, and Quincy Jones, spirituals from a variety of artists, or the gospel and folk music of Paul Robeson are good choices. Both the music and the artists might become the subjects for research in other units of study.

Poems from the collection, *Dreamer: Poems by Primus St. John* (1990) are likely to provide adolescents with a sense of the harshness experienced by slaves who were forced to journey to the Americas. Oral dramatic readings of selected poems may be an effective means of directing students' thoughts to the distant time and place, the unfamiliar torment of human beings. "We Come to Know Each Other" narrates the story of two men from different African cultures who meet and become brothers aboard a slave ship. "That Day" tells the story of a woman, captured, beaten and enslaved on a slave ship. "I Was to Become a Bajan" is spoken by a man who is captured and shipped to Barbados. "Dreamer" speaks to the passions of love and the loss of one's family and one's dreams. These poems allow modern students to hear the long-silenced voices of those who endured the Middle Passage.

Kinesthetic activities might be added to the study of the Middle Passage in order to help students vicariously experience a fragment of the frustration of restricted movement. For example, in order to give students a sense of the confinement the slaves endured on the ships, the teacher might crowd ten or so desks into a clump in a corner of the room, then draw on the floor a box around the perimeter of the clump. Ten students could be assigned those seats; once they are seated, the teacher can tell them that they are responsible for cleaning the floor and seats in the area, without moving out of the box, and that they will be given a short period of time, perhaps four minutes, to finish the job. The teacher would then distribute ten brooms and mops, and several pails of water, cleaning cloths, and other cleaning supplies. While the ten students strive to clean the floor, the other students could take notes about the scene. Once the cleaning is complete, all students could discuss what effects the constraints of space and time had on the workers' attitudes and their ability to complete the task. As an individual follow-up, students could be asked to write journal entries about the episode and the feelings it brought out among the workers, or entries about other times that their personal space had been invaded, and the emotional effects of such an invasion.

A provocative story that might be read aloud is a selection from Keens-Douglas and Gukova's *Freedom Child of the Sea*. Told as a folk tale, "Freedom's Child" is the story of a boy who was born in the sea immediately after his mother was thrown overboard during her Middle Passage. His face is beautiful, but his body wears the scars of all of the people who have suffered during their Middle Passage. Freedom's Child rescues troubled swimmers, and he and his mother continue to live in the sea until there is harmony among all people. Two other short stories may be useful and interesting additions to the unit of study. Both from Hamilton's *Many Thousands Gone: African-Americans from Slavery to Freedom* (1993), "Somersett" and "A Kidnapped Child" are especially appropriate choices. The first is the true account of a slave, Somersett, whose master believed he had drapetomania—the running away disease. His master placed Somersett on a ship in England to be sold in Jamaica, but with the help of the courts and English law he was set free. The latter tells the story of Olaudah Equiano, who was kidnapped in Nigeria in 1745, at the age of eleven. Sold and re-sold many times, Equiano eventually purchases his freedom and works in England to bring slavery to an end. These selections, which are easy for most adolescents to read and are potentially of high interest, are good choices for helping reluctant readers become engaged in the study of the Middle Passage.

Although few movies deal exclusively with the Middle Passage, an excerpt from *Roots I*, depicting Kunta Kinte's family from before his capture through the end of the sea journey, provides an excellent visual and oral complement to the literature-based study of the Middle Passage. We recommend that the teacher show the clip in its entirety one time and then show it again, pausing frequently in order to allow students to discuss what they are seeing. As a follow-up activity, students might assume the personae of passengers on a slave ship and write a letter, poem, or descriptive essay about their experiences. These pieces of writing, and others composed during the study of the Middle Passage, could be gathered into a class publication.

Once students have gained a basic understanding of the Middle Passage, they should be ready to read longer, more substantial works such as Fox's young adult novel *Slave Dancer* (1973) and Johnson's *Middle Passage* (1991). *Slave Dancer* is an excellent choice for reluctant readers, but can be read quickly by others as well. It is narrated by a thirteen-year-old boy who was kidnapped by unscrupulous slavers so that he can play music for slaves to dance to aboard the ship. With Jesse, readers travel from New Orleans to West Africa and see, hear, smell, and almost taste the horrors of the slaves' lives. Jesse comments on the inhumane treatment suffered by the slaves, and he shares their lament. *Middle Passage* is a novel that presents the extraordinary journey of Rutherford Calhoun, a freed slave who escapes from the consequences of womanizing and unpaid debt by unknowingly stowing away on a slave ship. Students often offer expressions of pain and disgust while reading these two novels. Such responses indicate that their awareness has been raised, and provide raw material for teaching, learning, and growth of understanding.

A Final Word

In leading students to explore the Middle Passage, teachers must consistently seek ways to bring conflicts and contradictions to the foreground of discussion and writing. Students' differing perspectives on the issues that emerge during the study of this theme should not silence discussion: instead, their differences should be critically examined in a safe classroom environment. The teachers and students will be able to work together to help each other transcend the boundaries of class, race, ethnicity, gender, and misinformation. Literature-based study of the Middle Passage can be an equalizer because it gives volume to the voices that have been silenced during the history of the United States. This is not a unit to be taught during February, as a bow to "Black History Month"; to do so would trivialize its importance. Instead, it is a unit to be taught whenever students of any race and ethnicity begin to separate themselves from "others" due to lack of information and understanding of those who are different historically and culturally from themselves. This unit might be taught as part of a series of short units on oppressed peoples; such a series would include attention not only to the Middle Passage, but also to the history of Native Americans after Columbus and of the horrors of the Jewish Holocaust. Themes such as oppression, survival, courage, and faith speak to both the universality and the particularity of human experience. Study of these themes also allows students to develop a vocabulary for contemplating and examining human behaviors, while encouraging them to critically interrogate the discourse of oppression. The history of oppressed people is a song of sorrow, but it is a song that must be sung, one that must be heard.

Works Cited

Bennet, L. Jr. (1962). *Before the Mayflower: A history of the Negro in America* 1619–1964. Baltimore: Penguin.

Equiano, O. (1985). The interesting life of Olaudah Equiano or Gustavus the African. In P. Edwards (Ed.). *The interesting life of Olaudah Equiano or Gustavus Vassa the African.* New York: Readex Microprint, 25–32.

Feelings, T. (1995). *The middle passage: White ships/black cargo.* New York: Dial.

Fox, P. (1973). *Slave dancer.* New York: Dell.

Franklin, J. H. & Moss, A. A., Jr. (1994). *From slavery to freedom: A history of African Americans,* (7th ed.). New York: McGraw Hill.

Hamilton, V. (1993). *Many thousands gone: African-Americans from slavery to freedom.* New York: Alfred Knopf.

Johnson, C. (1991). *Middle passage.* New York: Penguin.

Keens-Douglas, R. & Gukova, J. (1995). *Freedom child of the sea.* Toronto: Annick Press.

St. John, P. (1990). *Dreamer: Poems by Primus St. John.* Pittsburgh: Carnegie Mellon University Press.

Web Sites: Slavery, Civil Rights, and African-Americans

http://h-net2.msu.edu/~slavery/
http://squash.la.psu.edu/~plarson/smuseum/homepage.html
http://www.kaiwan.com/~mcivr/pioneer.html
http://www.mecca.org/~crights/nc2.html
http://www.seattletimes.com/mlk/index.html

Supplemental Resources

Short Stories/ Folk Tales

Abrahams, R. (Ed.). (1985). *Afro-American folktales: Stories from black traditions in the new world*. New York: Pantheon.
In this collection, these stories are particularly recommended:
"A flying fool." This is a brief and humorous tale that explores the pathology of racism and at the same time questions the traditional white conceptualization of Christianity. A black man dies, and because he has lived a good life he goes to heaven. When he learns that blacks are not admitted, he slips in, steals some wings, and has a flying good time before the heavenly police throw him out of the pearly gates.
"Horses stay outside." In this tale, a black man is told he can not enter heaven because he is walking. As he leaves, he meets a white man on his way to heaven and suggests that the white man ride him like a horse, so that they can both enter heaven. When they arrive at the gates, St. Peter tells the white man to hitch his horse outside.

Hamilton, V. (1995). *In her stories: African American folktales, fairy tales, and true tales*. New York: Blue Sky Press.
Recommended stories from this collection include these:
"Lettice Boyer: From way back" Lettice is 110 years old when she tells her story. She recounts her life as a slave and after "The Surrender." Her tales provide insight into her folk beliefs and superstitions.
"Lena and one big tiger". Hamilton reports that this unusual tale where animal change their shape, was told in the 1890s by a Sea Island, Georgia, woman. In this tale, Lena boasts that she will never marry a man marked or scarred and is tricked by a tiger. The

story reflects early African societies where women held the dominant position in their families and societies provided the family names for children and property owners. The situation changed in a way that was catastrophic for African women with the onslaught of slavery.

Other Print Resources

Douglass, F. (1968). *Narrative of the life of Frederick Douglass, an American slave, written by himself.* New York: Signet.
    Douglass' narrative of his life as an American slave, and of his escape, is widely acknowledged as one of the best descriptions of slavery and freedom, not only because it was written entirely by Douglass, but also because of Douglass' eloquent and powerful use of language. His narrative depicts how and why he learned to read, points to contradictions inherent in a democratic and Christian society built upon slavery, and examines the effects of slavery on the oppressed and the oppressor.

Douglass, F. (1962). My bondage and my freedom. In *Life and times of Frederick Douglass: his early life as a slave, his escape from bondage, and his complete history.* New York: Collier Books
    This short autobiographical piece, written by Douglass in 1855, is an updated version of the original written in 1845. Douglass explains how he learned to write, the corruption of the spirit among white slave holders, and the incompatibility of education and slavery.

Web Sites

Slavery Issues
    http://grad.let.rug.nl/~welling/usa/ch5-p6.html
    This site is dedicated slavery issues; two interesting features are a section devoted to President Lincoln's debate about slavery with Douglas, and a link to the Coalition Against Slavery in Mauritania and Sudan (CASMAS), which provides background information and articles that focus on the modern-day (current) slavery in North Africa.

Although not directly related to the Middle Passage as a particular time and set of events, the following sites can help students and teachers extend the focus to the concerns of those who still suffer from oppression.

http://www.kaiwan.com/~mcivr/pioneer.html
> Brief summaries of "African-American Pioneer" heroes including Maya Angelou, Martin Luther King, Jr., and Rosa Parks are presented.

http://www.seattletimes.com/mlk/index.html
> This site is devoted to Martin Luther King, Jr., with links to information on "The Man," "The Movement," "The Legacy," an electronic classroom, and more.

http://www.mecca.org/~crights/nc2.html
> This site provides information on several aspects of Civil Rights, including links to a virtual tour of the Civil Rights Museum and descriptions of historic events.

CHAPTER EIGHT

AGING: OUR UNDERSTANDINGS AND ATTITUDES

Larry S. Gordon

He Knew Hemingway
Belkis L. Cabrera

He knew Hemingway but spoke about his wife
And the portrait he never made
And how her brown hair caught the red in the sun
And the ballet dancers twirled in his now dim mind
As he sat a conductor who could no longer direct
And the Marias with their wrinkles and dried hair
And her
With her lollipop sucking the laughs
From the children downstairs
So far, now gone
The candied wrinkles
And the lives they trace
In stenciled sketches
Of strangers in buses
Of women and men
And sons who forgot
That they play the piano
And canasta
And dominoes
And bingo

And pay a quarter-meal for life
Impatience
Moving in stitches and stripes
And wheelchairs and walkers
In cycles and memories.

My Students Are So Young. Why Should I Teach a Unit on Aging? Goals and Rationale

As secondary teachers, we seem to cover virtually every stage of human existence in our language arts curriculum, from childhood to dying, but we often ignore the stage after adulthood and before death—old age. Perhaps we are somewhat myopic in stressing "coming of age" themes while neglecting the fastest growing segment of our population, the "over-sixty crowd."

Aging should be a particularly relevant issue for all students who, through advances in modern medicine, will be called upon to relate to unprecedented numbers of elderly. As medicine prolongs life, our students will find themselves in situations in which they will need to interact with, and perhaps care for, aging relatives. Thus, they should be sensitive to the concerns, attitudes, achievements, and goals of older members of the population. Advocates of "multicultural" teaching point out that the elderly should be included when we draw attention to populations that are underrepresented in literature, art, and the social consciousness. This thematic unit attempts to introduce secondary students to issues of aging.

Creating Empathy

Many of our high school students have grandparents who, by today's standards, are not yet elderly. Others live far from their parents' parents, and are essentially unacquainted with them; some do not know their fathers or their mothers, and thus have no relationships with the parents of their parents. Students also have friends or classmates who are being raised by their grandparents, in the absence of a parent. Whether contact with the elderly is limited or is a confusing part of our students' everyday lives, then, many feel an instinctive desire to distance themselves from people who are too different, in terms of age, experience, and perspective. Some of our students have admitted that they suffer the malady "gerontophobia," fear of the elderly. Nevertheless, they have assured us that despite, and perhaps because of, their misconceptions about the aging and the elderly, they benefit from studying the older portion of our population. We believe that like our students, yours may also benefit from this focus.

In order for students to become interested and involved in this unit, they first must be introduced to the aging population. During this initial process, students should explore their own "feelings" about the elderly and the aging process. An important initial instructional goal, therefore, is to create empathy and to facilitate emotional connections between students and the elderly. We have found that this is often best accomplished through presenting "accessible" multimedia materials to students —songs, movies on videotape, and television shows, for example —to which they can easily relate, and about which they are willing to engage in meaningful activities and discussion. The nonprint media enhance study of the literature that we build into this unit. We recommend that you pick songs, television shows, and movies with your own students in mind — works that you choose specifically for their potential to elicit responses that will help teens crystallize and articulate their perspectives on aging and the elderly. It is our intention to provide suggestions that will guide you toward choices that are appropriate for your students, not prescriptions that must be administered without modifications in dosage, timing, or combination with other ideas.

Introducing the Theme of Aging with Songs, Literature, Movies, and Television

Before beginning the literary study of the aging, we recommend a practice that we have found successful: play for students a cassette recording of Jimmy Buffet's "The Captain and the Kid" (1976), from the *Havana Daydream* album (MCA Recording Agency). This song celebrates a captain who is too old to sail anymore, but who relives his passion for the sea through memories he tells in stories to his grandson. The theme of aging is close to the surface of this pleasant song, at least from our perspectives as adult listeners who are hoping to find aging themes in the song. Next ask students to discuss all of the themes that emerge—for them as teen listeners—as they listen to the song. Finally, explain your reason for playing this song (or another that you select for this activity) as the introduction to a new literature-based thematic unit.

A slightly more structured approach for integrating a song into the classroom is described below. We have used this activity successfully with different songs in several units and have watched the sequence help students become engaged in actually studying songs as works of art:

1. Play the song and ask students to listen to it. When the song is finished, ask them to write for three minutes about their response to the

song. If students are new to this kind of activity, you might give them questions that will prompt responses, such as these:

- How does the song—its words or tune or both—make you feel?
- Which memories come into your mind as you hear this song? (If you do not think of any memory as you listen, think about what memories come to you as you listen to any music, and jot down those memories, instead.)
- Do you like the song or not?
- Do you recognize the artist, the style, the time when this song was most popular?

Allow five minutes for discussion of their written responses, and three more minutes to allow students to make additions or revisions to their initial responses.

2. Play the song a second time and ask students to note, in writing, any feature of the music itself that captures their attention, such as a relaxing or driving rhythm, an instrumental portion, and so on. Conduct a brief discussion of their responses to the musical qualities of the song.

3. Distribute a copy of the song's lyrics to the students and allow them to read them silently, then play the song a third time. This time, the teacher should ask students to highlight words or phrases that stand out as they hear the song. Allow them to discuss briefly the words and phrases they have highlighted.

4. Discuss their initial responses to the song, and to its musical and literary qualities. After allowing students to revise and crystallize their initial responses, discuss how the musical features and the literary features work together to achieve a particular effect for each of the listeners.

Discussion of this set of questions is designed to lead students to the realization that each listener "hears" the song in his or her own way. The parallels with the reader-response approach to literature instruction are strong; we like to ask students to articulate, during a class brainstorming session, the ways that different people who listen to the same song are like different readers who respond to the same piece of literature. Similarities that students are likely to comment on include these: (1) although everyone in the class hears the same music and words, the interpretations of the music and words that each student constructs is his or her own; (2) each student who pays attention to the musical and textual cues, without ignoring any cues and without allowing any particular cue to receive too much emphasis, can construct a "correct" interpretation of the song. While this activity reinforces the theoretical basis for a response-centered teaching and learning approach, it also has a theme-related benefit: through engaging in it, students will begin to think about the world of those who are no longer young.

If you wish to establish literature at the core of the thematic unit of study from its inception, you might choose to have students select one or more of the short stories or poems discussed below, instead of a song, to read and respond to as an introduction to the unit. These stories explore relationships between young people and their elderly relatives.

- Nikki Giovanni's book-length collection *Grand Mothers: Poems, Reminiscences, and Short Stories about the Keepers of our Traditions* (1994) is a paperback gem. If you are limited in time and/or resources to only one supplemental resource during the unit on aging, this book is our strongest recommendation. The variety of works within this 168-page paperback will offer something to all students; it may help readers understand the special impact that grandmothers, regardless of their culture and age itself, can have on the younger lives they touch.
- Toni Cade Bambara's, "Maggie of the Green Bottles" (1968) is a short story about Granny Maggie, as told through the eyes of her great-granddaughter, Peaches. Maggie was considered eccentric and a burden to the adults of the extended family who lived in Peaches' childhood home. To Peaches, however, Maggie is mesmerizing, and the two share a special, confidential relationship. That relationship and Peaches' loss of her sense of wonderment upon Maggie's death are fertile themes for student exploration.
- Paule Marshall's, "To Da-duh, In Memoriam," (1967) is a beautiful story about the speaker/author's trip to see her Barbadian grandmother, and the lessons she learned from that experience. Marshall tells us that her grandmother "died and I lived, but always, to this day even, within the shadow of her death," a profound comment on the effect of her experiences with her elderly relative.
- Grace Paley's, "A Conversation with My Father," (1974) discusses differences in tastes between the young and the old.

- Norma Fox Mazer's *Waltzing on Water* (1989) and editor Paul Janeczko's *Strings: A Gathering of Family Poems* (1984) are filled with poems that beg to be read aloud by students' voices.

Students will be able to further explore, through these works of literature, and particularly through guided consideration of their responses to the texts, how they feel about aging and the elderly, and how others deal with aging relatives, as well as fears that surround aging and even some of the special joys that accompany growing old enough to answer to no one but oneself.

If you are interested in integrating literature with movies, we have some suggestions for this unit. *On Golden Pond* (1981) and *Driving Miss Daisy* (1989), are both award-winning, timeless movies, now available in video cassette; each depicts difficult relationships between children and their aging parents, as well as the love and respect that is often shared between elderly pairs, whether they are married or are long-time friends. A different approach may be the cult classic *Harold and Maude* (1971), which is the story of the unlikely coupling of a young man who is bored with wealth and stagnation, and an old rascal, played by Ruth Gordon, who sees nothing but goodness and fun in the world. Another feature movie that is now available on video, one that we have used successfully as a part of a focus on aging, is *Cocoon* (1985). We have been impressed with students' insights that this story not only portrays the elderly as positive human beings, but also reflects human transitions over time (from the wonderment of childhood to the acceptance of old age) and how those transitions continue as we grow old. *Cocoon* shows time as the fire that changes, advances, and evolves us as we age, and it allows us to laugh with our students about the changes that most of us recognize from experience, and those that we can expect, as well.

You might also choose to have students consider videotaped episodes from television shows. One choice is reruns of the situation comedy that reached the zenith of its popularity in the late 1980s, *The Golden Girls*, in which three fully mature working women, and the outspoken, demanding mother of one of the women enjoy living independently in Miami, dealing with typical problems related to their jobs, social lives, and relationships with families. Stereotypes of older women can be explored using this medium.

You might also choose to ask them to respond to carefully-selected episodes of a currently popular situation comedy that features an aging character, such as *Frazier*. One semester during which we taught a unit on aging, our students decided to record episodes of *Frazier* and to develop group projects around the comedy. They formed two parties and launched opposing campaigns that functioned throughout the aging unit. During the campaigns, some students made short speeches and television videotape advertisements that spoke to the rights of Frazier, the liberal radio psychologist, to live his own life, without being pressured by the constant presence of his aggravating father. Meanwhile, other students chose to campaign for the rights of the retired, conservative father, a man who has swallowed his pride and moved into his son's posh but suffocating, staid Seattle apartment. The students studied the rhetorical patterns of several political speeches to craft authentic campaign speeches for their party. The campaign leaders from both parties decided at the beginning of the project that class consensus, with an overwhelming majority vote for Frazier or his father, was the goal for the class. The winners would be the party that had used more persuasive arguments and had won over those who began on the project as supporters of the other party. Such consensus was never reached, but the students realized that a greater benefit was that the project involved them in discussions and presentations that revolved around the benefits and constraints that surround the circumstances of a grown man sharing an apartment with his father. Even more important, they realized the importance of general issues about aging, which subtly were raised and explored. If you do not have the time or inclination to watch much television yourself, ask your students for help. They can name shows that feature at least one person who is a grandparent, or an elderly person. Record a few episodes of each show they mention, then set aside a few planning periods or evenings for special viewing sessions, during which you consider whether or not the episodes will be appropriate for your classes. You might also write a brief justification for bringing popular television programs into your classroom; although we have not experienced any trouble with this aspect of our teaching practices, we know teachers who have been questioned by their department chairs, principals, and the parents of students when they move beyond the predictable texts of the classroom and introduced popular media for academic study.

Examining Attitudes about Aging and the Elderly

While students are becoming acquainted with fictitious characters through canonical and/or young adult and other popular literature, and through songs like Jimmy Buffet's, they can further their understanding of issues related to aging by interviewing their older relatives—or friends of the family, and asking them questions regarding how these relatives feel about old age. A word of advice: encourage students to select older people with whom they have had conversations before, in order to reduce anxiety and the fear that they will not be able to connect, verbally, with the people they have chosen. Ask them to explore the interview subject's personal history. It may be necessary to guide students through their interviews by assisting them in formulating pointed questions that will provide real insight into aging issues. A suggested questionnaire may be generated by the entire class. Sample questions that students might ask aging interviewees to elaborate on include these:

- What kind of relationship did you have with your parent(s)?
- What is your favorite childhood memory?
- What about your childhood or teenage years makes you most proud?
- What concerned or worried you most when you were young?
- If you could change anything about your life, what would it be?
- What do you most look forward to in getting older?
- What worries you the most about growing/being old?
- What are some things that you would still like to do or see?
- If you could trade your age and experience for youth and inexperience, would you choose to be a teenager in today's world?

In addition to gaining insight into aging, students may receive the "fringe benefit" of better relationships with their particular interviewee. Ideally, students will likewise ask themselves some of these thought-provoking questions. To guarantee this kind of thinking, you might require that they write interview notes in a double-entry journal format, recording interview questions in one column on a page, and their own responses, whether to the question itself or to the interviewee's answer, in a parallel column on the same page.

After students complete their interviews and notes, their results should be written up in prose form. This could take the form of a mini-biography, a newspaper feature story, a memoir, a vignette, poem, or perhaps an essay about their personal reactions to the answers elicited in their interviews. See Cabrera's poem, "He Knew Hemingway," which begins this chapter, page 169, as an example of one teacher's reflection on a conversation with an elderly friend.

Students can also learn about attitudes toward the elderly and aging through sites on the World Wide Web. One promising site is that of the "Interactive Aging Network," which posts answers to seniors' questions about health, legal and financial issues, and entertainment resources. Students might peruse this site in order to learn what is of concern to the aging members of the population, from the perspective of those who are aging. Students might be surprised to find that in addition to information about predictable topics such as flu shots and retirement benefits, this site for the elderly provides information about other internet resources including *Golfweb* and the electronic version, or "zine" of the magazine *Wired*, named *Hotwired*, a magazine for computer enthusiasts of all ages. Senior citizens, high school students, and teachers whose goal is to better understand the world of the elderly, are invited to transmit messages, electronically, to the Interactive Aging Network at this Web address (the site was still partially under construction upon the publication of this text):

http://www.ianet.org.

Another resource that might help students learn more about the concerns of the elderly is the organization called "Little Brothers: Friends of the Elderly." The Hancock, Michigan, chapter has a completed Web site that provides visitors with a glimpse into the concerns of the organization, including its current activities, motto, volunteers' service statistics, and so on. The implication is that these elderly people are far from idle or addled. The site is located at the following address:

http://198.110.128.229/houghton/home.html.

Exploring the Aging Process: Activities Using Literature, Graphs, and Community Involvement

Often, students have not thought about human development, beyond their present status. Poetry, music, and even psychological studies may help these students better understand the aging process. Maya

Angelou's poems, "On Aging" (1986) and "The Last Decision" (1986) as well as Dudley Randall's "George" (1966) depict both the ravages of aging, and the strength and pride of Angelou's elderly woman, who tells us " . . . tired don't mean lazy/ and every good-bye ain't gone."

Students may learn more about aging, and may better understand their own attitudes toward the elderly, by reading aloud, writing initial responses, then discussing Shel Silverstein's poignant "The little boy and the old man" (1981). This poem speaks to the similarities of an elderly man and a little boy, and concludes with the old man holding the boy's hand, sadly telling him that they both understand what it feels like to be ignored by adults. After reading and hearing the poem read by several different voices, recording then discussing their responses to it, individual students or the class as a whole might generate an illustrated human lifeline, identifying key life events which denote a person's development. This could be combined with an explication of Jaques' "All the world's a stage" soliloquy from Shakespeare's *As You Like It* (Act II, scene 7, lines 139–166), which identifies seven stages of human development. The last full sentence of the soliloquy presents an ugly yet popular portrait of old age, and may provoke discussion among teenage students: "Last scene of all,/ That ends this eventful history,/ Is childishness and mere oblivion; Sans teeth, sans eyes, sans taste, sans everything."

While groups work on the illustrated human lifeline, you might offer some members of the class the opportunity to go beyond the literary treatment of the effects of aging by gathering information on psychological explanations of the phases of human development. Two theorists whose ideas are often included in general psychology textbooks are Erik Erikson, who espouses a theory of personality maturation within a social context, and Lawrence Kohlberg, who delineates and explains stages of moral development. You might find that students will best be able to conduct this kind of research if you coordinate with a science, health, or social studies teacher in a cross-disciplinary project.

Contemporary young adult novels are another wonderful source of fictional introduction to the problems of aging, and many are particularly effective in presenting the relationship between adolescents and their grandparents or elderly in general. Angela Johnson's, *Toning the Sweep* (1993) is a powerful and beautifully artistic short novel in which the relationships of three generations of women are explored and developed when the grandmother admits that she is dying. Short enough to read in four or five class periods, this culturally rich novel also introduces readers to attitudes and rituals associated with aging, death, and dying by some African-American communities such as, "toning the sweep."

Another novel that is accessible to secondary readers is Robert Cormier's, *Tunes for Bears to Dance To* (1992). This book explores the relationship between a young boy, who recently lost his older brother, and a Holocaust survivor. In addition to the good versus evil theme, the novel depicts the benefits of befriending an elderly individual.

Memory (1988) by Margaret Mahy, is a young adult novel, that is set in New Zealand. It tells the story of Jonny, a nineteen-year-old who is haunted by his sister's accidental death. In his search for his sister's best friend, Jonny meets Sophie, who suffers from Alzheimer's disease. Jonny follows Sophie to her squalid house and, feeling like an outcast himself, takes refuge with her. Through their relationship, Jonny comes to terms with his abusive past and learns to care about, and to take responsibility for, someone other than himself.

Several of the young adult novels by Sue Ellen Bridgers, including *All Together Now* (1979), *Notes for Another Life* (1981), and *Permanent Connections* (1987) portray adolescents who have weak or troubled parents, and who must live, at least temporarily, with their grandparents. Bridgers beautifully presents the special connection that those who, because they are too young or are too old, feel alienated from the middle generation of adults.

Valuable reading experiences can be made even more pertinent if combined with a class visit to a nursing or retirement facility where the students can visit the residents. Prior to visiting either of the facilities, students could read "Sila," (please see the poem below), followed by "The Moustache," by Robert Cormier (1989).

Sila
Belkis L. Cabrera

Her cream hair lies dormant in the windless house
And the curtains are drawn
Except for the kitchen shades
With maize and pepper print
The air conditioner kicks and the cat stirs
And then with a newly-drawn self-assurance
He eases down and settles at her feet.

Along the corners the worn wooden floor
With wind and rain
Bends
Like her back
I watched her grow by me
And my daughter grow by her
Watering dry roots with old photographs
As she presses her long fingers
Over the little one's forehead
Steadying the album over her lap
Combing her bangs
With a slight tremble in the wrist
I knew them when they were weaving hands
And smelled like mangoes in summer.
She's grown tired and her limbs
Once swollen with life
Hang from armrests
With scars seeped into wrinkles
And although she won't admit it
She's afraid of being moved
Into a home
Because she says that's why Elsa died
And the doctors couldn't treat her
'Cause only love can
And she goes on
Wrestling with the air
Trying to convince me
To convince herself
Besides she can't take the cat
She murmurs
Motioning to her sandals.

This poem is powerful; student readers are likely to respond to the image of a woman who must sacrifice her own home for an institutional one; the idea that nursing home residents had other lives, other homes, may be a new thought for many students.

"The Moustache" is a short story about a teenage boy who visits his grandmother at a nursing home. The young man feels guilty about not having visited his grandmother for a long time and discovers that she is a real person, wrestling with some guilt feelings of her own. Classroom activities surrounding the facility visit could center on students' writing personality portraits of elderly people they met during their visit. Their "portraits" describe the elderly person's physical appearance, what he or she did during the course of the visit and how he or she spends most of his or her time, concerns about which he or she spoke, and the elderly person's impact on the student. Of course, students could also be asked to respond to their "field" experiences either orally or in a journal. In *Seeking Diversity* (1992), former middle school teacher Linda Rief describes a language-arts class project in which her students visited and befriended residents of a local convalescent home. Her account offers convincing evidence of the opportunities for developing language skills when students are involved in a project to which they are devoted not only as students, but as people. Although the students in Rief's classes were middle school students, the ideas about this project, as well as many others in the fine book, can easily be modified for high school classes.

Using the Canon and Other Resources

A thematic unit on aging, with a focus on students' attitudes regarding the elderly, presents many opportunities to combine "traditional" literature in new and creative ways. Once students are focused on the unique challenges of aging, they may approach certain works from new perspectives. Additionally, classic literary works that are often ignored in high school may be introduced in this unit. For example, Shakespeare's *King Lear* provides fertile material for exploration of the problems of aging, the physical and mental obstacles faced by the elderly, and children's responses to their changing parents. The play presents the elderly in varying roles. The king, of course, is failing both physically and mentally, but is too proud to give up the title of king. The Earl of Kent, the king's aging friend, remains strong, intelligent and loyal. The children of the aging main characters reflect morals ranging from selfless to rapacious. Cordelia and Edgar remain loyal to their aging and extremely demanding and capricious fathers, while Goneril, Regan and Edmund take advantage of their parents' frail condition. These offspring, usually seen as evil ones, are abusive and depict the all too common situation of children who are anxious to inherit their parents' wealth. This brilliant play, which is often overlooked in the high school curriculum because of its complexities, presents a perfect experience for the exploration of aging.

After reading the play then performing segments of *King Lear*, the class might enjoy and benefit from viewing the film, *I Never Sang for My Father* (1970), starring Gene Hackman and Melvyn Douglas. This movie is about a son's remorse over his failure to reconcile with his aging, cantankerous father. Although the prospects are limitless, the following are a few additional examples of "traditional Western" literature that may be effective in a unit on aging:

- *Mr. Sammler's Planet* (1970) by Saul Bellow
- *The Old Man and the Sea* (1952) by Ernest Hemingway
- *Travels with My Aunt* (1969) by Graham Greene
- *Goodbye, Mr. Chips* (1962) by James Hilton
- *The Good Earth* (1977) by Pearl S. Buck
- *The Picture of Dorian Gray* (1918) by Oscar Wilde
- *The Lion in Winter* (1966) by James Goldman
- *Death of a Salesman* (1949) by Arthur Miller

Facing the Inevitable: Literature and Activities that Deal with Death

It would be disingenuous to ignore the issue of death in a unit on aging. Of course, the materials on this sensitive subject should reflect various approaches to this topic. For example, Dylan Thomas' "Do Not Go Gentle into That Good Night" (1996), first published in 1945, is an apostrophe directed toward the poet-speaker's dying father; the speaker urges him to resist death, to "rage against the dying of the light." The actual circumstance surrounding Thomas' writing of the poem may or may not be important for students to consider as they work to make sense of the poem for themselves as readers. We have found it interesting to work with students to explore the speaker's apparent attitudes toward death, before sharing with them any factual information about the poet or the poem. In contrast with Thomas' unrestrained tone is the calm and methodical preparation for death that is evident in the surprising, "A Summer Tragedy" (1992) by Arna Bontemps. In this short story, an elderly black couple prepare for their joint suicide in scenes that lead many readers to suspect that, though infirm, they are preparing to go on a Sunday outing to visit friends or family. It is a moving yet ultimately troubling story of an elderly couple's death with dignity.

We have been surprised by our high school students' frequent refusal to accept the premise of this story; they often feel compelled to rewrite the ending into a happier one. After we ask those who are uncomfortable with the double suicide to write a new ending, we then discuss what it is that makes them uncomfortable, both as readers and as human beings, with Bontemps' story. Fine discussions emerge when we give students the opportunity to express their feelings about this topic, using the story as a catalyst and a fictitious—therefore, safe—point of reference.

Multicultural approaches to death could also include Isaac Bashevis Singer's "Elka and Meir" (1988), the story of two workers at a burial society, who encounter the Angel of Death once too often. In the Native American tradition, Gabriel Horn's "The Spirit Journey and the Pipe" (1993) explores death as the pouring back of the human spirit into "the Mystery . . . like a drop of rain that falls back into the ocean where it originated." This story could act as a stepping-stone to group presentations/reports on different cultural mourning practices.

A powerful conclusion to this thematic unit could be a persuasive paper regarding the issue of who ultimately bears the responsibility for the care of the elderly—society or families. Students might conduct research on topics such as the following:

- 1997 Supreme Court findings related to doctor-assisted suicide;
- questions about the ethics of euthanasia;
- the practices for caring for the elderly in various cultures.

Each of these topics is appropriate for interdisciplinary study, and may complement your cross-curricular planning for teaching earlier portions of the aging unit, such as the activities that focus on the physical and psychological changes that occur as one ages. For help gathering data during this portion of the unit, you might arrange for students to visit the Web site of the Senate Committee on Aging and review summaries of the committee's publications and other materials, at this address:

http://www.senate.gov/~aging/

Research findings might be presented to the class in oral reports or written papers; some might choose to respond to information on any of the topics, the ethics of euthanasia, for example, in the form of a short story or poem rather in the the form of a traditional research paper.

Following the research presentations, the class could prepare a dramatic reading, perhaps a choral one, of John Keat's powerful poem "To

Autumn". Many readers interpret this ode as a statement that life's end can be marked with ripeness, completeness, and renewal. Students might be asked to respond in a creative way, either in making a collage of pictures taken from magazines, or by drawing original sketches, or by writing poems or stories, to the same questions that they asked older relatives or friends during the interviews at the beginning of the unit. When the unit is beginning to draw to a close, creative reconsideration of questions like these, perhaps in the form of student-created dramatizations, poems, songs, or movies, is likely to lead students to provocative reflections on their own stances: "What do you look forward to about growing old?" "What do you most fear about aging/growing old?" Students who have seriously considered the topics of this thematic unit are likely to find, through self-evaluation and reflection, that they have experienced changes in their attitudes toward aging and the elderly.

Works Cited

Angelou, M. (1986). The last decision. In *Shaker, why don't you sing?* New York: Random House.

Angelou, M. (1986). On Aging. In *And still I rise*. New York: Random House.

Ashby, H., Director. (1971). *Harold and Maude* [feature film/video]. Higgins, C., Lewis, M., and Mulvehill, C. B., Producers. Hollywood.

Bambara, T. C. (1968). Maggie of the green bottles. In *Gorilla, my love*. New York: Random House.

Bellow, S. (1970). *Mr. Sammler's planet*. New York: Viking.

Beresford, B., Director. (1989). *Driving Miss Daisy* [feature film/video]. Brown, D., Zanuck, L. F., Zanuck, R. D. (Producers), Hollywood, CA: Warner Brothers/Majestic Films.

Bontemps, A. (1992). A summer tragedy. In M. G. Secundy & L.L. Nixon (Eds.), *Trials, tribulations and celebrations: African-American perspectives on health, illness, aging, and loss*. Yarmouth, ME: Interculture Press.

Bridgers, S. E. (1979). *All together now*. New York: Harper.

Bridgers, S. E. (1981). *Notes for another life*. New York: Harper.

Bridgers, S. E. (1987). *Permanent connections*. New York: Harper.

Buck, P. S. (1977). *The good earth*. New York: Harper & Row.

Buffet, J. (1976). The captain and the kid. On *Havana daydream* [album/CD] New York:MCA Recording Agency.

Cates, G., Director and Producer. (1970). *I never sang for my father* [feature film/video]. Hollywood, CA: Columbia Pictures.

Cormier, R. (1989). The moustache. In J. S. Simmons & M. Stern,(Eds.). *The short story and you*. New York: National Textbook Company.

Cormier, R. (1992). *Tunes for bears to dance to*. New York: Dell.

Giovanni, N. (1994). *Grand mothers: Poems, reminiscences, and short stories about the keepers of our traditions*. New York: Henry Holt.

Goldman, J. (1966). *The lion in winter*. New York: Random House.

Greene, G. (1969). *Travels with my aunt*. New York: Viking.

Harris, R. (Ed.). (1983). *Best short stories: Middle level*. Providence, RI: Jamestown.

Hemingway, E. (1952). *The old man and the sea*. New York: Scribner.

Hilton, J. (1962). *Goodbye, Mr. Chips*. Boston, MA: Little, Brown.

Horn, G. (1992). The spirit journey and the pipe. In *Native heart*. San Rafael, CA: New World Library.

Howard, R., Director. (1985). *Cocoon* [feature film/video]. Brown, D., Zanuck, L. F., Zanuck, R. D., Producers. Hollywood, 20th Century Fox.

Janeczko, P. (Ed.). (1984). *Strings: A gathering of family poems*. New York: Bradbury Press.

Johnson, A. (1993). *Toning the sweep*. New York: Scholastic.

Mahy, M. (1988). *Memory*. New York: M. K. McElderry Books.

Marshall, P. (1967). To Da-duh, in memoriam. In *Reena and other stories*. New York: Feminist Press at City University.

Mazer, N. F. (1989). *Waltzing on water: Poetry by women*. New York: Dell.

Miller, A. (1949). *Death of a salesman*. New York: Viking.

Paley, G. (1974). A conversation with my father. In *Enormous changes at the last minute*. New York: Farrar, Strauss & Giroux.

Randall, D. (1966). George. In *Poem, counterpoem*. Detroit: Broadside.

Rief, L. (1992). *Seeking diversity*. Portsmouth, NH: Heinemann Boynton/Cook.

Rydell, M., Director. (1981). *On golden pond* [feature film/video]Carr, T. & Gilbert, B. Producers. Hollywood, Universal Pictures.

Shakespeare, W. (1996). *As you like it*. Excerpts in *Literature and language arts: The British tradition*. St. Paul, Minnesota: EMC/Paradigm.

Shakespeare, W. (1977). *As you like it*. In *The Oxford School Shakespeare: As you like it*. Oxford, England: Oxford University Press.

Shakespeare, W. (1994). *King Lear*. In *The Oxford School Shakespeare: King Lear*. Oxford, England: Oxford University Press.

Singer, I.B. (1988). Elka and Meir. In *An Isaac Bashevis Singer reader*. New York: Farrar, Straus, & Giroux.

Thomas, D. (1996). Do not go gentle into that good night. In *Literature and language arts: The British tradition*. St. Paul, Minnesota: EMC/Paradigm.

Wilde, O. (1918). *The picture of Dorian Gray*. New York: Boni & Liveright.

Supplemental Resources

Poetry

Agard, John. (Ed.). 1989. *Life doesn't frighten me at all*. New York: Henry Holt & Co.
This anthology has numerous poems dealing with the theme of aging including, "Father"—a son speaking about how his father has aged (Rozuvicz); "Another Dad"—a grandson who thinks of his grandfather as another father (Markham); and "Direction"— a Native American poem about a boy who turns to his wise old grandfather for advice and direction (Lopez).

Blake, William. (1993). Songs of experience. In M. H. Abrams (Ed.). *The Norton anthology of English literature*. New York: W.W. Norton & Co.
The poems in this work illustrate the notion that with age comes wisdom.

Elsland, R. (1984). In *Grandparents' houses*. New York: Willow Morrow &Co.
This anthology is a collection of poems dealing with the elderly, specifically, grandparents.

Martz, Sheila. (Ed.). (1996). *Grow old along with me—The best is yet to be*. Watsonville, CA: Papier-Mache Press.
An anthology of poetry, prose, and photographs by writers of various racial and ethnic backgrounds reflecting differing perspectives on aging. The common thread running through the collection is "the need to be loved, the importance of family connections,[and] an acceptance of the aging process."

Martz, Sheila. (Ed.) (1987). *When I am an old woman I shall wear purple*. Watsonville, CA: Papier-Mache Press.

An anthology of poetry and prose explaining women and aging, focusing on the relationships between and among mothers, grandmothers, grandchildren, and older women friends.

Whitman, Walt. (1991). Thanks in old age. In J. Canarroe (Ed.), *Six American poets*. New York: Vintage Books.

The theme in this poem is a jubilant one, as the title might suggest, the poet speaks of accepting death by appreciating the "little things" in life. This work could be used as a contrast to King Lear, who is reluctant to face old age.

Yeats, William Butler. (1983). When you are old. In T*he poems of William Butler Yeats: A new edition*. London: Macmillan.

This poem depicts the sad aspects of aging. While the poet asks the elderly to dream about the times when they were young and many rejoiced in their beauty, he cautions that the young abandon their elders.

Popular Songs

Chapin, Harry. (1976). Cat's in the cradle. On *Greatest* stories live [album]. Elektra Record.

The song tells how a father neglects his son as he is growing up and when the father begins to age, the son neglects the father.

Rogers, Kenny. (1983). Twenty years ago. On *20 greatest hits* [album]. Liberty Records.

An old man remembers his war buddies and begins to realize the importance of spending time with friends.

Stevens, Cat. (1972). Father and son. On *Greatest* hits [album]. A & M records.

A father discusses the hardships of growing old and advises his son not to grow up too fast.

Short Stories

Buck, Pearl S. (1962). The old mother. In *Hearts come home*. New York: John Day Co.

This short story explores the traditional Asian extended family paradigm and the benefits and difficulties of elderly parents living with their children.

Freeman, Mary Wilkens. (1979). The village singer. In *Short fiction of Sarah Orne Jewett and Mary Wilkins Freeman*. New York: Penguin Books.

    Candace Whitcomb, the leading soprano in a local church choir, is removed from her position because her voice sounds "too old" and is replaced by a younger soprano. Rather than "going away quietly," Candace fights against a society that discriminates against her.

Hawthorne, Nathaniel. (1974). Dr. Heidegger's experiment. In *Twice told tales*. Columbus: Ohio State University Press.

    A classic story involving aging and the elderly, with a focus on the psychology of a frustrated aging scientist.

Hawthorne, Nathaniel. (1974). The village uncle. In *Twice told tales*. Columbus: Ohio State University Press.

    Another gothic classic story involving aging and the elderly.

O'Conner, Flannery. (1955). A late encounter with the enemy. In *A good man is hard to find*. New York: Harcourt Brace.

    The story of General Sash who is 104 years old and his granddaughter, who is about to graduate from college at the age of 62.

Secundy, M. G. & Nixon, L. L. (Eds.). (1992). *Trials, tribulations, and celebrations: African-American perspectives on health, illness, aging, and loss*. Yarmouth, ME: Intercultural Press.

    An anthology of short stories, narratives, and poems exploring aspects of the life cycle from an African-American perspective. Includes literature from such notable authors as Alice Walker, Langston Hughes and Maya Angelou.

Singer, Isaac Bashevis. (1966). The Spinoza of market street. In *Selected stories of Isaac Bashevis Singer*. New York: Farrar, Straus, & Giroux.

    Poignant tale of elderly Jews in Warsaw, Poland; read along with another story in this collection, "The Old Man."

Walker, Alice. (1967). To hell with dying. In L. Hughes (Ed.), *The best short stories by Negro writers*. Boston: Little, Brown & Co.

    Walker recalls the life of a lively elderly gentleman who refuses to succumb to death. This piece would work beautifully with Dylan Thomas' poem "Do Not Go Gentle into That Good Night."

Books (Fiction and Nonfiction)

Marquez, Gabriel Garcia. (1991). *One hundred years of solitude*. (Gregory Rabassa, Trans.). New York: Harper Collins.

This novel traces seven generations of the Buendia family whose matriarch, Ursula lives to be over one hundred. Despite her age and status of a forlorn widow, Ursula is filled with energy, very intuitive, and hides her blindness to escape compassion. She is firm in her beliefs but still depicts the "little ole sweet grandma" because of the love and guidance she provides to all of her offspring and descendants. Ursula both fits and breaks every popular stereotype of the aged.

Miklowitz, Gloria D. (1983). *Close to the edge*. New York: Delacorte Press.

In spite of having all the advantages money can provide, high school senior, Jenny, sees little point in life until she volunteers to play the piano for a senior citizens' band and receives the benefit of the wisdom of the elderly.

Thomas, K. (1986). *Changing of the guard*. New York: Harper & Row.

After the death of her beloved grandfather, sixteen-year-old Caroline resists change, spending her time with an elderly grandmother alone, until a flamboyant new girl at school draws her reluctantly into a friendship.

Welty, Eudora. (1969). *The optimist's daughter*. New York: Vintage.

The story of Laura McKelva Hand, a young woman who has left the South and returns, years later, to New Orleans, where her father is dying. After his death, Laura and a series of characters look back on their lives. Their stories show the many transitions a life can take over the years, how people change and adapt as they age. Through these stories, Laura finally comes to an understanding of herself, and her father.

Wexler, N. (1993). *Mama can't remember anymore*. Virginia Beach: The Donning Co.

A biography of the author's struggles with an aging mother. This novel presents a view into nursing homes and the struggles of their occupants and family members.

Television Series

Frazier
The Golden Girls

World Wide Web Sites

http://www.ianet.org/progdev/train.htm
    Interactive Aging Network
http://198.110.128.229/houghton/home.html
    Little Brothers: Friends of the Elderly
http://www.senate.gov/~aging/
    United States Senate Subcommittee on Aging

Author Index

Abrahams, R., 166
Achebe, Chinua, 84, 110
Agard, John, 187
Alarcon, Francisco, 64, 71, 73
Allende, Isabelle, 110
Alvarez, Julia, 102, 110, 148, 149
Anderson, E., 66, 73
Angelou, Maya, 45, 49, 50, 55, 168, 178–179, 185
Anonymous, 45, 50, 119, 131
Apolinaro, A., 141, 150
Arkin, S., 78
Ashabranner, Brent & Melissa, 140, 150
Ashbery, J., 119, 131
Augenbraum, H., 153
Austen, Ralph, 161

Bambara, Tony Cade, 46, 52, 174, 185
Banks, R., 69, 73
Barrio, R., 134
Bassuk, E.L., 134
Beals, Melba Patillo, 34, 44, 46
Bellow, S., 183, 185
Bennet, L., Jr., 165
Berck, J., 127, 131
Berry, J., 123, 131
Bing, L., 78
Blacker, Terrance, 102, 110, 133, 134
Blake, William, 187
Bode, Jane, 144, 145, 150
Bonham, F., 76
Bontemps, Arna, 183, 185
Bridgers, Sue Ellen, 102, 110, 180, 185
Brown, M., 76
Buck, Pearl S., 183, 184, 185, 188
Bukowski, C., 132
Bunting, E., 134
Bunton, Iman, 157, 211
Buss, Fran Leeper, 150
Butterworth, W., 76

Cabrera, Belkis L., 27, 44, 61, 70, 81, 113, 117, 137, 169, 178, 180, 211
Carey-Webb, A., 73, 134
Carroll, Pamela S., 14, 27, 81, 209

Carter, Alden, 84–85, 110
Chesnut, M.B., 46, 55
Chopin, K., 20
Cisneros, Sandra, 20, 147, 150, 153
Clifton, Lucille, 75, 120, 131, 135
Collier, James Lincoln, 102, 110
Comer, James P., 34, 46
Comer, Maggie, 34
Conlon-McKenna, Marita, 140, 150
Conroy, Pat, 103, 110
Cormier, R., 77
Cormier, Robert, 180, 186
Crane, Stephen, 31, 46, 56, 135
Crew, Linda, 147, 150
Crutcher, Chris, 33, 44, 46

Danticat, E., 144, 150
Davis, R.C., 135
Dean, W., 77
DeCrevoceour, M.G., 139, 140, 150
Deloria, E.C., 135
Devito, Cara, 103, 110
Dickens, Charles, 135
DiPasquale, Emanuel, 149, 150
Douglass, Frederick, 46, 55, 167

Ebert, Alan, 40, 46
Edelman, B., 46, 55
Edgerton, Clyde, 84, 85, 110
Edwards, P., 160, 165
Eighner, L., 135
Elbow, P., 19
Elsland, R., 187
Equiano, O., 165
Erikson, Erik, 179

Fairbanks, C., 128, 131, 135
Feelings, Tom, 160, 165
Fisher, L.E., 143, 150
Fleischman, Paul, 103, 110
Fowler, Connie Mae, 85, 110
Fox, P., 164, 165
Franklin, J.H., 160, 165
Freedman, Russell, 140, 150
Freeman, Mary Wilkens, 189

Frost, Robert, 12, 19, 23

Gale, W., 78
Gansberg, M., 66, 74
Gardner, S., 69, 74, 77
Gaylord, S. K., 144, 150
Geiogamah, H., 75
Gere, A.R., 128, 131, 135
Gibson, William, 34, 46
Gillian, M.M., 151
Giovanni, Nikki, 8, 19, 23, 46, 50, 103, 110, 174, 186
Glenn, M., 65, 74, 75
Glueck, , 129
Goldman, James, 183, 186
Goodwillie, S., 67–68, 74
Gordon, Larry, S., 169, 211
Greenberg, J.E., 153
Greene, Graham, 183, 186
Gregg, Gail P., 1, 61, 113, 137, 209
Groom, Winston, 35
Guest, Judith, 104, 110
Gukova, J., 163, 165

Hahn, M., 133
Haley, A., 46, 55
Hamilton, V., 165, 166
Hansberry, L., 23, 47, 53
Harris, R., 186
Hawkins, R.F., 152
Hawthorne, Nathaniel, 20, 189
Hemingway, Ernest, 31, 47, 183, 186
Hesse, K., 47, 54
Hewett, L., 72, 74
Hilton, James, 183, 186
Hinojosa, M., 67–68, 74
Hinton, S.E., 70, 71, 74, 78
Homer, 47, 50, 71
Horn, Gabriel, 184, 186
Howes, A., 128, 131, 135
Hubbard, J., 117, 131, 135
Hughes, Langston, 47, 50, 53
Hurston, Zora Neale, 21, 31, 37, 47
Hutchinson, L., 135

Ibsen, H., 47, 53
Inez, C., 66, 74

Jake, J., 154

Janeczko, Paul, 175, 186
Janos, L., 48
Johnson, Angela, 179, 186
Johnson, C., 164, 165
Johnson, S., 135
Johnston, L., 131
Jones, A., 133
Justice, D., 75

Katz, S., 77
Keats, John, 184
Keens-Douglas, R., 163, 165
Kennedy, W., 133
King, B., 133, 135
King, Martin Luther, Jr., xiii, 67, 168
King, N., 7, 15, 16, 19
Kingsolver, Barbara, 85–86, 110
Kismaric, C., 135
Kohlberg, Lawrence, 179
Kosof, A., 133
Kozol, J., 127, 131, 135

Lamme, Robert, 40, 47
Landau, E., 134
Langer, J., 13, 16, 19
Laurents, Arthur, 75
Lazarus, E., 143, 150
Le Guin, U.K., 21, 24
Lee, Harper, 31
Lee, R.E., 47, 55
Lieberman, Elias, 143–144, 150
Lincoln, Abraham, 47, 56
Lopez, S., 77
Lowry, Lois, 18, 19, 21, 32, 47
Lyons, Mary E., 18, 19, 21

Mahy, Margaret, 180, 186
Mallory, T., 47, 54
Marchant, Geoff, 40, 47
Marques, Gabriel Garcia, 190
Marshall, Paule, 174, 186
Martz, Sheila, 187, 188
Mathabane, Mark, 135, 145, 148, 150
Mazer, Norma Fox, 104, 110, 175, 186
McCall, N., 67–68, 74
McConnell, C., 71, 74
McKay, C., 152
Mee, S., 9, 19
Mercer, C., 143, 151

Merriam, Eve, 6, 19, 23
Meyer, Carolyn, 34, 47, 54
Michener, J.A., 154
Miklowitz, Gloria D., 190
Miller, Arthur, 100, 153, 183, 186
Miller, Melinda, 137, 211
Milton, John, 141, 151
Mitchell, D., 15, 19
Mora, P., 152
Morales, A.L., 152
Moss, A.A., Jr., 160, 165
Mowry, J., 72, 74, 76
Myers, Walter Dean, 33, 47, 56

Namioka, Lensey, 104, 110
Nasaw, J., 133
Nelson, T., 122, 131, 135
Nemiroff, R., 23
Neruda, P., 146, 151
Newton, Miller, 29, 47
Nixon, J.L., 154
Nixon, L.L., 189

O'Conner, F., 76
O'Conner, Flannery, 189
O'Hehir, D., 119, 132
Ortiz, J., 154

Paek, M., 144
Painter, Kim, 40, 47
Paley, Grace, 174, 186
Parks, G., 123, 132, 135
Paulson, Gary, 104, 110
Peck, Richard, 105, 110
Philbrick, Rodman, 32, 44, 48
Platt, K., 77
Potok, Chiam, 105, 110, 148, 151
Purves, A., 96, 97, 111

Quarles, B., 46
Quindlen, A., 134

Ramirez, E., 154
Rand, Ayn, 11, 16, 18, 19, 20, 21
Randell, D., 186
Rich, Adrienne, 23, 145–146, 151
Rief, Linda, 182, 186
Rios, A., 64, 74
Rodriguez, L., 78

Rogers, T., 96, 97, 111
Roop, L., 128, 131, 135
Rosenberg, L., 134
Rosenblatt, L., 13, 20
Roy, Jacqueline, 105, 111
Rubin, N., 67, 74
Rylant, C., 132
Ryu, S.L., 146, 151

Salinger, J.D., 22
Schaafsma, D., 128, 131, 135
Secundy, M.G., 189
Shakespeare, William, 71, 74, 179, 182, 186, 187
Sherburne, Z., 48, 53
Shilts, Randy, 34, 48
Shusterman, Neal, 105, 111
Silverstein, Shel, 179
Singer, Isaac Bashevis, 184, 187, 189
Smith, Betty, 147, 151
Smith, Lee, 86, 111
Solzhenitsyn, A., 141, 151
Sophocles, 4, 11, 15, 20, 48, 53
Soter, A., 96, 97, 111
Soto, Gary, 67, 74, 75
Spears-Bunton, Linda, 157, 211
Spinelli, J., 123, 132, 135
St. John, Primus, 162, 165
Staples, Suzanne Fisher, 4, 20
Steinbeck, John, 86, 111, 124
Stern, S., 76
Swindels, R., 122, 132, 133

Takaki, R., 154–155
Tan, Amy, 105, 111, 148, 151
Taylor, Mildred, 32–33, 34, 48, 54
Tennyson, A., 48, 51
Terkel, Studs, 145, 151
Thomas, A., 63, 74
Thomas, Dylan, 48, 51, 52, 72–73, 183, 187
Thomas, K., 190
Tollentino-Davidson, Michelle, 113, 211
Twain, M., 22

Uchida, Y., 155
Ulibarri, S.R., 48, 54
Uris, L., 141, 151

Virgil, S., 153
Vollgracht, Nan, 137, 211

Walker, Alice, 48, 51, 86, 111, 189
Walters, A.L., 135
Watts, Elizabeth L., 1, 9, 211
Welch, J., 78
Welty, Eudora, 97, 190
Wersba, B., 135
Wexler, N., 190
White, T.H., 48, 54
Whitman, Walt, 48, 51, 188
Wilde, Oscar, 183, 187
Williams, Bard, xiv
Wolff, Virginia Euwer, 97, 106
Wormser, R., 74
Wright, R., 77, 133
Wright, Richard, 66–67

Yeager, C., 48, 56
Yeats, William Butler, 188

Zeitlin, Steven J., 88, 111

Subject/Title Index

"Ability to Tackle Harvard, The," 40, 48
"Adagio for strings," 3, 19
"Adirondack Iron," 69–70, 73
Adolescence, 29, 115
Adolescence: Guiding Youth Through the Perilous Ordeal, 29, 47
Adolescent students, need for examples of heroic behavior, 27
Adventures of Huckleberry Finn, 22
Aekyung's Dream, 144, 151
African Americans, music of, 162
Afro-American Folktales: Stories from Black Traditions in the New World, 166
"After Tonight," 67, 74
Aging
    activities using literature, graphs, and community involvement to explore the aging process, 178–182
    approach for integrating a song, 172–174
    creating empathy, 171–172
    establishing literature at the core of the unit, 174–175
    examining attitudes about aging and the elderly, 177–178
    facing the inevitable: literature and activities that deal with death, 183–185
    goals and rationale for teaching the unit, 171–172
    introducing the theme with songs, literature, movies, and television, 172–176
    our understanding and attitudes on, 169–191
    questions students might ask aging interviewees, 177
    situation comedy activity involving, 175–176
    supplemental resources, 187–191
    using the canon and other resources, 182–183
    World Wide Web sites listed, 178, 184, 191
"Ain't No Sunshine," 67, 74
Alex Haley's Queen: The Story of an American Family, 46, 55
"All the world's a stage," 179
All Together Now, 180, 185
Alta Vista search engine, 37, 108
Always Running: La Vida Loca: Gang Days in L.A., 78
"America," 150
"America" (from West Side Story), 152–153
America: Mother of Exiles, 137–155
American Dreams: Lost and Found, 145, 151
American Literature, 45, 50
American Me, 68–69, 70, 74
American Refugees, 135
American Voices: Multicultural Literacy and Critical Thinking, 131, 135
And Still I Rise, 45, 49, 50, 185
And the Band Played On: Politics, People, and the AIDS Epidemic, 34, 48, 56
Anders, A., 78
Animal Dreams, 85–86, 110
"Another Day in Paradise," 118, 131, 135
Anthem, 18, 20, 21
Antigone, 4, 11–18, 48, 53
    after reading, 16–18
    before reading, 12–13
    collage activity for, 17
    during reading of, 13–15
    supplemental work for, 18
    synopsis of, 11–12
Apollo 13, 35, 36, 47
April and the Dragon Lady, 104, 110
"Arkansas Nine," 34
Armstrong, Gillian, 19, 23
As You Like It, 179, 186
Ashby, H., 185
Ask Me If I Care, 67, 74
Associative jotting, 12–13

Avalon, 155
Avildsen, John G., 57
Awakening, The, 20

"Baby Mine," 106–107, 111
Barber, Samuel, 19
Batman, 35
"Beautiful Boy (Darling Boy)," 93, 94, 96
Bedford Reader, The, 134
Before the Mayflower: A History of the Negro in America, 165
Beggar's Ride, The, 122, 131, 135
Benetar, P., 46, 51
Beowulf, 45, 50
Beresford, B., 185
Bernstein, L., 152
Best of Comic Relief 3, The, 135
Best Short Stories of Negro Writers, The, 189
Best Short Stories: Middle Level, 186
Bette Midler, 47
"Big Green Lady," 137–138
"Black History Month," 164–165
Bland, B., 134
"Blue Bird's Offering," 135
Blues Traveler, 24
"Body Indian," 75
"Bold Americans, The," 50
Boyz N the Hood, 70, 79
Braveheart, 22
Brooks, G., 24, 46, 51
Brown vs. the Board of Education, 18
Bruce, T., 24
Buffet, Jimmy, 172, 177, 185
Bukowski, 132
But Seriously . . . The Video, 117–118, 122, 131
Butterflies on the Wind: An Anthology of Poetry by Chinese and American Writers, 150
Byrne, Debbie, 106

Cain, C., 78
"Can We Live in Two Cultures," 145–146, 151
"Captain and the Kid, The," 172, 185
Carey, M., 46
Carroll, Sissi, and personal experience with homeless woman, 124–126
Carter, Jimmy, 40
Carter, Thomas, 46, 58
"Cat's in the Cradle," 94–95, 96, 188
Catcher in the Rye, The, 22
Cates, G. 186
Centennial, 154
Changing of the Guard, 190
Chapin, Harry, 94–95, 288
Children of the River, 147–148, 150
Choice of Weapons, A, 123, 132, 135
"Choices," 8, 19, 23
"City of Angels," 132, 134
Civil Rights Movement, 37
    search example of, xiii
Class Dismissed, 75
"Climb that Mountain High," 47, 52
Close to the Edge, 190
Cocoon, 175, 186
"Code of the Streets, The," 66, 73
Collage, as activity to help students synthesize thoughts, 17–18
Collins, Phil, 117–118, 122, 131, 135
Color Purple, The, 86, 111
"Colors," 70, 74
Compound, The, 78
Connick, H., Jr., 46, 52
Contemporary American Poetry, 131
"Conversation with My Father, A," 174–175, 186
Coolio, 73, 74
Coppola, F., 150
Cotton Candy on a Rainy Day, 19, 23
Courage File, 39–40, 43, 44
Crews, 67–68, 74
Crystal, B., 135
Cybill, 98

"Dance, The," 24
"Dancing Nancies," 24
Dangerous Minds (movie), 56, 73
Dangerous Minds (TV series), 48, 58
Dateline, 48, 58
Dave Matthews Band, 24
Dead Poets' Society, 22
Dear America: Letters Home from Vietnam, 46, 55
Death of a Salesman, 100, 183, 186
December Stillness, 133
"Delta," 23

Demme, Jonathan, 46, 57
Des'ree, 19, 24
Diamond, Neil, 139, 140, 150
"Did You Know the Boy," 61, 70
"Do Not Go Gentle into That Good Night," 48, 51, 52, 72, 74, 183, 187
Do or Die, 78
Doll's House, A, 47, 53
Don't Look and It Won't Hurt, 105, 110
Douglas, Marjory Stoneman, 18
Down and Out in America, 134
"Dr. Heidegger's Experiment," 189
Dreamer: Poems by Primus St. John, 162, 165
Driving Miss Daisy, 175, 185
Durango Street, 76

Early and recent immigrant arrivals, a bridge across, 139
Eleni, 18, 22
"Elka and Meir," 184, 187
Ellis Island: Gateway to the New World, 143, 150
Emerging Voices, 152
"Employer, The," 40, 47
En Vogue, 19, 24
"Ending Poem," 152
Enormous Changes at the Last Minute, 186
Envisioning Literature, 19
Epilogue/Finale (from Les Miserables), 106
ER, 48, 58
Estafan, Gloria, 46
Exodus, 141, 151

Fallen Angels, 33, 47, 56
Family Installment: Memories of Growing up Hispanic, 154
Family Matters, 98
Family
    conducting oral history interviews, 90–92
    culminating activity: presenting oral family histories, 92–93
    gathering oral histories; possible interview questions, 90–92
    growing strong family trees, 81–112
    guidelines for beginning oral history project, 88–89
    oral history project for, 87–93
    other activities: popular music, 93–96
    other suggested resources, 101–110
    resources on the World Wide Web, 108–110, 112
    selecting a family-oriented topic, 83–84
    suggestions for whole-class or small-group reading, 84–86
    tableaux as response for literature, songs television, movies/videos, 96–98
    teaching and learning activities for, 87
    television family project, 98–100
"Fantine's Death" (from Les Miserables), 106
Far and Away, 142, 150
Far Dream, A, 155
Farm, The, 46, 52
"Father and Son," 188
Father of the Bride, 108
Favorite Poems Old and New, 150
"Feeding the Birds," 27–28, 44–45
Feury, J., 134
"Fire," 76
Fleming, Henry, 41 42
Florry of Washington Heights, 77
Fly Away Home, 134
Fools Crow, 78
Forced Out, 135
Forest Gump, 35, 37, 48
Frazier, 176, 191
Freak the Mighty, 32, 44, 48
Freedom child of the Sea, 163, 165
"Freewill," 24
Freewriting, 3–4
Frisco Kid, The, 155
From Exiles to Immigration, 154–155
"From Mother with Love," 48, 53
From Slavery to Freedom: A History of African Americans, 160, 165
Frost, Kid, 67, 74

Gandhi, 18
Gangs
    a bridge from violence to topic of, 67–68
    "glory" of life in, 63
    members of, 68–70
    some classic literature options for, 70–71
    suggested young adult novels about, 71–73
    and violence, a teenage crisis, 61–79
"Gangsta's Paradise," 73, 74
Genesis, 118, 119, 131
Genovese, Kitty, 66
"George," 179, 186
Gettysburg Address, The, 47, 56
Gibson, Mel, 22
Giver, The, 18, 19, 21, 32, 47
Glory, 48, 56
Godfather II, The, 142, 150
Golden Girls, The, 175, 191
Gone with the Wind, 124
Good Earth, The, 183, 185
"Good Enough for Me," 48, 53
Good Man Is Hard to Find, A, 189
Goodbye, Mr. Chips, 183, 186
"Goodbyes," 146, 151
Gorilla, My Love, 185
Grace Under Fire, 98
Grand Mothers: Poems, Reminiscences, and Short Stories about the Keepers of our Traditions, 103, 110, 174, 186
"Grandpa and the Statue," 153
Grapes of Wrath, The, 124, 132, 135
"Greatest man I Never Knew, The," 107, 111
Grow Old Along with Me—The Best Is Yet to Be, 187
Growing strong family trees, 81–112
Growing up Latino, 153

Hamada, S., 134
Happy Days, 98
Harold and Maude, 175, 185
Harris, Frank, 40
"He Ain't Heavy, He's My Son," 40, 47
"He Knew Hemingway," 169–170, 178

"He Knows Now," 1
Headman, 77
Hearts Come Home, 188
Herek, S., 47
"Hero," 46
Heroes and courage, study of, 27–60
    after reading activities, 44-45
    beginning the unit, 37–40
    books from school canon, 31
    categories of heroes, 30
    cross-disciplinary activity with social studies/history classes, 33
    decisions for teachers to make on balancing issues, 30
    five fictitious young adult books, 32–33
    mid-unit activity, character continuum, 41–42
    mid-unit activity, song lyrics, 42–44
    nonfiction books, 33–34
    popular movies and electronic media, 34–36
    preview activities useful as introduction, Courage File, 39–40
    preview activities useful as introduction, newspapers, 38–39
    sustaining activities, 41–44
    using World Wide Web as complement, 36–37
    World Wide Web sites on listed, 59–60
Hertzberg, P., 122, 131
High school students, seeking their identities, 2
Home Improvements, 100
Home Less Home, 134
Homebird, 102, 110, 133, 134
Homeland, 154
Homeless in America, 133
"Homeless Woman Living in a Car," 119, 131
"Homeless," 134
Homeless, The, 134
"Homelessness and Language Arts: Contexts and Connections," 134

"Homelessness and Reader-Response: Writing with a Social Consciousness," 135
Homelessness in literature, the media, and in our minds, 113–135
Homelessness
　activities that extend the classroom into the community, 128–130
　activity to increase empathy and introduce a classic American film, 123–127
　author's personal experience with homeless woman, 124–126
　creating lasting impressions and memories, 128–130
　developing the theme, 116
　interdisciplinary connections, 130–131
　introducing the topic and theme with music, videos, and photography, 116–119
　others' perspectives on, 119–121
　questions to prompt discussion, 116, 118–119, 120–121
　supplemental resources, 132–135
　teenage homelessness and the runaways, 117–118, 121–123
　as a topic, 115–116
House of Mango Street, The, 20, 147, 150
House of Spirits, 101
"How Long," 46, 52
How Porcupines Make Love, III: Readers, Texts, Cultures in the Response-Based Literature Classroom, 96, 111
How the Garcia Girls Lost Their Accents, 102, 110, 148, 149
How to Collect Your Own Family Folklore. A Celebration of American Family Folklore, 88, 111
Howard, Ron, 47, 107, 111, 150, 186

"I Am an American," 143–144, 150
"I Am" poem, 9, 19
"I Have a Dream," xiii
"I Hear America Singing," 48, 51
I Know Why the Caged Bird Sings, 45, 55

"I Leave South Africa," 145, 150
"I Need a Hero," 46, 52
I Never Sang for My Father, 183, 186
"I Was to Become a Bajan," 162
"I Won't Back Down," 48, 52
"I'll Remember," 132
Ice-T, 70, 74
Identity, introducing a unit on, 3–4
Iguana Killer: Stories of the Heart, The, 74
Imagemaking, 16–17
Immigrant Kids, 140, 150
Immigrants and exiles
　a bridge across early and recent arrivals, 139
　disappointment, disillusionment and loss of identity, 145–146
　family history project, 149
　a final activity or two, 149
　the harsh journey, 139–141
　life in their new "home," 143–145
　their arrival, 142–143
　young adult novels depicting immigrant life in America, 146–149
In Grandparents' House, 187
In Her Stories: African American Folktales, Fairy Tales, and True Tales, 166–167
Individuality
　activities investigating society's definitions of, 10–11
　explored as a theme, 3
　and language arts, 2
　questions to ask students, 4
　supplemental resources on, 20–25
　World Wide Web sites on listed, 25
Inside Life Outside, 134
Internet, definition of, xiii
Interview questions for Oral history project
　artifacts, 92
　characters, 90
　food, 92
　historical events, 91
　language, 91
　love, 91
　other questions, 92
　stories, 90

Into a Strange Land: Unaccompanied Refugee Youth in America, 140, 150
Introduction to the Short Story, 76
Ironweed, 133
Isaac Bashevis Singer Reader, An, 187
It Doesn't Always Have to Rhyme, 19, 23

Jacobs, Harriet, 18
JAG, 49, 58
Journaling, 4
Journey of the Sparrows, 140, 150
"Journey, A," 46, 50
Joy Luck Club, The, 105, 111, 148, 151
"Joy of an Immigrant, a Thanksgiving Poem," 149, 150
J3 journal, 14, 16
Juveniles in Trouble, 74

Kaffir Boy in America, 135, 148, 150
Keeping Christina, 102, 110
Keller, Helen, 34
Kennedy, John F., 37
"Kidnapped Child, A," 163
Kids on the Run, 123, 131
King Lear, 182, 187
King, Martin Luther, Jr., 18
King, Rodney, verdict, 65
Kirk? Krak!, 144, 150

"L.A. Prayer," 64–65, 71, 73
Land of Promise, 154
Language and Reflection: An Integrated Approach to Teaching English, 128, 131, 135
Language arts, and individuality, 2
Language of Literature, The, 48, 54, 152
"Last Decision, The," 179, 185
"Late Encounter with the Enemy, A," 189
Law and Order, 49, 58
Lee, Ang, 108, 111
"Legal Alien," 152
Lennon, John, 93
Leroy and the Old Man, 76
Let the Circle Be Unbroken, 48, 54
"Letter from Birmingham Jail," 67
Letter to his son (R.E. Lee), 47, 55
Letters from a Slave Girl, 18, 19, 21

Letters from Rifka, 47, 54
Levinson, B., 155
Life and Times of Frederick Douglass: His Early Life as a Slave, His Escape from Bondage, and His Complete History, 167
"Life Doesn't Frighten Me at All," 45
Life Doesn't Frighten Me at All, 187
Life in the Ghetto, 63, 74
"Like a River," 94–95, 96
Lion in Winter, The, 183, 186
Literature Across the Cultures, 151
Literature and Language, 150, 151, 152
Literature and Language Arts: the British Tradition, 187
Literature: An Introduction to Fiction, 74
Literature Instruction: A Focus on Student Response, 19
Literature: 150 Masterpieces of Fiction, Poetry, and Drama, 135
Literature, students evaluating own decisions through, 2
Literature: The American Experience, 46, 47, 55, 56
Literature: The British Tradition, 45, 47, 48, 51
"Little Boy and the Old Man, The," 179
Little Mermaid, The, 108
Little Women, 11, 19, 23
"Lola in a Cardboard Box," 113–114, 117
Los Angeles Times, 37
"Luka," 94, 96

Madonna, 132
Maggie: A Girl of the Streets, 135
"Maggie of the Green Bottles," 174, 185
Maggie's American Dream, 34, 46
Make Lemonade, 97, 106
Makes Me Wanna Holler, 67–68, 74
Mama Can't Remember Anymore, 190
"Mamma Says—A Tribute to My African Forefathers: Peace and Prayers," 157
Maniac Magee, 123, 132, 135
"Man on the Corner," 119, 131
Many Thousands Gone: African-Americans from Slavery to Freedom, 163, 165

Many Worlds of Literature, The, 150, 151
Marshall, Thurgood, 18
Mary Chesnut's Civil War, 46, 55
"Masculine Protest," 76
McIntire, Reba, 47, 52, 107, 111
McPhee, John, 18
Meet Me in St. Louis, 108
Melrose Place, 98
Memory, 180, 186
Menace II Society, 63–64, 74
Middle Passage, 164, 165
Middle Passage, the, 157–168
    confinement activity, 162–163
    a difficult yet essential feature of the secondary school curriculum, 159–160
    a final word, 164–165
    goals and rationale for a unit on the Middle Passage, 158–159
    opening students' eyes, ears, and minds, 162–164
    supplemental resources, 166–168
    a teacher's beginning, 160–161
    Web sites listed, 160–161, 166, 167–168
Midler, Bette, 106, 111
Miracle Worker, The, 34, 46
"Miss Rosie," 120, 131, 135
Mi Vida Loca, 70, 78
Monologues, having students write to clarify reading, 15
Morisette, Alanis, 107, 111
"Morning Noon and Night," 81–82
"Morning They Shot Tony Lopez, Barber and Pusher Who Went Too Far, The," 75
Morris, Gary, 106
Morrow Anthology of Younger American Poets, The, 75
Morte d'Arthur, 47, 54
"Most Famous Monument," 151
"Most Vulnerable People, The," 150
"Mother to Son," 47, 50
"Mothers of the Disappeared," 107
"Moustache, The," 180, 181, 186
Mr. Holland's Opus, 35, 47, 108
"Mr. Mack Pilgrim," 65
Mr. Sammler's Planet, 183, 185
Mrs. Doubtfire, 108

Multicultural Books to Make and Share, 144, 150
Muslim family life, 5
Muslim society, role of female in, 5–8, 10
"My Bondage and My Freedom," 167
"My Daily Dives in the Dumpster," 135
My Family, 142, 150
My Friend's Got This Problem, Mr. Chandler, 65, 74
My Name is Asher Lev, 105, 110, 148, 151
"My Promised Land," 141, 150
My Wonder horse/Mi caballo Mago, 48, 54

Nair, M., 151
Narrative of the Life of Frederick Douglass, an American Slave, Written by Himself, 46, 55, 167
NASA, Web search example for, 36, 59
National Geographic, 143
Nation of Amor, A, 71–72, 73, 74
Native Heart, 186
Native Son, 65
Nava, G., 151
Neufeld, M., 155
"Never Again," 161
"Never Marry a Mexican," 153
"New Colossus, The," 143, 150
Newcomers to America, 153–154
New Kids in Town: Oral Histories of Immigrant Teens, 144, 150
New Native American Drama: Three Plays, 75
19 American Poets of the Golden Gate, 132
No Place To Be: Voices of Homeless Children, 127, 131
North, The, 142, 151
Norton Anthology of English Literature, 187
Norton Anthology of Modern Poetry, The, 74, 75
Notes for Another Life, 180, 185

"O Canaan Land," 145, 151
Odyssey, The, 47, 50, 70, 74
"Old Lady Under the Freeway, The," 119, 132

Old Man and the Sea, The, 31, 47, 183, 186
"Old Mother, The," 188
Oliver Twist, 135
Olmos, Edward James, 68–69, 70, 74
"On Aging," 179, 185
Once and Future King, The, 48, 54
One Day in the Life of Ivan Denisovich, 141, 151
One Hundred Years of Solitude, 190
One of the Boys, 135
"Ones Who Walk Away from Omelas, The," 24
On Golden Pond, 175, 186
Optimist's Daughter, The, 190
Oral history project, 97–93
    conducting interviews, 90–92
    culminating activity: presenting histories, 92–93
    gathering histories; possible interview questions, 90–92
    guidelines for beginning, 88–89
Oral History, 86, 111
Ordinary People, 104, 110
"Orlando Martinez," 75
Outside Looking In, 102, 110
Outsiders, The, 70, 74

Paper Dance: 55 Latino Poets, 73
Paradise Lost, 141
Parenthood, 107, 111
Paula, 101, 110
Pearl, The, 86, 111
Perez Family, The, 142, 151
"Perfect," 107, 111
Permanent Connections, 180, 185
Petty, T., 47, 52
Philadelphia, 46, 56
Picture of Dorian Gray, The, 183, 187
Playing Their Part, 19
Plum Pickers, The, 134
"Poem by a Yellow Woman," 146, 151
Poem, Counterpoem, 186
Poems, 45, 50
Poems of William Butler Yeats, The: A New Edition, 188
Poetry Brief: An anthology of Short, Short, Short Poems, 75
Power of One, The, 46, 57

Prentice Hall Literature, 48, 51
Prince of Tides, The, 103, 108, 110
Proposition 187, 139
"Prospective Immigrants Please Note," 145–146, 151
"Proud upon an Alien Shore," 152
"Public School No. 18: Patterson, New Jersey," 151

Rachel and Her Children, 127, 131, 135
Raisin in the Sun, A, 23, 47, 53
Rats in the Trees, 76
"Raymond's Run," 46, 53
"Reach," 46
Reader's Digest, 129, 131
Reader, the Text, the Poem, The, 20
Rear-View Mirrors, 103, 110
Rebel without a Cause, 76
Red Badge of Courage, The, 31, 41, 46, 56
Reena and Other Stories, 186
Rene and Georgette Magritte with Their Dog After the War, 153
Rescue 911, 49, 58
Rite of Passage, 77, 133
"River, The," 46, 52
"Road Not Taken, The," 12, 23
Robin Hood: Prince of Thieves, 48, 57
Robinson, James G., 48, 57
Rogers, Kenny, 188
Roll of Thunder, Hear My Cry, 32–33, 34, 48
Romeo and Juliet, 70, 71, 74
Roots, 46, 55
Roots I, 163
Roseanne, 98
Rule of the Bone, 69, 73
"Runaway Train," 132
Runner's Literary Companion, The, 46, 52
Rush, 24, 25
Rydell, M. 186

Scarlet Letter, The, 20
Scorpions, 77
Scott, D., 74
Sea Gypsies, The, 108

Search engines
    Alta Vista, 37
    definition of, xiii
    example of search for Civil Rights Movement, xiii
    example of search for NASA, 36
    WebCrawler, xiii
    Yahoo, xiii
"Season's Greetings from the Heart," 40
Second Stone, The, 76
Seeking Diversity, 182, 186
Selah, A.T., 121, 132, 135
Selected Poems of Langston Hughes, 47, 51
Selected Stories of Isaac Bashevis Singer, 189
Sense and Sensibility, 108, 111
Separate but Equal, 18, 23
Shabanu, 4, 5–11
    after reading, 8–11
    before reading, 6–7
    during reading of, 7–8
    "I Am" poem of, 10
    other resources to complement study of, 11
    synopsis of, 5–6
Shadow of the Dragon, 77
Shakedown Street, 133
Shaker, Why Don't You Sing, 185
"Shed a Little Light," 48, 52
Shooting Back: A photographic View of Life by Homeless Children, 117, 127, 131
Short Fiction of Sarah Orne Jewett and Mary Wilkins Freeman, 189
Short Story and You, The, 48, 54, 186
"Sila," 180–181
Silent Dancing, 154
Silicon Songs, 133, 135
Simon, Carly, 94–95
Simon, P., 153
Simpsons, The, 98
Singleton, J., 79
Sinkler, S., 134
Sisters/Hermanas, 104, 110
Six American Poets, 188
60 Minutes, 48, 58
Slave Dancer, 164, 165
Slavery, 157–168

"Slumnight," 74
Smith, John, 56
"Someone Else's Dream," 24
"Somersett," 163
Something in Common, 47, 53
Something Permanent, 132
Sondheim, S., 152
Song lyrics, as focus on heroes, 42–44
Songs of Experience, 187
Soul Asylum, 132
Soul Daddy, 111
Soul Fire, 72, 73, 74
Sound and Sense: An Introduction to Poetry, 48, 51
Sound of Music, The, 108
South Central, 79
Spiderwoman's Granddaughter, 135
"Spinoza of Market Street, The," 189
"Spirit Journey and the Pipe, The," 184, 186
Spotlight on Literature, 46, 48, 50, 51
Spottiswood, Roger, 56
"Stand," 24
Star Trek, 35–36
"Starting Fast," 132
Statue of Liberty, The, 143, 151
Steel Magnolias, 108
Stevens, Cat, 188
Stevens, George, Jr., 23
Stone Cold, 122, 132, 133
Stone, O., 79
Storymaking and Drama, 19
Stotan!, 33, 44, 46
Street Family: A Novel, 133
Street Gangs in America, 69, 74
"Street Musicians," 119, 131
Streetwise, 121, 123, 132, 135
Strings: A Gathering of Family Poems, 175, 186
"Subdivisions," 25
Sugar Cage, 85, 110
Sullivan, Annie, 34
"Summer Tragedy, A," 183–184, 185
"Survival Kids Transform Classics to Murals," 129
Swing Kids, 46, 57

Tableaux as response for literature, songs television, movies/videos, 96–98

"Tamara Jackson," 65
Taylor, J., 48, 52
"Teaching Ideas: Ways into Literature," 19
Teenage crisis: gangs and violence, 61–79
10,000 Maniacs, 132, 134
"Thank You, M'am," 47, 53
Thanksgiving Poems, 150
"Thanks in Old Age," 188
"That Day," 162
That Was Then, This Is Now, 78
"The Interesting Life of Olaudah Equiano or Gustavus the African," 160, 165
The Middle Passage: White Ships/Black Cargo, 160, 165
Theban Plays, The, 20, 48, 53
Their Eyes on the Prize, 49, 58
Their Eyes Were Watching God, 21, 31, 37, 47
"Then They'd Watch Comedies," 64–65, 74
"They're Coming to America," 139
Things fall apart, 84, 110
Third and Indiana, 77
"38 Who Saw Murder Didn't Call the Police," 66, 74
"This Is Your Life," 4, 24
"Those Boys," 75
Three Sisters, 104, 110
"Thumbprint," 6, 19, 23
"To Autumn," 184–185
"To Da-duh, in Memoriam," 174, 186
"To Hell with Dying," 189
To Kill a Mocking Bird, 31
"Toning the Sweep," 179, 186
Touched by an Angel, 49, 58
"Tourist from Syracuse, The," 75
"Trapped," 65
Travels with My Aunt, 183, 186
Tree Grows in Brooklyn, A, 147, 151
Trials, tribulations and celebrations: African-American Perspectives on Health, Illness, Aging, and Loss, 185, 189
Triple-entry journal, 14, 16
"Tropics in New York, The," 152
Tunes for Bears to Dance to, 180, 186

Twentieth Century Interpretations of "The Graphs of Wrath," 135
"Twenty Years Ago," 188
Twice Told Tales, 189
2PAC, 65

U2, 107
"Ulysses," 48, 51
United States Marine Corps, 48, 52
Up Country, 84–85, 110

Vega, Suzanne, 94
Vietnam conflict, 37
"Village Singer, The," 189
"Village Uncle, The," 189
Violence
    exploring causes of, 63–67
    exploring individual's role in, 66
    and gang activities, reasons for studying in the Language Arts classroom, 62–63
"Virginia Pilgrim," 65
Virtue of Selfishness: A New Concept of Egoism, The, 11, 16, 19
Voices from the Future, 67–68, 74
Voices from the Street: Young Former Gang Members Tell Their Stories, 78
Voices in Literature, 153

Walking Across Egypt, 84, 85, 110
Waltzing on Water: Poetry by Women, 175, 186
Warriors Don't Cry, 34, 44, 46
"Warriors, The," 135
Way Past Cool, 72, 73, 74
Wayne, John, 27
We All Fall Down, 77
"We Come to Know Each Other," 162
WebCrawler, xiii
Weir, Peter, 22
Welcome to the Oasis and Other Stories, 153
West Side Story, 75–76, 152
What Daddy Did, 105, 111
"What Is an American?," 139, 150
When I Am an Old Woman I Shall Wear Purple, 188
"When You Are Old," 188

Where I want To Be, 103, 110
Where the Day Takes You, 122, 123, 131
White Lilacs, 34, 47, 54
Who Are the Homeless?, 131
"Why Does Family Homelessness Occur? A Case Control Study," 134
"Why I Live at the P.O.," 97
Wildflower Girl, 140, 150
"Willie," 45, 50
"Wings Beneath My Wings," 47
Wiseman, C., 24
"With Imagination (I'll Get There)," 46, 52
Wizard of EarthSea, The, 21
Woman Who Loved Worms, The, 66, 74
Women of Hollering Creek, 152
"Women," 48, 51
World Wide Web, xi–xiv, 37, 149, 160, 178
    definition of, iii
World Wide Web for Teachers, The, xiv
World Wide Web sites listed, 25, 37, 49, 112
    Advanced Counseling and Psychological Services, 109
    African-American heroes, 49, 59, 168
    civil rights, 168
    counseling, 109
    divorce and family structure changes, 109
    Greek mythology, 49
    heroes and courage, 59–60
    home and family, 109–110, 112
    individuality, 25
    Interactive Aging Network, 178, 184, 191
    interracial families, 109
    Library of Congress, 49, 59
    Little Brothers: Friends of the Elderly, 178, 191
    Martin Luther King, Jr., 168
    mythological heroes, 60
    NASA, 49, 60
    "slavery" in Yahoo, 160–161
    slavery issues, 161, 167–168
    slavery, civil rights, and African-Americans, 166
    sports heroes, 49, 60
    Stepfamily Association of Illinois, 109
    United States Senate Subcommittee on Aging, 191
    war letters, 49, 60
World's Best Poetry, The: Minority Poetry of America: An Anthology of Asian, Black, Hispanic and Native American Poetry, 152
Writing in conjunction with reading, 14–15
Writing without Teachers, 19

"Y," 67
Yahoo, xiii, 108, 160
Yates, Peter, 19, 22
Yeager: An Autobiography, 48, 49
"You Gotta Be," 4, 24
You'll Never Guess the End, 135
"Youth Violence and the Language Arts: A Topic for the Classroom," 73

Zanuck, D., 132, 135
Zemeckis, R., 48
Zwick, Edward, 48, 57

About the Editors

Gail P. Gregg, a former high school Language Arts teacher, is currently an Assistant Professor of English Education at Florida International University, Miami, Florida. She received her Ph.D in English Education from Florida State University in 1994. Dr. Gregg is a member of the National Council of Teachers of English, the Florida Council of Teachers of English, the Assembly on Literature for Adolescents (ALAN), the International Reading Association, and the Florida Reading Association. She was nominated for the Distinguished Instructor Award while at Florida State University, and as a high school teacher was awarded the Citicorp Excellence in Teaching Award. Currently serving as the multicultural columnist for the Florida English Journal, Dr. Gregg has also contributed numerous chapters in books, written many articles for professional journals, and has presented at international, national, and state conferences. Her teaching responsibilities at the graduate and undergraduate level include courses in Methods of Teaching English at the Middle/Secondary Level; Adolescent Literature; Multicultural Literature; and Classroom Management. Dr. Gregg is also responsible for Intern Placement and Supervision.

Pamela S. Carroll, a former teacher of middle and high school English, is currently an Associate Professor and Coordinator of English Education at Florida State University. She received her Ed.D. in English Education from Auburn University in 1990. Her articles have appeared in *English Journal, the ALAN Review, Middle School Journal, Multicultural Education*, and others. She has also contributed chapters in several books devoted to the teaching of young adult literature. Dr. Carroll is on the Board of Directors for the National Council of Teachers of English and the Florida Council of Teachers of English, the Executive Boards of SIGNAL and ALAN, and has been the Director of the North Florida Writing Project in 1990–1996 and 1997–1998. She is also on the Review Boards of *English Journal, The New Advocate*, and *English Education* and is Co-Chair (with Gail Gregg) of the Florida Council of Teachers of English Multicultural Commission. Dr. Carroll has been the recipient of the University Teaching Award and the Teaching Incentive Award at Florida State University.

About the Contributors

Elizabeth Watts—former high school English teacher in Broward County, Florida and currently an Assistant Professor of Secondary Education at Rowan University in Glassboro, NJ.

Larry Gordon—a lawyer who gave up his prosperous law practice to become a teacher. Currently teaching English in Ft. Lauderdale, Florida.

Michelle Tollentino-Davidson—currently a middle school Language Arts teacher in Ft. Lauderdale, Florida.

Melinda Miller—currently teaches Language Arts in a private school in Miami Beach, Florida.

Nan Vollbracht—formerly from New York and currently a substitute teacher in Dade and Broward County, Florida.

Belkis Cabrera—a Cuban immigrant who teaches high school Language Arts and Creative Writing in Hialeah, Florida.

Iman Bunton—a fifteen year old 10th grader, son of Linda Spears-Bunton.

Linda Spears-Bunton—an Assistant Professor of English Education at Florida International University in Miami, Florida.